The Accidental Library Manager

Rachel Singer Gordon

Information Today, Inc.
Medford, New Jersey

Third Printing, May 2008

The Accidental Library Manager

Copyright © 2005 by Rachel Singer Gordon

Library of Congress Cataloging-in-Publication Data

Gordon, Rachel Singer.
   The accidental library manager / Rachel Singer Gordon.
      p. cm.
   Includes bibliographical references and index.
   ISBN 1-57387-210-5
   1. Library administration. 2. Library personnel management. I. Title.
   Z678.G668 2004
   025.1--dc22

                                                        2004020283

Printed and bound in the United States of America

Publisher: Thomas H. Hogan, Sr.
Editor-in-Chief: John B. Bryans
Managing Editor: Amy M. Holmes
Copy Editor: Pat Hadley-Miller
Graphics Department Director: M. Heide Dengler
Book Designer: Kara Mia Jalkowski
Cover Designer: Ashlee Caruolo
Indexer: Sharon Hughes

Contents

Chapter 12: Philosophical, Legal, and Ethical Issues

Acknowledgments

Writing involves the effort and input of many people, and the book you are holding is no exception. Thanks are due, as always, to my editor John Bryans and the rest of the dedicated staff at Information Today, Inc. I'd also like to extend my appreciation to the library managers and library staff who took the time to provide their thoughts and comments; without their insights, the contents of this book would be much less useful. Lastly, thanks to my husband Todd and my son Jacob, who taught me the importance of prioritization, patience, and persistence in both management and life.

About the Web Page
http://www.lisjobs.com/talm

While this book references dozens of Web resources for managers and potential managers in all types of libraries (see Appendix B for a list of sites and URLs by chapter), Web pages come and go. In order to make *The Accidental Library Manager* a more useful and enduring resource for you, the valued reader of the book, it is being supported by a periodically updated directory of relevant sites.

Instead of typing numerous URLs into your Web browser, visit http://www.lisjobs.com/talm where you'll find clickable links to all the sites mentioned in the book.

Please feel free to e-mail changes and comments to rachel@lisjobs.com.

Introduction

Any librarian who spends a sufficient amount of time in the profession will inevitably be promoted into a managerial role. ... With these promotions come a host of varied new tasks for librarians: training, budgeting, writing office procedure manuals, writing and performing job evaluations, and disciplining employees. These bureaucratic tasks are not simple, but they are a part of many librarians' jobs.

Jess Nevins[1]

Why another book on library management? You do have many choices among useful and important resources that will help you throughout your managerial career. Few books, however, talk specifically to those who became library managers "by accident," without a planned step-by-step progression up the career ladder. Many books emphasize theory, history, and background, with less attention to day-to-day, real-world activities. The following pages focus on using your library skills, background, and training to become a more effective library manager, as well as on learning when thinking like a librarian might actually be a hindrance in your management position. You will find ideas on how to become a better and more effective manager, and ideas on what to avoid.

Librarians tend to enter the profession with the idea of specializing in subfields such as reference, youth services, or knowledge management. Only later do many librarians realize that they need to assume management responsibilities in order to move forward in their career. Librarians and other library workers enter accidental management in many ways. They may:

- Have management responsibilities thrust upon them by their administration

- End up running a one-person library or serving as the director of a small rural institution immediately post-graduation

- Enter a library management position from another field, with no previous library or management training

- Start gradually taking on responsibilities in their institution until they are formally moved into a managerial position

- Temporarily fill a management role when a supervisor steps down or retires

- Be asked permanently to replace a departing manager

- Or take numerous other paths. Most librarians and library workers have had little official management training at the time they take on their first supervisory or managerial responsibilities.

Librarian managers who were exposed to at least one "library administration and management" class in the course of their MLS may have found it heavy in theory and short on practical suggestions, or geared too heavily to administrators, with little attention to mid-level management issues. Others may not have given their full attention to such a class at the time, on the assumption that its lessons would never be needed. Students graduating from programs without a formal requirement, or those who did not attend library school, may have had no educational preparation for their new managerial role. In any case, there seems to be a general consensus among many library managers that their formal education and training failed to prepare them adequately for their career in library management.

Students who did enter the library field with every intention of becoming a manager—or who soon realized that management was for them—can treat this as good news. With a moderate amount of ambition, flexibility, and determination, any information professional should be able to move steadily up the career ladder, and your enthusiasm for management responsibilities will help you stand out. While the strategies and suggestions in the chapters that follow are geared particularly to accidental library managers, those who intentionally entered management will also find much applicable content.

Librarians who entered the profession with no thought to becoming a manager and later find themselves in management positions, however, need to develop both an enthusiasm and an aptitude for management, as do those who entered management before they had planned. Managers also need to make a commitment to lifelong learning that will enable them to develop and maintain their managerial skills, allowing their ongoing education and experience to interact and help make them better managers. The combination of existing skills and knowledge with the willingness to learn and grow in a management position creates the foundation for a successful career.

Whatever your environment, from a one-person corporate research center to a busy urban public library, the information and suggestions in this book will help you settle into (or prepare for) a career in library management—offering hope and encouragement along the way. While some ideas and examples will obviously work more or less well in specific library environments, the overall message of developing a management style that will empower you and your staff to serve the goals of your institution applies in all situations. Turn first to the sections in the book that seem most relevant to your own circumstances. Realize, however, that library managers tend to face similar issues, and that you may find pertinent information and advice where you least expect it!

Throughout the book, you will see quotes from the 244 respondents to a library manager's survey, which was posted and advertised online in Summer 2003. You will also find quotes from the 343

respondents to a second survey for library staff, which was posted
and advertised online in spring 2004. The questions for both surveys and some statistics are provided in Appendix A. Longer interviews with selected respondents to the manager survey are
included as sidebars in relevant chapters. Chapter 6 (on what
library staff members want from their managers) further highlights material from the staff survey, allowing respondents to
express in their own words the types of managerial behavior that
are best avoided and best emulated in any environment. The
words and ideas from these two groups help provide insight, both
into the working lives of library managers and into what library
staff need to see from their managers.

A number of the manager survey respondents emphasize the
accidental nature of their positions. Their stories include comments like:

- "My management responsibilities came on me sort of
  gradually—I supervised students and sort of unofficially
  managed circulation operations as a library assistant;
  then I supervised students for two years in a
  nonmanagement librarian position; and then I became
  an 'official' department manager."

- "Tripped into it: ran a one-person special library."

- "After finishing my MLS the director's position opened in
  a library close to my home. There was no chance for
  advancement at the library where I was employed so on a
  whim I applied and was offered the position."

- "I had not planned to become a manager so quickly out
  of graduate school, but I was committed to staying with
  the … district, so I took the opportunity when it came my
  way."

- "It really happened by accident, I was a reference librarian in a public library and was asked to consider being the manager of the town's HS library."

- "While I was in library school (and for a time after I graduated), I was the youth services librarian [at my library] ... I was not getting the mentoring I was looking for at the position, so I left to take another job. When the former director retired, the board called and asked me to consider coming back as the director."

- "The current manager left and they asked me to step in."

- "All the people who were senior to me left."

- "Basically I was having a wonderful time working reference when my manager surprised nearly all of us by announcing her retirement in June 2002 ... I had not planned to accept a management position this early in my career. I had worked many years in a business environment where management meant a certain set of values and tasks that to me were almost all negative. My career change was in part to find a work environment more in tune with my personal values, and I had found that in public reference librarianship. I was happy in my new career and reluctant to leave the work that was giving me so much joy. ... I felt the timing wasn't ideal, but it never is."

- "I had been hired as a reference and instruction librarian and the technology overtook the skills of the director. I was most comfortable with changes, so voila: assistant director."

- "Because of a staffing reorganization, the job duties of my immediate supervisor changed and I was the only other employee ... who had an MSLS."

- "By default—seniority and the willingness to get higher education while working."

- "I said I would never be a director. Never say never. I didn't think I wanted the stress and strain of directing—I didn't want the headache. I really enjoy it and am grateful I fell into my first director position."

The first principle of accidental library management, therefore, is to recognize that you are not alone!

Throughout the following chapters, you will find information to help you successfully settle into—and carry on in—any library management position, and thoughts on using your library skills to become a more effective manager. Chapter 1 discusses making the transition into library management, outlining different scenarios and providing suggestions for various situations, while Chapter 2 addresses different levels of management and their usual responsibilities. Chapters 3 to 5 talk about managing people, from staffing and professional development issues, to managing various groups, to communication and leadership, and Chapter 6 builds on these discussions to talk about potential managerial pitfalls and desired behaviors from the perspective of library staff. Chapter 7 explains various aspects of dealing with library facilities and technology, and Chapter 8 discusses managing change in today's library environment. Chapter 9, on managing money, covers issues from budgeting to fund-raising, while Chapter 10 talks about managing upward and outward, building relationships with your own administrator, board, larger institution, and/or community. Chapter 11 provides a whirlwind tour of management theories and principles, leading into Chapter 12's discussion of philosophical, legal, and ethical issues. Finally, Chapter 13 addresses the question of where to go from here in your management career, and the conclusion reemphasizes how accidental managers can successfully settle into their positions. Each chapter lists sources for further reading and self-education on the topics covered.

If you find yourself weary of reading theory-dense library management textbooks, fear not. View the information and discussions here as one side of a practical and friendly conversation with a colleague or mentor, helping to advise you as you build the foundation of a successful library management career. Not a manager yet? Congratulations on being forward-thinking in preparing yourself for your future career. Learning how management works, what it involves, and how libraries are managed in particular will help you be successful in any stage of your library life, and to realize that most librarians eventually do take on at least some managerial responsibilities. As one manager survey respondent notes: "Professors kept warning us that: 'You will be a manager.' A lot of my classmates denied it and said they weren't management material. Believe me, *you will be a manager.* If you don't want to be a manager, don't get an MLS."

While most of the content will be directly relevant to MLS librarians, any library manager can use the ideas in this book to move forward in their management career. Seeing the "librarian" perspective may also be useful to those who are non-MLS managers. The term "librarian" is used throughout in referring to library managers, not to minimize the value of the MLS, but in recognition of the fact that library managers of all types face similar issues and do similar work, regardless of their degree status. "Staff" throughout refers to those in any nonmanagerial library position, and library customers are variously referred to as customers, patrons, and clients.

If you have comments or thoughts on the pages that follow, I would love to hear your side of the conversation.

Rachel Singer Gordon
rachel@lisjobs.com

A note on bibliographies: Given the wonderful breadth of the library (and general) management literature, both the recommended reading sections following each chapter and the recommendations interspersed within chapters are selective rather than comprehensive. They represent some of the resources that have been helpful in influencing my thoughts about library management; supplement the recommendations with wherever your own reading takes you.

A note on what you will not find here: Unlike many library management books, this one lacks case studies. If you feel the urge to test yourself in this manner, open any management textbook, read *Library Journal's* "How Do You Manage?" column, or, simply, go to work each day.

Notes

1. Jess Nevins, "What Library Schools Still Aren't Teaching Us," in *Revolting Librarians Redux*, Eds., Katia Roberto and Jessamyn West. (Jefferson: McFarland, 2003) 48.

Chapter 1

Becoming a Library Manager

"But if I ran the zoo," said young Gerald McGrew,
"I'd make a few changes. That's just what I'd do..."
Dr. Seuss[1]

Chances are that at some point—while in library school, while working as a paraprofessional, while working as a front-line librarian, or even while utilizing your favorite library—you had visions of how you could arrange things better if you "ran the zoo."

Chances are that at some point after becoming a library manager, you realized that now that you *do* run the zoo—or at least the monkey house—it can be harder than you envisioned to implement those changes you have always wanted to make. Merely sitting in the zookeeper's seat, further, may transform both your perspective and your priorities.

Many of us are accidental managers; that is a given. What is not a given is the way you approach and grow into your management position. Parenting expert Dr. Spock once reassured parents everywhere with the classic line: "Trust yourself, you know more than you think you do." The same can be said for most accidental library managers. Everything you have learned—as a library worker, from previous supervisors, on the job, from mentors, from volunteer work, from committee involvement, in nonlibrary managerial positions, from classes, from workshops, from the professional literature, as a parent, or from coworkers—will be useful as you settle in. Start from the assumption that you know more than you think you do and that you can trust in your own common sense. You know how to treat people the way you would yourself like to be treated. You know how you would like the library, or your own small part of it, to work. You know how you respond to stress, to challenges, and to other people. Now, move forward from here.

Library management comprises more than just making the changes you have always wanted. You must make those changes (as well as manage ongoing operations) in the optimal fashion for your institution, in the context of its larger goals, other departments' activities, and your patrons' needs. You must learn to prioritize your own and your staff's tasks and goals, and to carry out these tasks in a logical order that allows each of your moves to build on your previous actions. Your interactions with and management of the various members of your staff always need to work toward allowing the institution (or your small part of it) to carry out its mission and to serve its customers. Management as a whole involves achieving institutional goals through the people and resources available to you.

Lawrence A. D'Urso, Manager of Adult Services, Mount Prospect Public Library, Illinois, explains: "My biggest challenge was learning what it means to be a manager. It's not just writing reports and keeping an eye on the budget, but it's also a lot of interaction with others. As an entry-level employee, I was very much accustomed to getting an assignment and doing it. Now as a manager, I had to think about overall goals, what other people think and how to apply their thoughts, how to implement the means to attain the goal and how to respond, negotiate, and interact with others who also are in some way or another involved in attaining the goal (that is, not just my one staff member but also the cataloging department, which had to make a change in their procedures to accommodate this unique project, the automation department technician who was developing software for our database, etc.). Learning how to accomplish and balance all of this was quite a challenge."

Library Skills and Managerial Challenges

Our skills and background as librarians can both help and hinder our managerial efforts. If we think consciously about these linkages, we can learn to become more effective in any managerial position. Positive connections include:

- *The ability to collect and analyze information.* Throughout your managerial career, you will need to utilize these skills in activities ranging from creating a budget, to strategic planning, to writing a marketing plan.

- *The urge to share information.* Any organization benefits from the free flow of information; close-mouthed managers foster inefficiency, rumors, and resentment.

- *The ability to organize knowledge.* Again, this will be useful in activities as large as strategic planning and as seemingly small as keeping updated and organized personnel files.

- *The tendency to build networks.* No manager can "go it alone," and librarians' propensity to share information, stories, experiences, and acquired knowledge with one another will stand you in good stead here.

- *The belief in the principle of equity of access and treatment.* As useful when it comes to staff as when dealing with library customers.

On the other hand, tendencies you need to be careful of as a library manager include:

- *The notion that "the patron is always right."* When you extend your wish to make life comfortable for your patrons to bending over backward to make life easy for

your staff, you run the risk of not pushing your people to
their fullest.

- *The wish to avoid conflict.* Studies and personality tests
  consistently show that librarians tend to tip the
  introverted and conflict-avoiding side of the scale. This is
  a generalization, but watch for these tendencies in
  yourself and be willing and able to step in to manage
  conflicts among your employees and with your patrons.

- *Emphasis of the philosophical over the practical.* Library
  school tends to foster a black-and-white worldview of
  philosophical idealism; managers eventually need to
  learn to compromise.

Additional linkages will be emphasized in the appropriate chapters, but always be open to understanding the ways in which your
background as a librarian affects your work as a manager. Make a
conscious effort to manage as a librarian.

Rachel's Laws of Library Management (apologies to Ranganathan)

Library resources are for use. Your job as any type of
library manager is to connect resources with users,
achieving the library's goals.

Every staff member his/her work. Learn people's
strengths and skills and deploy your staff accordingly.

Every task its doer. Encourage responsibility and
ownership of work; give credit for a job well done.

Save the time of your staff. Give them the tools, support, and encouragement they need to do their jobs
effectively and efficiently.

A library is a growing organism. This one needs no modification from the original. As a library manager, you need to be open to change and to helping the library evolve to meet the needs of your patrons.

These "laws" and other principles of library management will be explicated further throughout the book, and Ranganathan's original five laws are discussed in Chapter 11.

Overall, remember that you are a *library* manager, and that the ways in which you manage your people and institution (or part of it) need to be true to the principles and practices of librarianship. Ultimately, working effectively as a library manager demands developing a new way of thinking and behaving, while remembering your roots as a librarian or building a background in librarianship.

Making That Transition

As you adjust to your management role, the first transition from managed to manager can be the hardest. As a nonmanagement employee, you may have been provided with an orientation, directions, and fairly explicit instructions on your day-to-day duties when settling into a new position. As a manager, you may be thrown into a new job with little direction or instruction on how to proceed; management positions are often largely what you make of them. Although you will have a broad outline of your administrator's, board's, or institution's expectations, part of your job will actually be to define your own specific responsibilities and role within your department, library, or section.

Even after the first transition or two gives you an idea of what to expect, the transition into any managerial position can be tricky throughout your career. Transitional periods are inevitably stressful for both you and your new staff, as everyone involved is dealing with a fairly major change and needs to renegotiate relationships and work patterns. But while your staff members' daily work will most likely remain relatively constant, providing them with an underlying stability to draw upon while weathering the changes your arrival brings, you will face the additional task of redefining yourself as a supervisor, a department head, or an administrator.

The first few months in a managerial position can be critical in establishing your credibility, settling comfortably into your new role, and setting out your management style and strategies. This transitional period, while difficult, also presents the opportunity to begin as you mean to continue, to build relationships and alliances with your staff, supervisors, and colleagues, and to lay out your vision for your department, section, or organization. It is always harder to switch gears later than to chart your course from the outset. Take time, however, to get to know your staff, their personalities, their strengths, and their weaknesses before launching into a major change initiative (see Chapter 8).

In some ways it can be especially difficult to take over a position from a previous manager who seems to have run the zoo in a less than optimal manner. Library staff will have developed an understandable mistrust of those in a management role. Much of your time at the outset may be spent undoing the damage your predecessor left behind, rather than in moving forward with your own initiatives and ideas. As one manager survey respondent notes: "Be aware that your staff (especially if they've had bad experiences with managers in the past) may not trust you or your motives at first." This can be frustrating, so work on maintaining your own energy and enthusiasm. New library managers often come in brimming with ideas, but need to have the willingness first to learn the library's organizational culture and to lay the groundwork of trust needed for their initiatives' success.

Also think about the ways in which succeeding an ineffective manager can actually work in your favor. Any moves you make may lead to improvements—and there will be a general predisposition toward change. If you were promoted from within, having suffered with the rest, you will also have insight into what not to do when you move into a management role. Another manager survey respondent even explains her theory of management as: "Having seen library management done badly, I try to think: what would my old boss have done—and do the opposite." One staff survey respondent suggests: "Never forget what it's like to have a bad boss, and don't turn into one yourself." If you have experienced a history of incompetent or ineffective managers, though, it may take you some time to overcome your own distrust of management and realize that you are now one of "them."

Librarians who are promoted into a managerial position from within will find that their former coworkers will have particular preconceptions and expectations for their behavior as a manager, based on past conversations and behavior as an employee. Your former colleagues may no longer be quite sure how to interact with you. Oregon State University Librarian for Systems Applications Debbie Hackleman says that "the biggest surprise for me was that people I had worked with for more than five years viewed me as a different person simply because I had become a manager. They would sometimes agree to concepts that I presented, even though in reality they had very different views on the issue. I found this disconcerting because I wanted and expected them to express their honest opinions."

As any manager, your relationships and interactions with non-managerial staff members will inevitably change. Katharine Salzmann, Archivist/Curator of Manuscripts, Southern Illinois University at Carbondale, explains: "I don't know if it was exactly a surprise, but the biggest adjustment I had to make was simply realizing that I was a 'boss.' I wasn't fully prepared for the role and how people's expectations of me would change, or how my working relationships with individuals would change." This is not to say that you cannot have good, friendly working relationships with your staff members, but your relationships as manager and managed will tend to take on a different flavor than that of your relationships with your professional peers. You need to consider how important it is to you to be liked, as opposed to being respected as a manager. If you have tended to find most of your friends through work, you may need now to extend that circle outside your institution's walls.

If, on the other hand, you come from the outside to assume a management position in a given library, your first step before defining any new goals will be to familiarize yourself with the institution's existing mission and organizational culture, as well as with the people who will be working for you. You will need to settle into your new environment and to give people a chance to settle into the inherent change your arrival brings. You will of course have your own theories, ideas, and priorities—as well as responsibility for those imposed from above and outside. If you appear to be swooping in with a completely new agenda, however, you will undoubtedly meet with fierce resistance from existing staff. Find more on managing change in Chapter 8, but one key step for new managers is to realize that people's resistance to change often stems from a resentment of seemingly random edicts imposed from "on high." People need a compelling reason to move out of their comfortable routines, and need to feel as if they are a part of any change. Make it a point to learn from and work with your staff from the very beginning.

Realize also that the fact that your administration made the decision to hire from the outside rather than promote from within may mean that it is consciously looking for new perspectives and fresh ideas. Capitalize on this desire for change by enlisting administrative, institutional, and/or board support for your initiatives from the outset. Your goals have a greater chance of success if they receive consistent support throughout the management hierarchy of your organization.

Successful management is undoubtedly more complicated than just "doing the opposite" of what your previous less-than-competent boss used to do. A good first step, though, as you begin defining your role as a manager, is to think back to all of your experiences as someone who has been managed, inside or outside of a library environment. Identify both the role models you do, and those you do not, wish to emulate. Debbie Hackleman notes that "in some cases I learned by observing others—both what worked well and what I would choose to do differently. Observing negative examples is often quite useful."

Of course, it is always easier to identify negative experiences and to dwell on what not to do. This is a useful beginning, and you should always keep your previous managers'—and your own—missteps firmly in mind. Dwelling on the negative, however, fails to provide us with a solid foundation for deciding what *to* do, for making the decisions that help propel both our careers and institutions forward, and for establishing our own management style. The next task, therefore, involves deciding where to go and how to begin. Before implementing any changes, you will need to identify the goals for your institution, section, or department, within the larger goals of the organization, larger institution, or system. You need to provide yourself and your staff with a larger context for your work, in order to successfully define both what you do and why you do it.

Lastly, realize that, in any management situation, you will also be compared (whether favorably or unfavorably) to your predecessors. Whether comments tend to run along the lines of: "That's not how Ms. X used to do it," or: "We're so glad not to have to waste our time pleasing Mr. Y anymore," it will take staff some time to settle in and become accustomed to your way of managing things.

Remember, you are not the first person to ever face this transition—and, if you should ever leave your position, your staff will be equally as glad to explain to your successor just what she is doing differently. Do not get hung up on people's tendencies to bring up the past; libraries are long-lived institutions, and each library's history includes a long line of managers and management styles. Focus on carving out your own place and creating your own part of your institution's history.

What a Library Manager Does

The ways in which library managers spend their time of course vary among institutions and different levels of management—and in a sense, this is what this entire book is about! But there are some similarities among the roles and responsibilities of most managers. The basic job of any manager is to direct her resources and people toward accomplishing the defined goals of the institution. Higher-up managers may be responsible for defining these larger goals; section or department managers may set goals for their part of the whole in terms of the larger mission of the library; and libraries, as service institutions, need overall to define and to prioritize these goals in terms of the needs of their patrons or customers. As Cessa Vichi, a library division manager at the Josephine County Library System, Oregon, explains: "Fight for the patrons, and every decision that is made should be made because it will make it easier for the patron."

Any traditional managerial activity fits into this broad definition. You supervise and evaluate library staff in order to ensure that they work effectively to provide the services your patrons need and expect. You keep the technology and facilities in your institution humming along so that customers have a comfortable, safe, and useful place to work, as well as the tools to meet their informational needs. You help create a culture of customer service, realizing that your approach and that of your employees goes a long way toward creating an atmosphere in which you can effectively serve your community. The way in which you manage people largely defines their attitudes toward their work, which in turn defines how smoothly the organization (or your part of it) runs. You hold the authority to make decisions within your institution, and are responsible for making those decisions in the way that will best accomplish institutional goals. You are responsible for ranking the importance of various activities in terms of these goals, for prioritizing goals themselves, and for allocating resources (including staff and money) to best accomplish library goals.

Women in Management

Although librarianship is still a female-dominated profession, many observers have noted that men hold a disproportionate number of administrative positions, that they tend to receive higher compensation than women in the field, and that subfields of the profession with a higher concentration of male workers tend to be higher-paid. These discrepancies are beginning to change in some subsets of the profession; female Association of Research Libraries (ARL) directors, for example, now make slightly more than their male counterparts, although there are fewer of them overall. This change in the salary structure of the top positions at large research institutions, however, fails to extend to other management positions and library environments.

Female library managers can network with others to work to conquer these and other challenges. ALA's Library Administration and Management Association (LAMA, at http://www.ala.org/lama), for example, has a women administrator's discussion group. ALA also has a Committee on the Status of Women in Librarianship (COSWL), which has among its goals that of helping women advance into managerial positions, and maintains a Feminist Task Force. Although still underrepresented, especially in "top" jobs, relative to their presence in the profession, women make up an ever-increasing proportion of those in library management positions. This in turn results in an ever-increasing number of other female managers with whom you can network. You can also network with female managers in other professions; there are a number of organizations for professional women that will help you.

Women are also more likely to face interruption of their careers for family reasons. The lower pay in librarianship relative to that in many other professions means that (mainly but not exclusively) female librarians may be more likely to take time for child care, elder care, and other personal responsibilities than will their more highly paid nonlibrary partners. Work to create the same flexibility and opportunity for your staff as you would appreciate from your institution. Be open to job sharing, flexible schedules, and telecommuting options, when the type of position and an individual's personality and work ethic make these ideas a reasonable possibility. A number of library responsibilities can be effectively carried out off-site, including functions such as collection development and Web design. Libraries that fail to support flexible work options risk losing some of their best employees. Further, be supportive of pay equity efforts; do not dismiss them now that your own salary has increased with the assumption of your managerial duties.

Some argue that women have a distinct managerial style, that their ways of interacting with people inevitably differ from the "male" style of management and communication. Depending on who you read, you will find arguments that female styles of management are either a better or a less effective way of managing. Remember that you will need to develop your own style—as appropriate to your organizational culture, your staff, your own personality, and your library's goals.

Nonlibrarians as Library Managers

Non-MLS holders face particular challenges as library managers. Those new to the library environment may find that, although their existing managerial skills are transferable, it still takes time to understand and fit into the library world. Paraprofessional mid-level managers may encounter a prejudice for the MLS among degreed administrators and other department heads.

Non-MLS (or any) library managers must develop a deep understanding of the functions of their institution, especially of the particular section or project for which they are responsible. As one manager survey respondent stresses: "I think it is essential for a library manager to know the basics of the functions he or she is managing. For example, I wasn't familiar with the specific tool my cataloger used at my last job, but at least I knew cataloging, so I could help her when needed and know when she was or wasn't doing her job." You need to understand the work your staff is doing in order to properly evaluate whether they are doing this work well and efficiently. The process of developing this insight may be as simple as taking the time to observe and ask questions, or it may take some reading or coursework, depending on your situation and background. While MLS librarians value the degree, they also generally value experience and expertise. The best way to impart that value and to elicit their respect is by example.

Paraprofessional Managers

Paraprofessional managers occupy a unique place in a library's hierarchy. Although you may fill a managerial position that appears in an equivalent level on an organization chart as your MLS peers, you may have a more difficult time promoting your ideas to those administrators that have an unconscious (or even stated) preference for the degree—and you may receive a lower salary. This observation is not intended to rekindle the ongoing debate over the value of the MLS, but rather to make you aware of some of the issues you might face as a paraprofessional manager in many library environments.

If your organization will help cover the costs of a degree and you can see a clear career path for yourself, you can consider going back to school and earning your MLS. The fantastic combination of a library degree and your previous library and management experience should equate to higher salaries and more options in your future, if you intend to stay in the library field. Many librarian managers got their start in paraprofessional positions and then earned the degree after working in the field for a number of years, enabling them to move up and to advance their careers in library management.

In any case, realize that library school, while it may prepare people to be librarians, rarely prepares them for a career in management. Your MLS counterparts have no particular advantage *as managers.* The library skills and outlook that help create a good library manager, further, are by no means unique to degree holders.

Volunteer Managers

You may be entering a library management position in a small and/or remote library as a volunteer manager, on a full- or part-time basis, without specific library experience—and without compensation! Much of the information in this book will also be applicable in a volunteer situation, but you will need to adapt any advice, as appropriate, to smaller libraries and to your unique circumstances. As a volunteer manager, you also may be responsible for all library activities, from organizing a collection, to checking out materials, to managing others. Non-MLS library managers thrown into or assuming one of these library management positions should investigate Dave Sutton's *So You're Going to Run a Library: A Library Management Primer*, which is a useful guide for any manager new to libraries, especially in small institutions.

If you are a volunteer manager, congratulations on feeling so strongly about the value of libraries that you are willing to donate your time and effort to keeping one going (or starting one) in your community or in your institution. One of your first steps should be to try to find a more experienced library manager to serve as your mentor and to help answer your inevitable questions about both librarianship and management. Again, here, a willingness to learn and to grow in your position will serve you well. Part of being a good volunteer manager may also include inspiring others to volunteer, as well as constructively directing and praising their energies. (See the section on managing volunteers in Chapter 4.)

Nonlibrarians (New to Libraries)

If you enter library management from another profession, you may be taken aback by the amount of controversy the appointment of a nonlibrarian to a library administrative—especially a director—position in a larger institution can cause. This can be especially difficult if you begin calling yourself or are hired as a "librarian." (This is much less of an issue at the numerous small and/or rural public libraries in the U.S. that are staffed entirely with non-MLS personnel.)

As a non-MLS administrator, realize that you have walked into an ongoing argument about the importance of the MLS degree. Some of the professionals who have spent the time, money, and effort to earn a master's in library and information science feel strongly about the value of the degree, pointing out that non-M.D.s who work in doctor's offices are never called doctors; public school employees without degrees and certification are not considered qualified to work as teachers. Institutions that call nondegree holders "librarians" and award them with administrative posts, in this view, merely contribute to an erosion of the value of the MLS degree. This feeling is exacerbated by a general public perception that all library workers are "librarians" and questions such as: "You have to have a master's degree for this?!" as well as an ongoing internecine argument about the value of the degree and about the quality and rigor of some graduate programs. Your assumption of an administrative position can stir up all of these feelings and arguments, but realizing that the tension stems from a number of factors can help you take criticism less personally and prepare yourself to field people's concerns.

If there seems to be an argument or an undercurrent of feeling among staff that you are less entitled to your position due to your lack of an MLS (or even your lack of a library background), you may begin to feel defensive about your ability to do the job. This is a situation in which you will do best by expressing your willingness to learn from your staff. As Mary Pergander, Head Librarian, Lake Bluff Public Library, Illinois, notes of her pre-MLS management experiences: "I did not know as much about libraries as my staff did. I trusted them to teach me, they trusted me to lead them. It worked out fine." Although you may understand the basic similarities among the duties involved in administrative positions in different environments, only time will demonstrate your ability to serve effectively as a *library* administrator. Acknowledging the strengths and knowledge base of your employees, while also demonstrating the unique perspective and skills you bring to your position, is the best combination to begin winning over your staff. Any good manager learns from her staff in any environment; you will need to do so more overtly, and will need to rely on your professional staff in areas where your knowledge is lacking.

Make a point of learning about the issues that affect today's libraries. Keep up to date, for example, by reading Weblogs and library news sites each morning. Start with major resources such as the LISNews.com Weblog and general journals like *American Libraries* (http://www.ala.org/alonline) and *Library Journal* (http://www.libraryjournal.com), each of which posts breaking library-related news stories online. (Note that Weblogs, such as

LISNews.com, tend to pick up on stories several days—or weeks—before more traditional journals, and be willing to turn to a variety of sources to remain up-to-date.) Then, branch out further to include a couple of resources in your library's area of specialty. See the section on lifelong learning later in this chapter for further suggestions.

Librarians value information and the informed. Your interest in issues important to the field will help you assimilate into the library culture. As one respondent to the staff survey states: "My current manager does not have an MLS, nor does he have much knowledge of libraries. While I do appreciate his dedication to his work and his willingness to take action, I wish he would take more opportunities to understand and observe our work." Also be sure to join relevant local and national associations and to network with other managers, library workers, and librarians. (More on networking can be found in Chapter 10.)

Managing Yourself

Beyond this commitment to learning, there are also a number of personal qualities that will help you become a better manager—as well as those you should try to curb.

Habits and patterns to overcome include:

- Procrastination. Many libraries are able to hum along for quite a while even when some managerial tasks are put off, masking the fact that their internal foundations are crumbling. Do not let a façade of well being allow you to put off potentially unpleasant tasks such as managing conflicts or making needed budget cuts.

- Impatience. Although in certain situations impatience can be quite useful in getting tasks done on a timely fashion, it has little value when dealing with library staff. As Amanda E. Standerfer, Library Director, Helen Matthes

Library, Effingham, Illinois, suggests: "I would tell a new library manager to be patient. Not everything is going to work out in the first few months or years. I wanted to fix everything right away, and it just wasn't possible." (Find more on implementing gradual change in Chapter 8.)

- Defensiveness. New managers sometimes develop an unfortunate tendency to take comments personally, or to jump to lay blame on others. While defensiveness may grow out of uneasiness in your new position, your staff will be more concerned about your behavior than the reasons behind your actions. Accept that you will make mistakes; be willing to take blame as well as credit and to learn from your errors.

- Miscommunication. Effective communication goes beyond communicating clearly and providing staff with pertinent information, and includes watching your own behavior and communication style. There is no room for sarcasm toward your staff, for example.

Habits to cultivate include:

- Listening. (Find more on listening and communication in Chapter 5.) You need to pay attention to, and learn from, your staff, peers, customers, and administration. As Kari Baumann, Branch Manager, Centennial Park Branch Library, Greeley, Colorado, says: "I think the most important thing any new manager can do is to listen—to her staff, and to library staff that she doesn't supervise—to understand the organization as a whole."

- Assertiveness and self-confidence. Many new library managers have difficulty transitioning, not only into dealing with staff as a manager rather than as a peer, but into dealing with their own bosses and colleagues in a self-confident and effective manner. Take charge from the beginning. Start out as you mean to continue. Understand the power that you have in the organization, and do not be reluctant to use it to influence people and influence change in your library. (Although do not take this as a license to use your power capriciously!) Librarians with a tendency to be less extroverted can find this more difficult, but a certain level of assertiveness is necessary in order to maintain your influence in the organization.

- A willingness to be proactive. Why wait for problems to pile up or for complaints to find you? Look for ways to improve library service, working conditions for staff, workflow, or funding, and then act on achieving your goals in these areas.

- Communication. Find more on this in Chapter 5, but realize here the importance of maintaining open and frequent communication with anyone you supervise—or report to.

- Lifelong learning. See more on this later in this chapter; no library manager can afford to stagnate in her position.

People skills are essential to any effective manager—especially in libraries!—and much of the discussion here and throughout the book reflects that fact. Of course people skills are also important in most subfields of librarianship, but they are especially necessary for managers in any library setting, type, or department.

Charting a Management Path

The earlier you start consciously charting your career path as a library manager, the more successful you will be in your career as a whole. Some schools are proactively meeting the concerns of students seeking additional education in the management aspects of library science. If you are just joining the profession (or currently hold a paraprofessional management position), and you have a clear vision of a library career path that includes management, you can investigate graduate library and information science programs that offer a heavier emphasis on the administrative side of the field. Several schools now have joint programs that offer a heavier exposure to the management aspects of librarianship; Kent State and UCLA, for example, each offer a joint MLIS/MBA degree program, which can be especially useful to those whose career goals include management of a very large institution. Find more on creating and working toward career goals as a library manager in Chapter 13.

Mentors and Role Models

Earlier, the discussion focused on deciding whom *not* to emulate during your career as a library manager. Equally, if not more important, are the qualities of those you do choose to emulate. If you have lacked good managerial role models in your career so far, you can consider enrolling in a formal mentoring program—either within your own institution, or one sponsored by a library-related or other organization. Alternatively, seek out more informal mentors—online, through networking at local events, through contacting people writing on issues that interest you. Seek out expertise wherever it lies, and be willing to ask your mentors for their support and help.

Realize also that it can be useful to find multiple mentors to help you with the various facets of and different decisions involved in your position. Everyone has his or her own area of expertise, and a mentor can be anyone with experience or knowledge that you lack. Author and Webmaster Priscilla Shontz advises: "Find yourself some good mentors, either at your organization or elsewhere. This is important in any position, but in a management position you can sometimes feel very alone—especially if you manage a small library where you are the only manager. It can be incredibly helpful to have friends, mentors, and colleagues to whom you can turn when you have a question (especially as a new manager) or when you just need to vent! For example, if you manage a branch library, you may want to develop relationships with other branch managers, so that you can ask for advice when facing a decision or problem." Kari Baumann suggests that new managers "find a mentor to help show you the ropes in your organization and give you pointers on management skills."

Lifelong Learning

Most library managers tend to feel inadequately prepared by library school or by other formal education for their first management positions. While some were actually pleased by their management coursework, especially those from schools with a strong business component, other respondents to the manager survey shared comments such as:

- "All of my management experience was gained on the job."

- "Everything I learned I learned during working and hands on. Library school was nice but it only gave me the theoretical approaches … not the real nitty-gritty day-to-day grind and sweat needed to operate a library in a truly professional and successful manner."

- "I don't think the school could have prepared me better for management because I didn't view myself then as ever wanting to go into management."

- "'Administration of Libraries' was a complete waste of time. The professor was approaching retirement and had not worked in a library for at least 25 years. I learned about Industrial Age theories of management, but absolutely nothing practical. I had learned more on the job as a paraprofessional!"

- "I took an administration class and it was very theoretical. It didn't even cover how to do performance reviews, the hiring process, or the firing process. My suggestion would be to hire an instructor that is actually a director or assistant director. It would be much more effective to teach us managerial skills through real-world examples."

- "My library school experience dealt with nuts and bolts and theory of working in a library. There was no training on working with personalities (staff, patrons, board members, etc.) or the business aspects of running a library."

- "Not one class in library school prepared me for library management."

- "I feel that library school did not adequately prepare me for management responsibilities. There should be more opportunities in library school to learn about supervising others, basic HR policies (librarians should at least learn enough so that they know when to go to the HR person), and budgeting."

- "The course I took was very heavy on the history of management and very light on any practical information or practices. Although theory certainly should inform our practice, teaching theory exclusively (or almost exclusively) was a disservice to the students."

A one- or two-year graduate program, of course, can be hard pressed to fit in all the coursework needed to prepare someone to become a librarian, let alone to teach management skills as well. However, the lack of practical information presented in even the most basic library management courses was overwhelmingly cited as a problem by manager survey respondents—and, given the predicted upcoming wave of library retirements, this should be a concern for schools charged with preparing future library managers to fill these anticipated upper-level vacancies. Many respondents to the manager survey suggested that more hands-on courses would have been useful, especially those incorporating role-playing, job-shadowing, and/or presentations and advice from actual working managers in different library settings. Others suggested internships or other real-world activities.

A number of library managers do take advantage of continuing education opportunities to fill in the gaps left by their alma maters, or to build up their skills in specific areas. As a manager, you will likely need to take responsibility for your own ongoing learning and professional development. There may be no one above you that will suggest you take a class, attend a conference, or otherwise push yourself professionally, whereas as a nonmanagement librarian you may have been used to your supervisor suggesting (or requiring) that you engage in these activities. Never fall into the trap of assuming that, because you have progressed to a certain point in your career, you need no further professional development. (Find some specific examples of professional development opportunities in Chapter 13.)

Realize also that more official professional development activities such as workshops and meetings serve as excellent networking as well as professional development opportunities, and can keep you energized and focused on your career and your profession. Cessa Vichi, a library division manager at the Josephine County Library System, says: "Attending any training is always beneficial for ideas, new ways of looking at old problems, inspiration and growth as a leader. As a leader, the responsibility for organizational/division growth falls on you. New ideas, fresh input, and different approaches are vital to learning and growing as a leader."

You can locate official professional development and management training opportunities in a variety of ways, from reading your local library system's newsletter to attending ALA conferences. Also, be open to learning through your professional reading. Professional development includes all of your lifelong learning, from reading to on-the-job experience. Lifelong learning means precisely that: learning through all of your experiences, whether planned or not.

Some Suggested Sources for Reading on Management Issues

ALA's Library Administration and Management Association (LAMA) offers a free e-mail publication, "Leads From LAMA." To sign up, go to http://www. ala.org/lama and select LAMA Publications, then Leads From LAMA. You need not be a LAMA member to subscribe.

From Emerald, library managers can sign up for Emerald Now: free, biweekly, topical e-mail updates on management issues. Each issue includes free guest access to their selected "journals of the week," several selected thematic articles, book reviews, Web sites, and so on. Subscribe at http://www.emeraldinsight.com/ now.

Sign up for monthly updates from the Informed Librarian at http://www.informedlibrarian.com. Each issue links to the latest issue of a number of library and information-related publications that are available at least in part online; many offer free access. A limited version is available for free, or pay for premium access to receive information on an increased number of journals, guest articles, book reviews, and so on.

The Journal of Academic Librarianship publishes periodic guides to the professional literature. Topics have included management, information ethics, marketing, censorship, and other issues of particular interest to academic library managers.

Library Administration & Management published an annotated library management bibliography in their summer 2002 and winter 2003 issues, focusing on heavily cited classics. Find it in LAMA/LOMS Comparative Library Organization Committee (CLOC) and CLOC Bibliography Task Force, "Required Reading for Library Administrators: An Annotated Bibliography of Influential Authors and Their Works," in *Library Administration & Management* 16:3 (Summer 2002): 126–136 and 17:1 (Winter 2003): 11–20.

Library Management also publishes a yearly annotated and subject-organized roundup of the library-related management literature each fall, which you can look into as part of your aim to keep current. Note a mild U.K. focus, as well as a preference for peer-reviewed literature, however. The management literature for 2002, for example, was covered in fall 2003 in Patricia Layzell Ward, "Management and the Management of Information, Knowledge Based, and Library Services 2002," *Library Management* 24:3 (2003): 126–159. Ward is editor of *Library Management* and coauthor of *Management Basics for Information Professionals*. Note that this yearly roundup excludes monographs and Web sites.

See additional suggestions of current awareness Web sites earlier in this chapter, and be sure to peruse additional resources in your particular area of management (systems, collections, etc.).

Always try to think beyond your current job, and about how you can learn, grow, and move forward in your library career. Take advantage of professional development and networking opportunities. Look at these not as an imposition on your time, but as an opportunity to reenergize, learn, and open to new possibilities. Libraries, especially today, do not remain stagnant—you need to stretch yourself to keep up! Warren Bennis and Robert Thomas note: "The ability to learn is a defining characteristic of being human; the ability to continue learning is an essential skill of leadership. When leaders lose that ability, they inevitably falter. When any of us lose that ability, we no longer grow."[2]

As a librarian, you possess an inherent advantage over managers in other types of organizations. A major task of any manager is to identify and assimilate the information that will help her do her job. Who better to take on that task than information professionals? The only difference here is that, instead of compiling this information on behalf of your patrons, you are doing so for yourself and as is relevant in your own context. Most managers are made, not born, and you can use your library skills to help make your own way.

Notes

1. Dr. Seuss, *If I Ran the Zoo* (New York: Random House, 1950, 1978) 2.

2. Warren G. Bennis and Robert J. Thomas, *Geeks and Geezers: How Era, Values, and Defining Moments Shape Leaders* (Boston: Harvard Business School Press, 2002) 1.

Recommended Reading

Caputo, Janette S. *The Assertive Librarian.* Phoenix: Oryx Press, 1984.

Cooke, D. M. "Library management from A to Z." *Book Report,* March/April 1991: 13–15.

Evans, G. Edward and Patricia Layzell Ward. *Beyond the Basics: The Management Guide for Library and Information Professionals.* New York: Neal-Schuman, 2003.

Evans, G. Edward, Patricia Layzell Ward, and Bendik Rugaas. *Management Basics for Information Professionals.* New York: Neal-Schuman, 2000.

Hildenbrand, Suzanne. "Still Not Equal: Closing the Library Gender Gap." *Library Journal,* March 1, 1997: 44–46.

Hill, Linda A. *Becoming a Manager: Mastery of a New Identity.* Boston: Harvard Business School, 1992.

Howard, Joanna. *Managing More With Less.* Oxford: Butterworth-Heinemann, 1998.

Info Career Trends. Nov. 1, 2003. Special issue on library management <http://www.lisjobs.com/newsletter/archives/text/nov03.txt>. 25 April, 2004.

Info Career Trends. Jan. 2, 2004. Special issue on balancing work and family <http://www.lisjobs.com/newsletter/archives/text/jan04.txt>. 25 April, 2004.

Pymm, Bob and Damon D. Hickey. *Learn Library Management.* Lanham, MD: Scarecrow Press, 2003.

Sutton, Dave. *So You're Going to Run a Library: A Library Management Primer.* Englewood, CO: Libraries Unlimited, 1995.

Todaro, Julie. "What's a New Manager To Do?" *Library Administration & Management* 15:4 (Fall 2001): 249–251.

White, Herbert S. "Library Managers -- Female and Male." *Library Journal,* Feb. 1, 1987: 58–59.

Chapter 2

Levels of Management

Management is the art of maintaining direction while managing chaos.

Joan Giesecke[1]

While library managers of all types share some similar responsibilities, your place in your institution's particular hierarchy (or lack thereof) will necessarily impact both your job duties and aspects of your management style. The following descriptions outline the differing responsibilities at some of the most common levels of management in libraries. Job titles will vary by institution from what is presented here; some, for example, prefer to call department heads team leaders, while some, instead of hiring library directors, prefer to employ administrators, managing librarians, or head librarians. The specific title matters less than the responsibilities of your position, although sometimes job titles indicate the management philosophy of the institution's administration. Those hiring "team leaders," for instance, pretty clearly demonstrate a preference for a team-based style of management. Thinking about the language used in job ads and descriptions and about these institutional priorities can be helpful in targeting your efforts when applying for or settling into a new managerial position.

You may during your management career fill positions at one or more of these levels. You will move up, down, or laterally as your own circumstances change. (See more on stepping back and moving up in Chapter 13.) In each position you fill, even before entering library management, you will acquire skills that will serve you well in all of your future jobs. As Northeast State Community

College Librarian, Blourtville, Tennessee, Chrissie Anderson Peters states, "Every library position I have had in my 10 years in the field has done something to prepare me for each job that came after it. And I'm immensely thankful for that fact." Another manager survey respondent explains that: "I've held just about every library job there is in just about every type of library. They all helped prepare me [for management] because I learned first-hand the issues that staff have to deal with day to day." Successful managers build creatively on their existing skills and experiences, while always being open to new ideas and learning. As Frank Herbert writes in *Dune*, "... every experience carries its lesson." The key lies in understanding these lessons and integrating them into our everyday activities as library managers.

Whatever level of management you find yourself propelled into—or settling at—the combination of your mastery of management skills and your commitment to the principles of librarianship is the key to your success. Even before you become a manager, learning the best ways to manage yourself, your own performance, and your relationships with both your coworkers and your managers will help you to stand out and to move confidently up the library career ladder. And, no matter your level of management, you play an important role in making the library an effective organization and comfortable workplace for all. Kathryn L. Corcoran, Library Services Director, Munson-Williams-Proctor Arts Institute Utica, New York, explains: "Even if you never become a head librarian or a department head, you may end up managing a project, becoming an interim or temporary manager, or managing student employees or volunteers. Or you will need management skills in your involvement in professional organizations (committee chair, conference planning, etc.)."

At any level, let your previous skills, knowledge, and experiences guide you. As Joan Magretta notes: "Unlike most other professions—law or medicine or accounting, for example—you don't need a license to practice management. In fact, it's the only field we can think of where practice precedes formal training."[2] One respondent to the staff survey also emphasizes: "This is probably the one remaining profession in which being a generalist is the best thing you can do. Learn about as many different areas of knowledge as you can. They can be applicable in library work and management at the most interesting times!" So, take heart—accidental managers abound in any profession, but your library skills and background give you the edge here.

Directors

Congratulations—you run the zoo! Well, sort of. Every director is responsible to her larger institution and community, as well as to a board, dean, or other set of bosses. (See Chapter 10 for more on interacting with these various groups.) Directors, however, assume the main responsibility for daily planning, institutional decision making, and the ongoing operations of their library or library system. More than other library managers, you will be responsible for setting the course for your institution as a whole, as well as for budgeting, maintaining staff morale, and more political functions such as fundraising and marketing.

As an accidental director, you may assume an administrative position at a smaller or rural library right out of library school, or have a directorship land in your lap due to the unexpected departure of your previous administrator. In smaller libraries, you may retain many front-line librarian and/or clerical tasks, while also taking on the responsibility of running the institution as a whole. ALA and other professional organizations are predicting an upcoming wave of director-level retirements within the next 10 to 15 years; even if you have not intended to move into a director-level position, you may have an opportunity to do so in the near future.

Interview with Meredith Goins
Meredith P. Goins is an MIS librarian
in Knoxville, Tennessee.

Please explain how you became a director right out of library school. Had you had any previous management experience?

It was sheer luck, my personality, and my drive to succeed. My best friend from undergrad school, Stacy Dunevant, had moved back to her small-town home (Roxboro, North Carolina), which was in need of a library director. They had advertised for two months straight, with no applications. I had fond memories of going home to her house during Christmas and spring breaks and thought it would be a good place. It didn't help that Stacy's twin brother Steve was my husband's best friend and former roommate, either! Stacy's father, a former county commissioner and church deacon, was well-known and respected in the community, and was happy to give me a reference. The job also had the interesting perk of offering free housing for the library director, a three-bedroom, two-bathroom brick rancher, that was willed to the library for this specific purpose ... and the county maintained the house—what a dream!

I had no previous "formal" management experience, but was responsible for supervising and training student workers in my previous positions before becoming Library Director.

What advice would you have for others in similar situations?

When they tell you to network, they mean it! Not only did it help me find a job, it helped me start my own "support circle" of like-minded librarians that could help with the various problems that arose. I became friends with my direct supervisor, the county manager, and would often go to him for advice on how to handle situations. I think it flattered him to help me succeed. I also became very active in the community, a must for new folks in small towns. Anything that could possibly benefit the library, I was a part of:

Smart Start: learned of resources in the community and teamed with them to become a resource center. Because of this, they funded a Hispanic collection for all ages, including a one-hour bilingual story time every week.

Kiwanis Club: helped fund programs in the library and gave me a free outlet to advertise our programs.

Council for Women: helped identify powerful women in the community that I could model after.

The local newspaper: we received a free page every other week in the "B" section, in which we promoted our programs, listed new items received, shared book reviews and explained our policies, outlined new programs and introduced our staff. Cheaper than a newsletter, and easier too! The newspaper benefited because they needed to fill space, and it made it easy on the staff!

Other county department heads: I befriended those that would mutually benefit from our services; the health department and social services were two biggies. Both loved to display our items, and I could donate withdrawn items or book sale items to their special-needs areas (homeless shelters, foster children programs, etc.).

Get involved in your library organizations, local, state and national—the best support group you will ever find!

Did you feel that library school prepared you adequately for your director position? What else could your school have done to help prepare you?

I believe University of Tennessee, Knoxville prepared me well for my directorship. I especially was grateful for my public relations and grant-writing electives I took, a must for all libraries. Most that go into librarianship are analytical and organized, a must for all directors.

However, I could have used training in filling out E-Rate forms, and how to handle unimaginable circumstances such as finding two 12-year-olds having sex in our foyer ... I guess I should have had a class in social work, too!

What was particularly challenging about your position?

One challenge I faced was bigotry, which I was not prepared for. I had lived in the South my entire life, but I had never seen it first hand. I had white staff members who would not help African-American or Hispanic patrons because "they didn't deserve help." I gave a verbal warning when it was brought to my attention, but that brought out more of the same. I had the county manager discuss this with one woman, who said I couldn't understand because I was the "big city girl" who didn't know how small towns work. I do have to say I had a difficult time with that person the rest of my career there. However, the county manager suggested we remove the person from the bookmobile and into cataloging so that she had less interaction with the public. When given that option, she was thrilled and grabbed the opportunity gratefully. I don't care what a staff member believes when they are at home, but when they are in the library or representing the library, all humans, races, religions, sexes, etc., have equal rights!

I also had to fire my first and last person, our children's librarian that just stopped showing up. That was a lot harder to do than I thought, but healthier for the library. In return, we hired an energetic, creative, eager, always-there librarian, who is still there, even after I left. Personnel issues take much more time than you could ever believe. When you think you have everything figured out, someone throws a curveball at you and you have to reconfigure the library all over again!

What was particularly rewarding about your position?

Canceling a retired teachers' meeting and taking over our meeting room on September 11, 2001, so I could open it up to the public so they could watch what was happening. (We received over 1,000 reference requests in three days during that time period. Most folks wanted to know how they could help and how they could locate their relatives.) Becoming *the* place to get information during such a traumatic event meant that folks began to realize how important the public library was in that small, 38,000 population community ... and I had only been there a little over a year!

I also remember a boy that had just graduated from high school. He asked me to sign his yearbook because I didn't give up on him. He's now a lawyer and still e-mails me to thank me for letting him play on the computer (where he applied for financial aid and college, and

received both!) and all of our teen books and magazines. That is why I do what I do. I've made a difference,
and it makes me want to continue!

*Do you have any hints for those managing staff mem-
bers significantly older than themselves?*

This was one of the hardest things I had to overcome. I had to watch my language so that I didn't use
age-biased terms, which is harder than it sounds. I had
to modify job duties so that lifting, stooping, and carrying were minimized. I had to have the entire library
tested for mold due to a threat of a lawsuit because the
person had worked there 20 years and swore we were
responsible for her allergies. (We weren't; she was aller-
gic to the trees at her house ... we even paid for her
allergy testing and all the mold testing!)

I was also the only college-educated staff member, which
the older staff felt resentful of. They didn't understand that
cataloging was more than just downloading records from
the Baker & Taylor site ... that you don't just buy the first 90
books you see so you spend your part of the collection
development money. It was really difficult explaining why
we were weeding ... but they did know everyone in town,
and there was good customer service constantly.

*Is there anything else you would like to share about
first-time library directorship?*

Stop the gossiping from the staff the first day you get
there. It's evil and will undermine everything you do. I
am of the philosophy of informing the staff as much as
possible, so that they can better make decisions on their
own, empowering them to do a better job.

Many accidental library directors assume their first director-level positions in small libraries, in many cases as the only professional employee. Directing one of these smaller institutions, especially right out of school, can be a challenge—but an exciting one. Remember that you have a lot to learn from your library's long-term employees, whether degreed or not.

Assistant Directors

In many institutions, assistant (or associate) directors find themselves in an odd limbo between administration and middle management. As an assistant director, you may be groomed to take over the director position when yours retires or moves on. You may be part of the administrative team: attending board meetings; engaging in long-range planning; raising funds; managing building or other large-scale projects.

Assistant directors often have responsibility for building maintenance (see Chapter 7) and/or supervise department heads. They can serve as the liaison between the director and other upper-level management and library staff, so communication skills are particularly important. In larger institutions, multiple assistant directors will specialize in various areas such as budgeting or technology; in smaller libraries, one assistant director suffices. Effective assistant directors possess similar skills to both directors and department heads.

Department Heads

Now you are responsible for your own little corner of the zoo—which you may think of as the monkey house, the snake pit, or whatever analogy strikes your fancy and suits your situation. As a department head, you are responsible for the smooth running of a section of your larger institution, as well as for its interactions with other departments in the pursuit of the library's common goals. You can in one sense think of the other department heads in your library as comanagers, dividing up responsibility for the various sections and functions of your institution. This requires an ability to cooperate with other departments and managers in working toward a common purpose, and an understanding of how the different departments work together in keeping the institution going.

Joan Giesecke, management expert and author, discusses the importance of department heads and other middle managers in libraries, saying: "Today's middle managers are crucial for holding the organization together. This group helps tie frontline staff to top management. You provide the working leadership for the organization, helping to translate the overall organizational vision into the work of the department, unit, or team. You help link your group to the other units in the organization."[2] One of department heads' and other middle managers' primary roles is that of liaison, making their communication and people skills essential. (See more on communication in Chapter 5.)

In addition to creating these linkages, department heads will have similar responsibilities to those of a director, just on a smaller scale. You will need to plan the direction of your department, define its goals, manage its budget, and so on. To be successful in a department head position, you also need the ability to advocate for your own department and your own people, especially in conjunction with the library's larger mission. You will need to get funding for services, argue for raises for your employees, and get them the tools they need to do their jobs effectively. You will need always to balance the needs of your staff with those of the larger institution. As Debbie Hackleman says: "Middle management is a difficult position—representing and supporting your staff is sometimes at odds with representing and supporting the upper levels of administration."

Department heads and other library middle managers must learn when to delegate up. When you lack the direct power to make a decision or to get funding for a particular program, you will need to enlist the support of your library's director, of others further up the organizational chart, or of those with unofficial power within the organization. This is one reason to cultivate productive relationships with all different levels of colleagues and to promote your department's and staff's accomplishments to your own supervisors.

Supervisors

Some library managers can find themselves given management responsibilities without a concomitant increase in salary, or change in job title. This can happen in a number of different ways. You may be assigned an assistant, or asked to take responsibility for scheduling student workers, or assume budgetary responsibilities for technology as you begin working more heavily with library computer systems. You may assume temporary management responsibilities when a manager leaves or retires.

If this happens to you, try not to feel intimidated about asking for a new job description, title, or salary. Your ability to carry out your new management duties effectively will create a clear basis for your request. You need to look after yourself as well as your job duties and your employees, and, if your duties have changed, your job description and salary should reflect that change. One manager survey respondent shares her experience: "Our branch librarian retired and I was the only one with an MLS at the library. ... At the same time, I was a Librarian I, which was lowest on the librarian pay scale. ... The Administration would not call me a manager, but a Librarian in Charge, in order not to pay me anything extra for my assumed duties." Another notes: "It certainly makes it easier to lobby for a greater salary increase if you have a job title that implies you are in charge."

Your responsibilities for your staff and other specific responsibilities as a permanent supervisor will to a great extent mirror those of a department head, although you may not manage a budget or carry out other department-level functions. Other supervisors are never formally assigned a supervisory role, but share similar duties to those managers in formal supervisory positions. Your responsibilities here mirror those of other middle managers in libraries, and you can use your supervisory position as a way to see how you can settle into management, learn whether you wish to work up the career ladder from here, and so on.

Co-Managers

Some libraries have begun using management models in which two (or more) managers share complementary responsibilities for a particular department, section, or project. This idea of shared leadership mirrors the practice of working in teams, recognizing the unique strengths of individuals and the usefulness of being able to balance those strengths with others in pursuit of particular goals. Co-managing also gives you someone to bounce ideas off of and to share responsibilities with, so that you feel less overwhelmed by your managerial duties.

Interview with Valerie Viers
Valerie Viers is an academic librarian at Ripon College

Could you explain the type of co-managerial position you are in, and how it came about?
We started out as a three-person managerial team in the summer of 2002 when our director took another position. She recommended that the three of us work

together in a co-directorship until the college was in a better financial position to hire a director. Our college's financial situation improved the next year, but the arrangement was working so well that we recommended keeping it. When our dean asked us to find out what kinds of management models other academic libraries were using, we asked around and found many interesting arrangements at other schools. We finally recommended a library governing committee with a rotating library department chair. Having a designated chair satisfied the need to have a departmental contact person and someone who would be in a position to make tough decisions when there was lack of consensus among the committee members.

What are some of the challenges of your co-director position?

One of the biggest challenges in the beginning was finding out what work had to be done and who should do what. After the first year, it was much easier to delegate tasks. We wanted to make sure everyone on the team had experience in all aspects of the directorship.

What kind of support do you lend each other?

We bounce ideas off of each other when we have to make decisions concerning our respective departments. We also evaluate each other at the end of each academic year and offer support and constructive criticism.

How do you feel that co-managing has worked out in your institution? What are some ways in which others might successfully implement co-management positions?

I think it has worked very well and the larger college community seems to be very pleased with our arrangement.

I think successful implementation of a co-directorship requires flexibility on the part of all those involved, especially in the beginning. You're put in a new situation and it takes a year or so to settle into it. As with all relationships, good communication with your co-directors is critical. If you don't meet and talk regularly about new issues and tasks that have come up, you may find that they're either not getting done or that one person is doing all of them. An additional benefit of all this base-touching is that you get support you probably wouldn't have if you were the sole person in charge.

Steve McKinzie wrote a wonderful article on the management system they had at Dickinson College: http://www.webpages.uidaho.edu/~mbolin/mckinzie.htm. I would especially recommend his paragraph on rotating departmental responsibilities.

Is there anything else you would like to share about working effectively as a co-manager?

Learn to recognize and work with your colleagues' strengths and weaknesses. Delegating tasks to someone knowing they will excel at and enjoy it is satisfying for all involved. Helping people push their limits is a more challenging, and more rewarding, skill. Learning this balance is very important in any managerial situation: Help your colleagues grow without expecting them to be something they're not.

You may also find yourself in a flex-time or job-share managerial position, where you and another person each work part time and share management responsibilities, effectively splitting a job down the middle. These arrangements require a special commitment to communication and the willingness to present a consistent front to staff and administrators. Job sharing a management position allows you to stay on your career track while still attending to family or other responsibilities, and you can look into this possibility at your institution should your circumstances change and you need to scale back on your full-time management position.

One Person Library (OPL) Managers

As an accidental OPL manager, you truly do run the zoo—you are it! Your main task as an OPL manager (or solo librarian) will be to find the right balance between your duties as a librarian and those as a library manager. This also can be difficult because you lack workplace colleagues to bounce ideas off of, to delegate to, or to share your workload. Networking is particularly important to OPL managers, both to exchange ideas and experiences and to combat potential feelings of professional isolation. The Special Libraries Association (SLA) has a solo librarians division and sponsors the SOLOLIB-L e-mail discussion list (http://listserv.silverplatter.com/archives/soarcmsg.html; you do not need to be a member to subscribe), while ALA's Association of Specialized and Cooperative Library Agencies (ASCLA) has an Independent Librarians' Exchange. You might also consider subscribing to *The One-Person Library: A Newsletter for Librarians and Management* (information at http://www.ibi-opl.com/newsletter). Be sure to check out local opportunities as well, such as the Chicago-Area Solo Librarians (at http://casl.chilibsys.org); sometimes there is no substitute for in-person networking.

A good chunk—an estimated one-third to one-half—of SLA members are solo librarians. This even omits nonmembers and those in noncorporate environments. So, although you may be solo, you should not feel alone.

Interview with Judith Siess

Judith Siess is publisher/editor,
The One-Person Library newsletter,
author of *The OPL Sourcebook: A Guide for Solo and Small Libraries*, and first chair, Solo Librarians Division, SLA.

Could you talk a little bit about the unique manage-ment challenges facing solo librarians?

There are eight major challenges: time management, justification of the OPL's existence, lack of support (management, personnel, or monetary), professional isolation, attracting and keeping customers in the face of the Internet, being perceived as a professional or peer, reporting to a nonlibrarian, and lack of control over one's destiny.

There are benefits, however. The OPL often does not have to go through layers of administration to get approval for purchases or new programs. The OPL knows exactly what is going on in his or her library: what is being checked out, the questions being asked, who is using the library, and such. The OPL is often per-ceived as the "information guru" in the organization—the one to whom everyone comes for answers. Finally, any and all successes (and, of course, failures) of the library are also those of the OPL. He or she can make of it whatever is in their vision and power.

OPLs in public libraries (nearly 80 percent of public libraries serve populations of under 25,000 and are staffed by only one professional) face unique issues such as building maintenance, raising money for new buildings, bond issues, and other related matters. OPLs in school libraries may serve two or more school libraries, with volunteers (often students) staffing the library when the librarian is not there. All professional school librarians must also have a teaching certification. They are seen as an extension of the classroom and often assist teachers with special projects as well as run the library and teach library skills to the students. Some have additional duties, such as holding story hours, teaching reading or English, providing computer instruction, advising student groups, running the bookstore, and supervising the lunchroom. Hospital OPLs may also supervise more than one facility, creating difficult time-management problems.

A major problem common to all OPLs is the continuous need to communicate your value to those who control the purse strings. This value nearly always must be expressed in dollars. I could go on for hours on ways to do this. (Read my book: *The Visible Librarian: Asserting Your Worth With Marketing and Advocacy*, Chicago: ALA Editions, 2003.)

What are some ways in which OPL managers can network with their peers? What can they gain from staying connected with colleagues in other institutions?

Networking can be informal or formal. Formal networking involves the use of established organizations. OPLs usually are small, have limited resources, and have very specialized collections. Networking is a major factor not only in reducing the OPL's feeling of professional isolation, but also in reference, document delivery, interlibrary loan, acquisitions, and continuing education. All libraries and librarians depend on the support of others. Informal networking involves contacts among personal friends, within the organization, with former colleagues, and with former fellow students. Interpersonal networking is arguably more important than its formal counterpart. We rely on contacts with other professionals to make decisions on which books to buy, which vendors to use, and which meetings to attend. We call other librarians when we have a reference question that is out of our scope or need an answer in a reference book we do not own.

Our professional societies are the best sources of networking contacts. In addition to national meetings, you can attend local meetings, which usually occur more frequently. Even if the topic is not of immediate interest to you, go to the meeting. First of all, you never know when you will need to know about outsourcing, acquisitions, or whatever the topic is this month. Secondly, you need to renew your contacts with your fellow librarians, both to maintain your own sanity and to make sure they remember you when you call with a question or request. One of my colleagues referred to a consortium meeting as a "support group." By this she meant that the members could share their complaints, fears, and concerns, feeling confident that the others understand and probably have the same feelings as she has. Talking with someone who has "been there" is frequently the only way to deal with some new frustration or challenge on the job.

Are there particular courses or resources you would recommend for potential or new OPL managers? Do you have tips on getting employers to fund professional development opportunities?

Most library schools don't even mention solo one-person librarianship, so you are unlikely to have learned all you need to know in school. What do we need to learn and how can we learn it?

Organizational culture: Observe the organization. Talk to others. Read whatever in-house documents you can find.

Management, including financial management: Take courses offered by library conferences or local or regional associations, business schools, or management professional associations. Read some of the many excellent management books available. Observe others to see both good and bad examples of management.

Communication and presentation skills: Take courses from private vendors or communications or speech departments of local colleges and universities.

Information technology: Contact your institution's computer department or consult the Web for courses from major software vendors. Don't forget courses from library schools and training offered at a very low cost by library automation and database vendors.

Library and information skills, including knowledge management, research methods, and the information audit: These are available from library schools, many via the Internet. Library associations also offer courses at their conferences, in regional locations, or through self-directed learning.

Subject knowledge: Learn this on the job from your customers, in-house seminars or sit in on courses at your local college or university.

Personal development skills, such as assertiveness, time management, and dealing with problem people: There are good and low-cost courses offered by private companies, and courses are also offered at library conferences. There are also many good books available.

To get your management to pay for continuing education (CE) you must let them know how the organization will benefit. Show how you will be able to (in order of priority): save money, save time, provide better information, serve more customers. Be prepared to make an economic case for the course. However, if your employer won't pay for a course or conference, *pay for it yourself!* Ultimately, you are the one getting the education. (And, start looking for a job where the employer *will* pay. Negotiate support for CE just after you are offered the position. Few employers will say, "oh, in that case, I won't hire you" if you ask to be sent to one conference a year.)

What advice would you have for those moving into an OPL position?

Do all of the above, then tell yourself that you are only one person and you can only do so much. Put in your required 40 hours—then go home! There's nothing wrong with taking work home or working unpaid overtime occasionally; in fact, it is a sign of a professional. However, if you regularly do so, you will never get any help. No sane employer would hire you an assistant or another librarian as long as you are "donating" your time. You are doing yourself and the profession a disservice.

Don't take your job and yourself too seriously. I've never heard of a firm going bankrupt or a law firm losing a case or a hospital patient dying because of what a librarian did. You should enjoy your job and look forward to going to work—at least most of the time. If you don't, find another job.

Is there anything else you would like to share about one-person librarianship?

It's a demanding job, but if you are a person who likes to have control over your own job, time, and destiny, being a solo is a great way to go. Personally, I never wanted to do anything else.

As the only "professional" librarian in a smaller public library or school library, you might face issues similar to those facing OPL managers, although you may have clerical staff or others to help carry out some of the tasks involved in running your library. Independent information professionals, as one-person operations, also share similar concerns—although they may not manage a facility, they hold sole responsibility for managing their own business. Associations for independent professionals include ALA's ALSCA's (Association of Special and Cooperative Library Agencies), Independent Librarian's Exchange (ILEX) Section, and Association of Independent Information Professionals (AIIP; http://www.aiip.org).

As an OPL manager, you will need, even more than other library managers, to schedule your time carefully, in order to accomplish everything necessary to the smooth running of your library. You will also need to devote extra time to marketing yourself and your library, because your nonlibrarian boss(es) may not fully understand what you do. (See more on marketing in chapters 9 and 10.) One last difficulty solo librarians face is that of promotion—there is nowhere for them to go in their own institution, and those outside their environment may have trouble recognizing their experience as managerial when it comes time to move on. It becomes your responsibility to show how your solo librarian experience transfers to other environments. As Michelle Caulk, Electronic Services Librarian, St. Charles Public Library, Illinois, explains: "I was ... a solo librarian, so I did everything from interlibrary loan to acquisitions to reference. The variety of jobs helped me with time management, which really comes in handy with supervising the aides [in my current position]."

Solo librarians, though, are in a perfect position to build exceptional relationships with their customers. If yours is the only face they see, e-mail they receive, voice they hear, your patrons will inevitably connect you with the library. By the same token, you will get to know your customers as individuals, and will be able both to provide personalized service targeted to their unique needs and wants and to respond quickly to changing circumstances, with no need to build consensus, climb through bureaucratic channels, or get coworkers on board. Solo librarians tend to get used to the independence and variety inherent in their positions, and many find it difficult to later move to a bigger institution with more levels of management, to be a smaller fish in a bigger pond. Others can bring their independent spirit and multitasking expertise to other environments and thrive.

Project Managers

You may be going along contentedly as a rank-and-file librarian, and then find yourself put in charge of completing a temporary— but large—project. Project management requires you to assume new responsibilities, and brings unique differences to your workplace role. As a project manager, you are now responsible for the work of people over whom you may not normally have authority. This can lead to some odd working situations, and can present challenges when others have trouble recognizing your new authority.

Every manager at some time also serves as a project manager, as new circumstances arise. Even if you already have management responsibilities, however, you may not be accustomed to working with a particular group of people or in a particular area, and may not currently manage the people who have been placed on (or that you have chosen for) your project team. You will also need to face the challenge of balancing your normal job duties with your new responsibilities.

Projects are generally assigned for a fixed period of time, until a certain objective is met or task is completed. You may be assigned, for example, responsibility for overseeing the implementation of a new automation system, or for setting up a literacy program in accordance with the requirements of a grant your institution has just been awarded. Complex projects of this nature often need to draw upon the skills and perspectives of individuals in various parts of the library, bringing them together to work as a team for the duration of the project. You as project manager will then have the responsibility of managing the group involved in the project, ensuring its completion on time and to specifications.

Successful project management involves a good deal of planning and patience. A typical broad (and overly simplified) project outline might look like this:

- Identify the end result (outcome) needed at the project's completion. This may be imposed from above or from without, by your administration or by the terms of a grant, for example.

- Summarize the general scope of your project. You will need to clarify exactly what your group intends to accomplish, and break this down into its specific components.

- In conjunction with your group members, clarify who will be responsible for what aspects of the project. Establish good working relationships with their usual managers.

- Make sure everyone is clear on their responsibilities and has a step-by-step outline of the project, with specific dates for completion of each stage. Emphasize how steps build upon each other and that each step relies on the successful completion of the previous step.

- As the project progresses, you as project manager will then be responsible for ensuring the deadlines are met for each step, that each team member lives up to his responsibilities, that work is done well and efficiently, and that the project completes on time and accomplishes its stated goals. Your project outline gives you a general timeline and guidelines to work from, but can be modified as necessary during the process to reflect unforeseen circumstances.

Remember learning "outlining" in school? You can approach and break down a project in the same way. Any project can be broken down into large chunks (or subdivisions), and each subdivision then further broken down, until you reach the level of very specific tasks. Subdividing your project in this manner can help you get a handle on what exactly needs to be done and who needs to do it. It makes a larger project seem much more manageable, and shows you where you need to start.

If you think more visually, try using a graphical method of plotting out the tasks and timetable involved in your project, such as a Gantt Chart or PERT Chart. You can use software such as Microsoft Project to create these, or merely a pen and paper. (Examples of both types of charts can be found online at: http://www.doc.mmu. ac.uk/online/SAD/T04/projman.htm.)

Project managers in some institutions may be called "team leaders" or "group leaders," yet still have the same function of being responsible for a small group of people with a defined charge. Project management skills themselves will be useful in any management position, and your successful management of large projects shows both current and potential employers your aptitude for management. As Janet Crum, Head, Library Systems & Cataloging, Oregon Health & Science University, shares: "My library hired a consultant in the summer of 2001 to make recommendations re: restructuring. I had been the systems librarian for five years (and a cataloger for part of that time), during which systems became a bigger and bigger job. Many systems-related responsibilities were spread over several departments—Web management in reference (then access services, then collection development), workstation support in access services, etc. Meanwhile, I had been given my biggest assignment ever—managing our migration to a new automation system. I never saw the consultant's report, but apparently she recommended that systems and cataloging be consolidated into one department under me. My director and the other managers were pleased with my project management work, so they agreed."

Other Managers

You may be hired as a manager of collection development, library systems, or to fulfill another function that differs from what we think of as traditional management positions in libraries. You may not be required to manage people, or you may have a place outside of the traditional library hierarchy. In this case, you can take the time to build up the specific skills that you need for your job (such as budgeting or advocating for your department). You can also take any opportunity to shore up the management skills that are not specifically required in your position. (Serving as a project manager, for example, will give you experience managing people on teams, which may later help you become more marketable as a different type of manager.)

Differing Institutions

Expectations of library managers obviously vary widely depending on the type of institution they find themselves working in. While most discussions in this book are general enough to apply to a number of management situations, realize that specific duties and environments must differ—this is part of the marvelous breadth and variety of librarianship. Even in nonlibrary but related organizations, such as vendors and consortia, your library management skills will serve you in good stead.

Librarians' advantage in navigating multiple management positions lies in their ability to adapt disparate bits of knowledge, information, and background to fit different situations. This adaptive ability will be useful to you in any stage of your managerial career; you can turn the accidental nature of your position to your advantage at any level. In order to run any part of a library, it is essential to be invested in knowing how it works, to empathize with your employees, and to want to make a difference. On-purpose managers sometimes can stray further from their librarian roots because they are focused on their career ladder, emphasizing pure management skills and getting ahead over the principles and practices of librarianship. Those who have never before worked in a library or in a front-line position will have to make a special effort to stay in touch with their staff and their new profession.

Notes

1. Joan Giesecke, *Practical Strategies for Library Managers* (Chicago, ALA Editions, 2001) vii.

2. Joan Magretta and Nan Stone, *What Management Is: How It Works and Why It's Everyone's Business* (New York: The Free Press, 2002) 3.

Recommended Reading

Giesecke, Joan. *Practical Help for New Supervisors*. Chicago: LAMA, 1996.

—, ed. *Practical Strategies for Library Managers*. Chicago: ALA Editions, 2001.

Jordan, Mary Wilkins. "Surviving Your First Year as Library Director." *Public Libraries*, July/Aug. 2003: 215–217, 223.

Pergander, Mary. "Experiences of Early-Career Public Library Directors." *Public Libraries*, July/Aug. 2003: 252–254.

Sager, Don. "Evolving Virtues: Library Administrative Skills." *Public Libraries*, Sept./Oct. 2001: 268–272.

Siess, Judith A. "Flying Solo: Librarian, Manage Thyself." *American Libraries*, Feb. 1999: 31–33.

—. *The OPL Sourcebook: A Guide for Solo and Small Libraries*. Medford, NJ: Information Today, Inc., 2001.

Young, Arthur P., Ronald R. Powell, and Peter Hernon. "Attributes for the Next Generation of Library Directors." ACRL Eleventh National Conference, April 10-13, 2003. <http://www.ala.org/ala/acrl/acrl events/hernon.pdf> 23 April, 2004.

Chapter 3

Managing People: Personnel Issues

The talented employee may join a company because of its charismatic leaders, its generous benefits, and its world-class training programs, but how long that employee stays and how productive he is while he is there is determined by his relationship with his immediate supervisor.
Marcus Buckingham and Curt Coffman[1]

Ask any manager what consumes most of his time and gives him the most headaches, and personnel issues are likely to top his list. In many libraries, this is often partially due to circumstances not fully under your control, such as compensation scales, or due to the ways in which people had been accustomed to being managed (or not!) prior to your arrival. Respondents to the manager survey tended to specify various personnel matters as one of their top concerns, saying:

- "The biggest surprise was [that] the employees at that university would come in late to work, be gone for extended periods of time, and lie on their time sheets. There was a high level of incompetence. Work was being done over and over. Or, as one department head said: 'We keep doing the work until we get it right.'"

- "When I was assigned my first branch, I encountered several personnel who should never have been hired in the first place. Trying to motivate and train them and eventually having to fire several of them was one of the biggest challenges I have faced in the management of my branches."

- "It's fine to be friends with your staff, as long as you treat everyone fairly, but remember that they are your employees and you can't always be their 'buddy.' There are times when you have to make difficult or unpopular decisions or policies, or perhaps correct them or give them constructive criticism in a performance review."

- "The biggest thing in my position was learning when to make suggestions to help guide my staff and when to allow them to do what they needed to do to get the job done. My methods were sometimes very different from theirs and could work wonderfully for me, but not for them at all. I also had a lot of turnover in the part-time staff position below me (three people in just under three years)—in part due to low pay, difficult hours, and administrative woes in the top offices."

- "Several of the staff had been here for over 15 years and one long-term employee was experiencing performance problems. After less than a year in the management position, I was required to lay off staff due to a companywide staff reduction. Reorganizing roles and keeping morale up were both challenges."

- "The biggest surprise was what takes most of my time and energy is personnel issues, good and bad. Also that I am less and less a librarian every day, and more and more a manager."

- "I was also surprised to be put in the awkward position of giving some staff bad news about their performances when I had not been supervising them for more than a few months. I had to do staff evaluations after being on the job less than six months and was asked to comment on incidents that occurred before I was hired."

- "Although the four aides that I currently supervise are very hardworking and easy to get along with, that wasn't always the case. It surprised me that people thought it was acceptable to come in late five days in a row without repercussion. One aide fell asleep while shelf reading. I was surprised that this could happen in the workplace."

- "It is frustrating that not everyone understands that, if you are going to collect a paycheck, it's necessary to perform the job duties for which you are employed."

As a new library manager, you will most likely inherit one or more problem employees, as well as ongoing interpersonal conflicts. Whether you inherit an employee who has become accustomed to doing as little as possible, one who holds prejudicial attitudes toward coworkers or patrons, or one who is temperamentally unsuited to her position, whether you inherit staff members with a long-standing grudge against each other, one who has grown stagnant in his job, or one who is jealous of your new position, you are responsible for resolving the situation in the best possible way for your institution. You can do nothing about the way people have been managed prior to your arrival, all you can do is begin from now. You will find that managing staff and resolving these sorts of issues are among your most important managerial tasks.

The next few chapters talk about some of the different aspects involved in managing people, starting with personnel issues. Your library at its heart is about the people that work there—whether you are a one-person organization, or a 200-person operation. The value you create for your customers/patrons/constituency depends almost entirely on the actions of the library's staff and on the interaction of their various contributions in running your institution and providing its services.

Your main responsibility as a manager is to help your staff to work together, balancing their differing abilities and turning their activities and contributions into a coherent whole. To do this, you must make the effort to learn about your employees as individuals, try to empathize with their points of view, and show that you genuinely care about their progress. This also means learning when to be flexible and when you need to put people over policy, realizing when rules can bend and when policies can be modified. Show the same respect for your staff as for your customers, treating them as individuals, and providing them with the tools, information, and support to be effective in their positions.

It has been said that most employees quit their managers, not their jobs. Retaining good staff requires being a good manager, balancing the needs of your staff with those of the organization, and finding a match between those needs whenever possible. It requires recognizing that library employees are at least as important as library patrons—they are, in one sense, your institution's first customer—and meeting their needs is just as crucial. It also requires recognizing when one of your employees is not meeting the institution's needs, getting to the reasons why, and taking action to resolve the problem.

In a library environment, most managers are promoted into their positions because they have been good at their previous jobs; they move up based on their technical skills. As one staff survey respondent points out, though, "Just because you can catalog anything under the sun, or are a great reference librarian, does not mean you know anything about managing people." Understand what parts of your skills and background are transferable and in what areas you will need to work harder.

Hiring

Beyond hiring people for their existing skills and what they are able to bring to your library or department, you will need to examine how they will fit into the library's culture. Hiring the right people involves more than looking at just a list of classes a candidate has taken or previous jobs she has held, it also entails looking at a person's capacity to learn, to fit into the library's environment, to adapt to change, to work toward the goals of the library, and to grow with the rest of your staff. (Find more on identifying such capabilities in the section on interviewing later in this chapter.)

While many managers are initially intimidated by (or grow weary of) the process of finding, interviewing, and hiring the right candidate, hiring new people presents a wonderful opportunity to add new life and perspectives to your team, department, and/or library. Each new staff member enters with a unique background and skills—new graduates might bring technical skills your staff currently lacks, younger hires can bring energy and new ideas, and veteran librarians bring the depth of their experience and a wealth of knowledge about the ideas, programs, and services that have worked well at their previous institution(s). Take hiring decisions seriously; the person you hire now could be with you for years, so think long-term. As Kathleen Low succinctly puts it: "The best way to avoid problem staff members is never to hire them into your library."[2] In many libraries, you will have inherited "problem" employees with your position; avoid adding to your own personnel dilemmas.

When you have an opportunity to hire, also take the time, if possible and if allowed in your management situation, to review existing job descriptions and modify them as necessary to meet the changing needs of your library. Changes in job descriptions may need to be made in conjunction with your director and/or HR (human resources) office, and may require a reexamination of pay scales as well. Union agreements can also affect job descriptions and pay ranges, so be sure to understand all of the factors involved before beginning this reexamination process. Realize also that, if you bring in a new hire at a higher salary, your existing staff are likely to be perturbed.

While hiring does offer the chance for your library to incorporate new skills and new ideas, as you begin to surround yourself with good people, you will then want to work to minimize turnover. Beyond the time you personally expend in hiring and training new employees, the hiring process is costly for your library, especially when it comes to hiring qualified and experienced librarians. Further, the time between when a staff member departs and when you are able to hire and train a new candidate places stress on an understaffed department or institution. Minimize departures by keeping your staff motivated and happy in their work. (See more on motivation in Chapter 5.)

Retention and hiring will also be affected by whether your library is able to compensate librarians and library staff fairly. Be willing and able to fight for your employees, and understand that your pay scales will affect your ability to attract quality candidates. John Buzas, Branch Manager, Norfolk Public Library, Virginia, expresses his frustration when he notes that his biggest library management surprise was "the difficulty in finding quality, energetic people with the verbal and intellectual skills needed to help others in a library setting when I am only permitted to pay them less than what they could earn at a fast-food outlet or for the most menial of jobs." One respondent to the staff survey expresses the importance of fair salaries to quality service, noting: "Administrators have to fight against the trend in which money is willingly thrown at new technology and facilities, but nickel and dime staff to death, so that each new contract results in loss of real wages and benefits. Staff makes or breaks a library, and in order to provide the great patron service that all libraries say is top priority, administrators are going to have to put some money where their mouth is. Staff that has insecurity about basic needs will not have their mind on patron service or loyalty to the library."

As a higher-level manager, you may be involved in setting the salary structure and policies for your organization, deciding on salary ranges, percentage increases, whether the library will pay an annual cost-of-living increase in addition to (or instead of) merit increases, and so on. As a mid-level manager, you should at least have input into these decisions, and need to be informed about what comparable institutions are paying for similar positions. Understand that the need for new technical and other skills is blurring the traditional lines between MLS and non-MLS library staff, as well as their pay ranges. Try not to get locked into traditional job descriptions and salary schedules merely because this is the way in which your institution has managed in the past.

Finding good candidates will become easier as you gain a reputation for being the kind of organization people want to work for. Librarians talk—on e-mail discussion lists, to others in their personal networks, at conferences, or on forums such as the Contrarian Librarian (http://groups.yahoo.com/group/contrarianlibrarian). Over time, potential candidates gain a sense of the working environment at various institutions and apply accordingly. This becomes a mutually reinforcing process, as good people create a good institution, attracting more good people, and so on. The process of surrounding yourself with good and competent people also helps reinforce the culture of customer service mentioned in Chapter 1: Effective and happy staff create happy patrons; effective customer service cannot take place absent a positive institutional culture.

Larger institutions with separate HR departments, or those that are part of local government, may have very specific procedures to follow throughout the whole hiring process. HR personnel might do the initial recruiting and screening of all candidates, for example. You will want to find out about the procedures at your institution and to work closely with HR to avoid stepping on any toes. In some libraries, application forms will also be required by the municipality or institution prior to the hiring process, while in others they serve as more of a formality and are often even completed after a candidate has been hired. Application forms can also include more open-ended questions that give candidates the opportunity to demonstrate their philosophies and backgrounds.

You may also be involved in creating and/or placing job ads for candidates, either throughout your institution or for your section of the library. The position for which you are recruiting will determine the wording and placement of your ads; ads for clerks and other support staff, for example, may only be posted internally or in local newspapers, while ads for MLS librarians and technical staff might be posted in targeted journals or other nationwide resources. Your job ads, as all your recruitment activities, give you a chance to market your library to potential candidates; give some thought to your wording and content.

You should investigate the option of posting job ads online, through your local library system or state association, on targeted e-mail discussion lists, or nationally at Web sites such as http://www.lisjobs.com. When you are searching for professional-level staff, posting online allows you to draw on a larger pool of candidates, Internet postings are often low-cost or even free, and you can take advantage of more space and hyperlinks to explain more thoroughly the position and the library environment. Also, never underestimate the power of the Internet in helping you evaluate candidates. In the same way people Google potential boyfriends, you can research potential employees to see what they might have said when participating on e-mail lists, if they have a personal blog, if they have an online resume. Often what people say online is less guarded than what they reveal in an interview, and this can help you gain a fuller picture of a candidate's personality, interests, and strengths.

Larger libraries might participate in conference placement centers or library school job fairs. Again, here is your chance to market your institution to candidates, drawing on your communication skills and library background to paint a positive picture. Highlight the good points of working at your library—do you offer flexible

hours? A competitive salary? A nice climate? Good retirement benefits? Professional development opportunities? A casual work
environment? Think of what might help attract applicants, and
include these features in your pitch.

Interviewing

While the basic purpose of an interview is to identify whether a
candidate will be a good fit for your library in terms of her skills,
aptitude, and personality, remember that interviews also provide
potential staff members with the opportunity to get to know you
and your library. Give interviewees a realistic picture of the library's
culture and goals, the work they will be expected to do, and their
potential working environment. Never misrepresent the work environment, duties, or other aspects of the job just to get someone on
board. Allow them to make an informed decision about working in
your institution, and allow them an opportunity to ask their own
questions. The care you take to introduce potential hires to your
organizational expectations and culture, further, can go a long way
toward giving them a positive image of your institution—whether
or not they end up working for you at this time.

In some larger public and most academic institutions, your
interviews for professional-level staff will be conducted by a group
or formal committee. Try to keep these group interviews a manageable size to avoid intimidating your candidates, and to allow
everyone the chance to interact with potential hires. If you are
leading a group interview, keep it on track using similar tactics to
those you would use in facilitating a meeting—you may wish also
to meet beforehand to work out what questions each of you will
ask, in order to avoid duplication.

In some cases, you will wish to get a realistic picture of a candidate's skills in a certain area by having them actually demonstrate
those skills for you. Whether you ask a potential page to put a cart
of books in Dewey order or ask a potential bibliographic instruction

librarian to demonstrate part of a class, you will need here in all fairness to give the same opportunity to each candidate in order to evaluate them on the same basis.

If you ask for references, check them. Realize, though, that personal references are necessarily subjective, and that someone at a person's current institution might even give a glowing review because they want to be rid of their coworker! Use references in conjunction with interviews and other methods, and learn to trust your own impressions of candidates.

In the U.S., there are a number of questions you are legally proscribed from asking during an interview. These include a candidate's age, marital status, whether he has children, his religion, and other private matters that should not affect your hiring decision. Make sure you familiarize yourself with the legal requirements for conducting an interview as well as with any special requirements imposed by your institution. Yale University's Library Human Resources Department provides a useful online sampling of questions that interviewers are proscribed from asking, as well as some of those they may ask, at http://www.library.yale.edu/jobs/Employment/interviewguidelines.html.

Interviews allow an opportunity for you to see how your potential hire can communicate her ideas to others—an important skill in any library. Take the time to conduct interviews of a reasonable length, and be sure to allow candidates time to answer your questions fully. Let candidates do most of the talking; avoid getting swept up in what you are telling them so that your interview becomes overly one-sided and you leave without a realistic picture of their abilities and personality. Especially when hiring professional staff, ask open-ended questions that require a candidate to think, be courteous in allowing the time to do so, and do your best to put interviewees at ease so that they can answer more naturally.

Some sample interview questions from Indiana University can be found at http://www.indiana.edu/~libpers/interview.html.

Make yourself a consistent list of questions to use during the hiring process for any particular position, so that you can fairly compare candidates' answers to the same queries. It is fine to take notes during the interview so that you can refresh your memory of each candidate's answers at a later date, and you might also want to jot down notes to refresh your memory of the candidate herself ("red shirt, long hair"). This will help you match answers with candidates' names later.

Interviews will of course differ based on whether you are hiring a professional librarian or a paraprofessional assistant, a student worker or a new page; the questions you ask and the skills, personality, and abilities you are looking for depend on the position for which you are hiring. In general, though, especially when hiring professional-level staff, you will be looking primarily for flexibility, a willingness to adapt and learn, and the ability to fit into your library's environment, rather than for specific skills. Skills can always be taught and the requirements for any position change over time; the right combination of attitude and aptitude is harder to find. As McKenna and Maister write: "The most important hiring lesson to remember is that you should hire for attitude, and train for skills. Skills you can build. Attitude and character are harder to change. You need to have a sense of who is and who is not your firm's kind of person, and hire to fit the culture. You should look for people with enthusiasm, excitement, sparks, energy, spirit, a sharing style, personality, and compatibility."[3] Pay the same attention when hiring an MLS librarian or part-time circulation clerk; each represents the library to your patrons and carries out tasks essential to the smooth running of your institution.

This is of course a flexible rule, and the right combination of skills, potential, and attitude is different for each position—someone who works with the public or with students, for example, needs to possess communication and interpersonal abilities, while you will prize fluency in a foreign language monographs cataloger.

Once you make a job offer, especially for a professional level position, be prepared to engage in some negotiation with your potential hire. Do you have a little wiggle room in terms of salary? Start date? Flexible hours? Be prepared and know your options in the event that these questions come up. Again, union or institutional rules may lock you in to a greater or lesser extent, especially in a larger institution. Smaller libraries may have more leeway here, but may have less funding available to meet candidates' requirements.

Coordinating and Scheduling

After a candidate accepts your offer of employment, you will be responsible for integrating your new person into the workflow of your institution or department. In a larger institution, your human resources department may have developed its own mandatory, standardized orientation sessions on library policies and procedures. In a smaller institution, you may be responsible for any orientation your new employee receives. In any library, you will need to provide personalized orientation to prepare each new hire for his new duties and responsibilities.

Thoughtful orientations both help new employees get up to speed more quickly and help increase retention by making them feel part of the organizational culture from day one. Do not just let new hires muddle through; this wastes everyone's time. Take the time to introduce your new person to her coworkers, tour the facilities, provide her with any documentation she needs—and eat lunch with her that first day. Make sure everything is ready when she arrives; have her PC set up, get an e-mail account, give her a key to the building (if applicable), and have paperwork ready for her to fill out.

Once your new hire is more up to speed, he can be integrated more fully into the schedule and workflow of your department or library. Effective coordination and scheduling requires learning the workflows and rhythms of your department or organization. Perhaps the reference desk in your academic institution, for example, requires additional staffing when final papers are due near the end of a semester. Maybe your technical services department needs to turn all of its attention to processing materials at the end of the fiscal year when there is a rush of last-minute ordering as people spend down the remaining materials budget.

You can also consider creating documentation for new employees to help them quickly get up to speed and take their place in the day-to-day activities of your library. Much routine library work is especially easily documented. You can easily outline the procedure for unlocking doors and logging in PCs each morning, for example, or create a list of people in different departments and their areas of responsibility. Providing people with the information necessary to settle into and do their jobs effectively dovetails nicely with your library background and skills; this is merely staff rather than user instruction.

Effective scheduling and coordinating also includes the ability to analyze your department's (or library's) true staffing needs. As your library's everyday activities change over time due to changing demands for your services, you will need to reallocate staff, hire new staff, or allow the numbers of your employees to dwindle through attrition, by not replacing retiring or leaving staff members. As always, the more data you can collect to back up your decisions about staffing levels and allocation, the better. You may also need to change the mix of activities your staff engages in as demand for certain services changes or dwindles, as demand arises for new and innovative services, or as automation or other factors reduce the necessity for certain types of work. Part of your responsibility as a manager is to keep a handle on workflow and ensure that your staff is working in the most effective way possible to support the mission of your library. The PLA publication *Staffing for Results* (see recommended reading at the end of this chapter) outlines a number of ways to collect this data and to help balance workloads in public libraries. If you are a mid-level manager, you will need to provide this workflow data, and your recommendations on when and why to increase, decrease, or reallocate staff, to your own administrator.

Union or institutional rules may affect the way you are able to staff your department or institution and whether you are able to expand people's horizons by assigning tasks outside of their normal job descriptions. This is especially true if these tasks have historically been done by more highly compensated employees. (See more on developing a good relationship with library unions in Chapter 10.)

You will also need to address your staff members' concerns about any change in staffing patterns, particularly if their daily duties or departmental workflow are affected. (See more on dealing with change in Chapter 8.) Recognize that, as their manager, you have not only the right but the responsibility to assign duties and arrange workflow as best suits your library, even if this means making changes to the way things have "always been done." This also, though, means that you have the responsibility to research and think about your reasons for any such changes, and never to proceed arbitrarily with disruptions to your employees' work lives. Providing explanations and showing how workflow will improve will help build the necessary foundation of trust.

Think also about providing more flexible working options when applicable. Telecommuting, flex-time, and flexible scheduling are all appropriate options for many library positions. A willingness to be flexible can help you retain good staff members who are looking for work-life balance, whether these are younger staff just starting a family, or baby boomers caring for aging parents.

Reviewing

In most libraries, you will be responsible for conducting a performance review (evaluation, or appraisal) of each of your staff members at least once a year. Since your staff's raises are often contingent upon a positive review, many will take this process quite seriously. Be sure to conduct these reviews privately and at a time when you are unlikely to be interrupted. Your institution may have a standard appraisal form for you to use; if not, consider creating one for your library or your department. This form can include categories as basic as punctuality, assimilation of new skills, and attention to customer service, and as broad as personal goals.

You will likely have the chance to review new employees more often, after three months and/or after six months, for example, in order to evaluate how they are settling into their new positions. Many institutions use a probationary period during which an employee can more easily be let go. (Be sure to let your new hires know if they have a three-month review in their future!) This also allows you to ensure that your new staff member gets a feel for her own performance; it can sometimes be difficult for new staff to settle in and to feel as if they are doing their best work.

Before even getting to the review stage, make sure that each of your staff members has specific goals to work toward, on which he or she can later be evaluated. Make sure that these goals are clear to both of you—and, especially for professional-level employees, give them the opportunity to help define their own goals. If you go through a restructuring or reorganization, revisit people's job descriptions and sit down with them to help define new goals and outline new responsibilities. In addition to personal goals set by you and your employees, goals can also include competencies set at the departmental or institutional level for all employees. (See the discussion of competencies later in this chapter.)

Let your employees know year-round that you are paying attention to them and to their work. Include rewards if possible for professional development and other activities that relate to a person's job performance. Make sure, however, to do your formal reviews on time—do not let an anniversary date go by unremarked, because you will give people the impression that their job (and raise) is of little importance to you or to the institution as a whole.

Also ensure that people have an ongoing understanding of their progress, in order to avoid huge surprises at review time. It will be more useful to correct and guide people along the way, than to once a year tell them that they have been proceeding in the wrong direction for the past several months. Debbi Schaubman, coordinator for InMICH, a Michigan based library resource-sharing program, says: "Never let a performance evaluation be a surprise—communication with staff should be frequent and in-depth enough that the formal evaluation process is a formality. The staff should already know what you think are their strengths and challenges." Frequent communication also allows you to catch problems before they escalate. One respondent to the staff survey notes: "If there is a problem, address it early when it is still a low-key issue. Don't wait for the yearly evaluation and a surprise for all." Many respondents to the staff survey found these sorts of surprises at evaluation time extremely frustrating. Another shares: "Annual evaluation was a complete surprise, as I had not heard anything during the year to support the conclusion she reached in the evaluation … I would like my evaluations to not be surprises—how am I supposed to improve if I'm not told what is wrong?"

Think during the year about how you can encourage your staff to meet their goals, and continually act on your thoughts. At their reviews, discuss concrete ways in which they can improve and set new goals for them to meet. This will best be done in conjunction with your employees; get their ideas on ways they could improve and goals they wish to achieve, and work with them to jointly develop these goals. Using goals allows you to be less subjective at review time, since you then have a specified set of standards on which to evaluate each employee.

When you do a review, try to start the meeting with specific examples of what the employee has done well. Even if the review from that point must be more negative, if you find nothing to praise, you give your employees no motivation to do better and no examples of what they should continue to do. Providing specific examples of a job well done helps keep your employee from thinking that you are "just out to get them" or "never notice anything they do." Also have specific examples to back up your overview of any areas that need improvement, and be prepared to discuss your reasoning with your employee. You above all wish to avoid fostering resentment.

There have been a number of innovations in performance reviews that purport to give a better picture of an employee's true strengths and weaknesses. One is peer review, where people's colleagues get the chance to provide input on their performance. People's peers should be more familiar with their performance and day-to-day work because of the opportunity to work with and see them every day, but realize that you see the problem of bias and of people giving negative reviews because of a personal dislike of or grudge against their coworker. Peer feedback can sometimes, though, be very helpful to employees—especially newer employees—who are unsure how their colleagues perceive their performance or how they are fitting into the organizational culture. Another idea is allowing employees to review their own performance, then comparing and discussing their perceptions of their work with your perceptions as their manager. This can be more difficult for individuals who are more modest about their own accomplishments or who have difficulty tooting their own horns.

Three-hundred-and-sixty-degree feedback combines all of these methods, so people are evaluated by everyone they interact with—coworkers, their manager, their direct reports, and so on. In 360-degree feedback, each group is evaluating an individual on the same criteria. These different perceptions can then be compared. This does tend to bring the same problems as peer review, where people sometimes evaluate their peers on personal likes and dislikes rather than on performance.

Academic librarians in a tenure-track environment will also be subject to evaluation by a tenure or promotion committee. As a person's direct supervisor, you may be one member of that committee, but will work in conjunction with other committee members from elsewhere in the institution.

Individuals also will require different tactics for successful reviews and for year-round feedback. Some are inherently more self-motivated than others; some need more specific guidance from you; some may tend to get off track more easily than others. Again, the key here is to know your employees as individuals and to realize how much "management" each needs to be successful.

Promoting

Use your power to promote sparingly and wisely. Chapter 11 talks about the Peter Principle, where people are promoted up to the level of their incompetence—and there they stick, unable ever either to move up or to serve effectively in their position. Once you get to know your staff, you will get a sense of the level of responsibility and the types of duties they are willing and able to handle. A perfectly competent cataloger, for example, may not be pleased at a promotion requiring her to give up some of her cataloging duties in order to manage technical assistants. Also understand that some people may want to move up purely for a bump in pay; ensure that they also possess the personality and skills to do well in their new position. As Rose Moorhouse, retired librarian for the

Department of Defense, notes in the staff survey: "Make sure an employee wants to be upgraded to a particular job because they want the job, not just the salary increase."

Get to know your staff and the career paths they have in mind; get to know who can be pushed to move up the career ladder and who is comfortably set in her position. Think about how someone will likely react to increased responsibility, and about whether they have the people skills to manage staff. Think about "growing your own," and give staff the opportunity to learn and push themselves. Help prepare them to move up the career ladder in the future, and groom future leaders for your institution or for the profession itself.

Reprimanding ... and Firing

Much as you would like your staff always to take responsibility for their own actions and productivity, there will be times when you need to step in. Understand that people make mistakes, allow for this, and build flexibility into the way that you deal with others. Look here, however, for patterns of behavior that point to an underlying or long-term problem, or for times when people simply refuse to learn from their mistakes. You do not need to lie in wait for your employees to slip up, but you cannot afford to overlook problems, either. If your workplace is undergoing a great deal of transition, previously highly reviewed employees might also have difficulty adjusting or refuse to live up to new expectations. You can help them do so, but must be willing to hold people accountable for their actions when they resist change and refuse to move forward. (See more on managing change in Chapter 8.)

Even thinking about reprimanding, disciplining, or firing an employee can be difficult for library managers. Many libraries have long prided themselves on the differences between their organizational culture and that in much of the corporate world—but, unfortunately, often at the cost of keeping people whose attitude, behavior, or lack of performance would see them swiftly removed from any other environment. While most adults are actual grownups, some will take advantage of any situation that lacks consequences, or that fails to place any external controls on their behavior or standards on their work. This is the same reason that libraries institute fines! Librarians, by training or by temperament, like to say "yes." You need to learn when to say no, when to be assertive as a manager, and how to deal with problem situations.

Your responsibility to your library requires you to overcome any natural reluctance to confront poorly performing or badly behaving staff. Managers cannot afford to make only popular choices; they need to base their actions on what will be best for the institution. Never let your own need to be liked allow you to postpone dealing with problem employees; the situation is unlikely to resolve itself, but is instead much more likely to escalate. Ruth Metz explains: "Ignoring poor performance won't make it go away. It only makes it worse for the individual, for his self-esteem, for other workers affected by the poor performance, and for organizational morale. To the affected coworkers and subordinates, there are few things more demoralizing than believing that management ignores poor performance."[4] One manager survey respondent concurs, saying: "Managers have to manage work habits and performance. If you, or your leadership, make decisions about staff that are based on fear of hurting someone's feelings instead of decisions that are based on what is good for the library and its community, you will get caught in the popularity game."

When you find it necessary to correct one of your staff members, though, be sure to do so privately. While good work deserves public recognition, reprimanding members of your staff in front of others merely creates an opportunity for embarrassment and anger, diverting their attention from your real concerns about their behavior. Try to be objective about your employees' behavior, and never base a negative review, comment, or reprimand on a personal dislike of or problem with a staff member. Never put them down or attack them personally; address only their behavior, in terms of what they need to do to improve. If your employee takes your reprimand as unwarranted criticism, he will focus on that rather than on what he needs to do to resolve the situation.

While you will need to avoid postponing dealing with personnel issues, you also want to avoid reacting in the heat of the moment out of your own anger at an employee's behavior. Set aside a time for a performance interview, in which you outline the problem(s) and stress the specific actions that your employee needs to take to resolve the situation. Be very clear in outlining each step that needs to be taken and a specific timeframe in which the behavior needs to be corrected. Explain the consequences of not changing the particular behavior or performance—vague notions of "you have to change" will not give her an incentive or a clear path toward resolving the issue.

Again, specific goals are important in giving the staff member something to work toward. See if you can work out these goals cooperatively with the employee. Chances are that she really knows she is having problems, and may appreciate the chance to explain her side of the matter and/or to work toward positive solutions. Make sure she understands your specific concerns—it may be helpful to get her to repeat the gist of what you have said by asking something like: "What have you heard me say so far? Do you have any additions?" Never reprimand an employee without a discussion of how the issue can be resolved; recognize that there is a problem and work out how it can be corrected.

As the person begins to turn around, provide immediate and positive reinforcement for any behavior you wish to encourage. Part of your job as manager is to bring out the potential in everyone—and this includes bringing it out in your problem employees as well. In fact, people with the most potential can be the most frustrating to managers when they refuse to use their talents in supporting your library's mission. But, if you work to find items to praise as well as to criticize, you can build on these small successes.

Be sure to document these reviews and conversations so that there is a written record of your efforts to turn around your problem employee. Also document any specific incidents of poor behavior; you will need this documentation to back you up if you need to take further steps to resolve the situation. As one manager survey respondent suggests: "Document *everything!* From documenting your achievements (great for annual reviews and preparing for the next position) to documenting negative employees (you will need dates, times, and behaviors to counter their entrenched position as popular incumbent). A written record protects you. And if you don't think you will ever need such protection, you are truly naive." Make sure that you have institutional support for your efforts to discipline a poor performer, especially if it becomes necessary to build up a record leading to her dismissal. Ensure that you comply with all legal and institutional requirements, in the event that your efforts fail to make an impact on a problem employee and you do need to take more drastic action.

In larger institutions, you may become involved with an HR mediator or be subject to a union grievance if you take steps to negatively review or reprimand an employee. This is yet another reason to document a poorly performing, harassing, or otherwise troublesome employee's behavior, as well as your conversations, reviews, memos, and other communications with them.

As a last resort, realize that you may end up having to let a staff member go if he throws away all of his chances to improve his own performance or behavior. Think about firing both in terms of removing someone who is not a good fit for your library's culture and of providing an opportunity for that person to find a place where he does fit, a job to which he is more suited—or as a wakeup call when previous warnings have failed to make an impression. You can also think of it as necessary out of fairness, both to the library and to those staff members who are performing well in their jobs. One staff survey respondent suggests: "… if someone isn't working well, or is a sloth, fire them and get someone who can pull their weight so the library and its services don't suffer." This is a step that should be taken only when you have made every possible effort to turn around a person's performance and/or behavior. Make sure that he always knows what he needs to do to improve, and that, if he fails to so, that termination is a very real possibility.

Professional Development

Some institutions and managers fall into the trap of failing to support the professional development of their staff members, on the assumption that those who learn additional skills will become overqualified for and dissatisfied in their positions—and leave. Successful institutions, though, realize the importance of training and developing staff, allowing people to improve their skills, reenergize, and become ever-more-valuable parts of the library. If you meet your employees' needs in other ways, they are less likely to take their new skills elsewhere. The opportunity for people to keep their skills sharp and their minds fresh also helps keep them from stagnating in their positions and becoming bored with their jobs, increasing your ability to retain motivated staff. Professional development also opens the door for employees to develop the skills they need to move up in the organization; if you fail to invest in developing your staff, you will find yourself always needing to go outside the institution to hire new managers and higher-level employees. A commitment to professional development lets your employees bring new skills and ideas back to your library, energizing themselves, others, and the workplace as a whole.

Support outside education when applicable and possible, providing institutional aid and/or time to attend library school, join associations, attend conferences and workshops, or gain pertinent certifications. If your institution has limited funds, consider taking turns—taking pains to apportion limited dollars fairly and to provide support especially for those who have expressed interest in furthering their careers and knowledge. Trade off conference attendance on a year-to-year basis, and give attending staff the chance to share their experiences and the knowledge that they have gained. If you can send multiple staff, encourage them to attend different sessions to maximize the content they are able to bring back. Look for less expensive continuing education opportunities from your library system/consortium or from your institution. Encourage people to bring back what they learn and to share it with others through meetings, written reports, or formal training.

Always be on the lookout for opportunities to help your staff develop and grow in their careers. Some states, systems, or institutions require a specific number of annual continuing education hours; if yours does not, you might want to institute a requirement of your own. It is your job as a manager both to encourage individuals to take advantage of opportunities and to create an environment in which professional development is valued and seen as an important component in any employee's success. This will be most easily accomplished if support for professional development is part of the culture of the entire organization; however, use whatever power you have to create this supportive environment for your own staff.

Also pay attention to your need to keep up with your own professional development. Chapter 1 talks about the need to keep growing and learning as a manager, and you need to balance your own lifelong learning needs with those of your staff. There are two major traps here: You will need to avoid spending all of your scarce professional development dollars on yourself, and you will need to avoid giving all of your funding to your staff at your own expense.

Core Competencies

The term "core competencies" refers to the basic skills and knowledge library staff need to carry out their duties effectively. New staff members or changing work conditions require a constant reappraisal of necessary competencies, and create a concomitant need for training and staff development. (See the next section for more on training.) Some libraries have developed elaborate lists of core competencies for each job description, and you may be responsible for evaluating your staff on their assimilation of these competencies. Other institutions may never have formalized these, which provides you with an opening to start from scratch and to thoroughly evaluate and clearly lay out what your employees need to know. Competencies can also serve as guidelines to the skills and/or qualities you would like to identify in new hires, and some libraries base merit increases on the mastery of various competencies.

You may wish to expand out your list of concrete competencies to also include more intangible personal characteristics, such as a commitment to lifelong learning, personal responsibility, and flexibility. Also realize that your own supervisor or your institution may set their own separate competencies for managers, which you will need to master.

Examples of core competencies can be found online from both associations and individual libraries, with those from associations being somewhat more general. These include:

- "Competencies for Information Professionals of the 21st Century" (SLA): http://www.sla.org/content/learn/comp2003/index.cfm

- "Core Competencies for Librarians" (New Jersey Library Association): http://www.njla.org/resources/competencies.html

- "Core Competencies for Libraries and Library Staff" (sample chapter from *Staff Development, a Practical Guide*, 3rd ed., by Elizabeth Fuseler Avery, Terry Dahlin, and Deborah A. Carver: http://archive.ala.org/editions/samplers/sampler_pdfs/avery.pdf

- Tampa Bay Library Consortium: Core Competencies: http://www.tblc.org/training/competencies.shtml

You can use these as guides when creating your own list of competencies, or talk to your colleagues at similarly sized libraries to see what they are using.

Training

Library training (or "staff development programs") can help individuals meet their core competencies and go beyond basic skills. Training is both a professional development issue and an ongoing necessity for maintaining high levels of service and productivity in any library. This is especially true when it comes to technology and to customer service. Because libraries are constantly changing environments, staff need to continue to learn and grow in order to meet the challenge of keeping up with changing technology, changing collections, changing job duties, and the changing needs of their constituents. "Librarianship" is not a fixed body of knowledge, but is instead a field, which continually assimilates relevant skills and knowledge from a number of interrelated specialties. Librarianship as practiced in your institution needs to remain relevant by constantly adapting to changing circumstances.

Pay special attention to providing training on technological and customer service issues. Institutions that have made an investment in technology—both equipment and software—need their staff to be able to use the system effectively. As Bruce Massis points out: "A library can install the most sophisticated and technologically advanced equipment available, but if the staff is not properly trained or does not wish to be trained, then that equipment becomes merely decorative."[5] Library users also have ever-increasing expectations of technological expertise, as well as an ongoing need for assistance and training in their own use of the library's technical tools. Especially if you have a large staff, you will wish to provide training to impress upon everyone the primacy of customer service in your organization. Customer service workshops can range from the perennially popular dealing with difficult patrons to conducting effective reference interviews.

Beyond internal training, there are a number of trainers providing workshops and presentations on various aspects of customer service in libraries. You can look at outside trainers to bring in for yearly in-service days, or perhaps partner with other libraries in your system or consortium to bring in outside training and share the costs. Many library organizations do offer these regular staff or in-service days, which allow staff the opportunity to reenergize and learn new ways of thinking about their jobs. There are a plethora of resources to help you, your trainers, and your institution design effective training for library staff during an in-service. A full day set aside for training allows both full- and part-time staff to participate, and relieves you from the scheduling headaches of covering the desk or carrying out your normal duties while also trying to get everyone trained. These days can include a mix of activities—from videos, to outside speakers, to small group hands-on workshops, to conference reports, and so on. Buy pizza, play games, make the experience fun, and ensure that everyone gets to participate.

Training has unfortunately gotten a bad rap in many institutions because it has often been so poorly done. But, if done properly, training is an inherent and ongoing process that allows library staff to remain up-to-date and able to carry out the goals of the institution. In addition to providing special training when your institution adds new technology or institutes new systems and procedures, consider making training a regular part of every employee's work life. As a director, you can implement this from the top down; as a department head or mid-level manager, you can implement or take advantage of regular training opportunities for your own staff.

You may not be labeled as a "trainer" in your institution, but, as a library manager, there are a number of ways you will be involved in the training process. First and foremost, you will need to convey your support and enthusiasm for the institution's training program to your staff. Although formal training can lead to complications in terms of scheduling and coverage while employees are being trained and practicing the skills they have learned, you need to look at this as an opportunity rather than merely an inconvenience. Avoid falling into the trap of not sending your best people (or yourself) to training because you cannot afford to spare them—without the chance to keep their skills fresh, they may not remain your best people for long.

You will also need to work with trainers to help develop and evaluate competencies and to give insight as to how your people could most benefit from training. You will need to know what staff are learning, so that you are able properly to evaluate them on their assimilation of new skills, and so that you can encourage them to share their skills with others.

You may be called upon to provide training in the day-to-day functioning of your department or institution. New employees, those being cross-trained, and those just shoring up their skills will look to you for guidance. As a manager, in many situations you should exemplify the skills needed within your institution, or within your department or section of the library. Be sure to provide new employees with the background and skills they need to do their jobs, beginning with an orientation that introduces them to their coworkers, to their duties, and to their work environment. Again, your institution may have a standard orientation process, if not, provide one for your own employees.

Beyond training in day-to-day activities, you may find that you need to invest in training for special and specific circumstances, such as when your library begins migrating to a new automation system. This is a natural candidate for an in-service day or for taking advantage of vendor-provided training opportunities. Also, give staff input into the creation of training programs or in deciding what would be useful for them to learn.

Although it may seem as if you have enough to deal with just training people for their own positions, think also about the possibilities presented by instituting training across departments. Cross-training can reenergize your employees and provide a better understanding of workflow across departments or throughout the institution, and the experience they gain in training can allow people to fill in cross-departmentally when necessary. In unionized institutions, however, check whether union rules may govern your ability to cross-train or deploy staff across different departments. Also avoid cross-training if your staff is already overworked and expressing feelings of burnout; you wish here to alleviate rather than add to their stress.

A thorough discussion of all of the steps involved in creating an effective training program are beyond the scope of this book. Organizations and resources you may wish to investigate in formulating yours, however, include:

- Avery, Elizabeth Fuseler, Terry Dahlin, and Deborah A. Carver, coordinating eds. *Staff Development: A Practical Guide, 3rd ed.* Chicago: ALA Editions, 2001.

- Ballard, Angela F. "Ahead of the Curve: Insuring Success of a Technology Training Program for Library Staff." Computers in Libraries (conference), March 2004 <http://www.infotoday.com/cil2004/presentations/ballard.pps> 25 April 2004.

- CLENERT (http://www.ala.org/ala/clenert/clenert.htm)

Be sure to invest in the development of all staff, not just MLS librarians. Every library employee needs to develop the skills that equip her to work in a rapidly changing library environment. Look also for ways in which you can integrate what people learn into the day-to-day life of your institution. If an employee attends a workshop, for example, and brings back ideas for new programs or services or a new workflow, listen to their suggestions and be open to innovative ideas from your employees.

Mentoring

As a library manager, you have the opportunity to serve as either a formal or an informal mentor to more junior staff members in your institution, or to others in the profession as a whole. Take the chance to give back to the library profession while also benefiting your institution, your staff, and yourself. The younger and newer librarians and library workers of today are the library leaders of tomorrow, and institutions that fail to nurture talent at all levels will eventually find themselves at a distinct disadvantage. If you mentor individuals in your own institution, you have the opportunity to allow them to hone their skills in temporary leadership positions, on a team, or in charge of a given project, for example.

The purported "graying" of the library profession means that we now more than ever need to encourage new leaders. Help those you mentor to think of themselves as leaders within your library, even if they are not serving formally in a leadership position. Mentoring helps prepare them to continue where you leave off, and to enhance the skills and outlook they bring to your institution or to the profession as a whole. In an academic environment, mentoring also can include helping to guide others through the tenure and promotion process.

Mentoring provides an individual connection that can be invaluable in career development and success. Although earlier you were urged to find your own mentors, think also about the type of mentorship you could provide to your own juniors. Learning from your own mentor and mentoring others help keep the profession moving forward. As Mary Pergander, Head Librarian, Lake Bluff Public Library, Illinois, suggests: "Seek out mentors and resources. Get involved with your library system. Identify strong leaders. Get to know and emulate them. Ask them how they would handle your challenge of the day. ... Don't wait to be approached. In the same turn, approach others who are even newer than you are. Share with them and grow together. Pass on what you learn and keep the ladder reaching forward and backward."

Your needs and experience and outlook will change at different stages of your library career, and you can mentor your younger or junior colleagues just as more experienced managers have mentored you. Help them follow your path up the library career ladder—or to blaze their own. Mentoring also encourages you to grow in your own position, because now you serve, not only as a manager, but as a role model. It allows you to gain insight from your younger or less-experienced colleagues as well, as they can bring a fresh perspective to a variety of issues.

When it comes to staffing and personnel issues, librarians' experience in matching information to users' needs will come in handy. In the same way that you make these matches for patrons, endeavor to match your staff to the library's needs. Balance the skills, knowledge, and personalities available in your library as needed. The same skills that make you a good librarian help to make you a good manager—you want your staff to succeed, and can provide the resources and information necessary for them to do so.

Notes

1. Marcus Buckingham and Curt Coffmann, *First Break All the Rules: What the World's Greatest Managers Do Differently* (New York: Simon & Schuster, 1999) 11–12.

2. Kathleen Low, *Recruiting Library Staff: A How-To-Do-It Manual for Librarians* (New York: Neal-Schuman, 1999) xi.

3. Patrick J. McKenna and David H. Maister, *First Among Equals: How to Manage a Group of Professionals* (New York: The Free Press, 2002) 227.

4. Ruth F. Metz, *Coaching in the Library: A Management Strategy for Achieving Excellence* (Chicago: ALA Editions, 2001) 36.

5. Bruce Massis, *The Practical Library Manager* (New York: Haworth, 2003) 5.

Recommended Reading

Aluri, Rao and Mary Reichel. "Performance Evaluation: A Deadly Disease?" *Journal of Academic Librarianship* 20:3 (July 1994): 145–155.

Avery, Elizabeth Fuseler, Terry Dahlin, and Deborah A. Carver, coordinating eds. *Staff Development: A Practical Guide, 3rd ed.* Chicago: ALA Editions, 2001.

Baldwin, David A. *The Library Compensation Handbook: A Guide for Administrators, Librarians, and Staff.* Westport, CT: Libraries Unlimited, 2003.

Blanchard, Kenneth and Spencer Johnson. *The One Minute Manager.* New York: Berkeley Books, 1983 (paperback ed.).

Buckingham, Marcus and Curt Coffman. *First, Break All the Rules: What the World's Greatest Managers Do Differently.* New York: Simon & Schuster, 1999.

Giesecke, Joan, ed. *Practical Help for New Supervisors.* Chicago: American Library Association, 1992.

Lawler III, Edward A. *Treat People Right! How Organizations and Individuals Can Propel Each Other Into a Virtuous Spiral of Success.* San Francisco: Jossey-Bass, 2003.

Low, Kathleen. *Recruiting Library Staff: A How-To-Do-It Manual for Librarians.* New York: Neal-Schuman, 1999.

Lubans, John Jr. "I've Closed My Eyes to the Cold Hard Truth I'm Seeing: Making Performance Appraisal Work." *Library Administration & Management* 13:2 (Spring 1999): 87–89.

Mayo, Diane and Jeanne Goodrich. *Staffing for Results: A Guide to Working Smarter.* Chicago: American Library Association, 2002.

Mullins, John. "People-Centered Management in a Library Context." *Library Review* 50:5/6 (2001): 305–309.

Rogers, Michael. "The Money Tradeoff." *Library Journal*, Nov. 1 2003: 40–41.

Robbins-Carter, Jane and Douglas L. Zweig. "Are We There Yet? Evaluating Library Collections, Reference Services, Programs, and Personnel, Lesson 5." *American Libraries*, Feb. 1985: 108–112.

Rogers, Shelley C. "Out of Theory and Into Practice: Supervising Library Employees." *Journal of Academic Librarianship* 19:3 (1993): 154–157.

Turner, Anne M. "When Firing Someone Is the Only Choice." *Library Journal*, March 15 2004. <http://www.libraryjournal.com/article/CA 386763> 6 May 2004.

White, Herbert S. "What To Evaluate and What To Reward." *Library Journal*, April 15 1999: 62–63.

Wimer, Scott. "The Dark Side of 360-Degree Feedback." *T&D*, Sept. 2002: 37–42.

Chapter 4

Managing People: Managing Different Groups

*Managing library facilities, people, and programs
calls for the weaving together of many diverse
ideas, philosophies, and personalities.*

Lucile Wilson[1]

While you will develop your own particular style and priorities as a library manager, you also must understand that each person you are responsible for comes with his own background and issues. You will need to make adjustments to your own approach in order to manage different people effectively, rather than expecting each to respond to the same management style in the same way. Generalizations are, of course, always dangerous, and each of your employees is an individual, but an understanding of some of the broader issues involved in managing various groups will be helpful nonetheless as you settle into your position.

Managing employees as individuals requires managing with an understanding of their varying backgrounds and perspectives, which are in part (and to differing degrees) influenced by the multiple groups of which they are members. Do not use these to define people, rather, recognize these affiliations and backgrounds as part of the entire constellation of factors that helps you understand them, their perspectives, and their priorities, and how these perspectives and priorities influence their actions and reactions. Managing different groups of employees also requires an honest acknowledgement of your own biases and of the ways in which your background influences your perspectives of and reactions to your employees, as well as a commitment to controlling these biases as much as possible. Pay attention to treating people as individuals.

Your own approach to diversity issues in your library is necessarily impacted by your previous experiences. For example, John Buzas, Branch Manager, Norfolk Public Library, Virginia, explains his background and opinion: "... OCS with the Navy, five years of active duty with the Navy, 15 years with the Naval Reserve, and an MBA somewhere along the way. Every librarian should be required to serve on active duty in the military (as should every citizen) to appreciate the diversity of our population and also the challenges our nation faces." Working or interacting with diverse groups of people in any situation gives you a different perspective on the subject than if you have tended to work primarily with people similar to yourself.

In any library, if you are in charge of people, you will eventually, inevitably, end up managing someone who is in some major way unlike yourself—older, younger, of a different gender, of a different ethnic background, of a different religion. You will need to manage mixed groups in which the members are in some ways unlike one another; you will need to direct your staff's efforts toward serving groups of which none of you are a member; you will need to cultivate respect for cultures and backgrounds and beliefs unlike your own. All of these activities are a natural part of both management and librarianship.

Given that libraries employ a diverse workforce, the questions then become: how best to manage in a diverse environment; how to leverage diversity to spark creativity and innovation; and how to weave diverse backgrounds and perspectives into the creation of a strong organization. Managing diverse groups involves both the way in which you directly manage different individuals and your contributions to an overall institutional commitment to integrating diverse backgrounds, groups, perspectives, and points of view into your library's management structure and decision making, as well as a commitment to recruiting, hiring, and retaining a diverse pool of employees. (ALA offers tips on recruiting for diversity online at: http://www.ala.org/ala/diversity/divrecruitment/recruit ment diversity.htm.)

Diversity Issues

Diversity has become such an overused buzzword that people's instinctive negative reactions to its ubiquity tend to obscure the true importance of cultivating and utilizing a diverse workforce. The basic commonsense premise of valuing diversity, however, is that people of different backgrounds each bring their particular strengths to an institution; the blending and interactions of these strengths and perspectives create an inherently stronger organization. The integration of a variety of backgrounds and points of view allows libraries to thrive and to adapt to changing circumstances, rather than getting stuck in one pattern of thinking as when everyone comes from a common perspective. Zemke, Raines, and Filpatrick talk about the concept of "difference deployment," which they define as "... the tactical use of employees with different backgrounds, experiences, skills, and viewpoints to strengthen project teams, customer contact functions, and, at times, whole departments and units."[2] Libraries, most of which of necessity serve a diverse clientele, may wish to pay particular attention to the ways in which the makeup of their staff does or does not reflect that of the population they serve and the ways in which they can use a diverse staff to strengthen service.

While we may intellectually realize the value of diversity, interacting with people whose backgrounds and perspectives differ from our own can be difficult, because it moves us outside our comfort zone and forces us to confront our own biases. The effective management of diverse groups requires learning to recognize when and why this discomfort occurs, and working to balance it with an appreciation of the contribution diverse perspectives bring to the library. Diversity issues involve any number of groups, and only a few major categories are specifically discussed here. This is not intended to slight any particular group that is not mentioned, but just to give some examples of the types of situations in which diversity issues can come into play.

Understand that local statutes, federal law, administrative policies, and other outside influences impact the way in which you hire, deploy, and manage a diverse population of employees. Take caution from the 2002 Atlanta-Fulton Public Library System reverse-discrimination lawsuit, for example, in which several white employees won a multimillion-dollar argument that they were demoted or reassigned because there were "too many white faces in management"—for reasons completely unrelated to their abilities as library managers. A failure to rein in an openly prejudiced staff member could also lead to lawsuits against both that person and the library itself, not to mention contributing to a toxic work environment for library employees and/or patrons and thwarting your efforts to hire and retain good people. Some libraries or their larger institutions will have official diversity offices or officers, an official diversity statement, and/or verbiage about the institution's commitment to diversity that must be included in every job ad.

Your commitment to the value of diversity in your library requires:

- An acknowledgement of your own conscious and unconscious biases about various groups

- A realization that, while people are influenced by their heritage, they are not entirely defined by that heritage

- A commitment to helping library staff members recognize and work to overcome their own biases so that they can work effectively with, for, and among people of different backgrounds, beliefs, ethnicities, abilities, and orientations

- An expectation that all of your staff members will work up to their potential, no matter their backgrounds, education, or job level, with a concomitant commitment to help bring out that potential in everyone

- A willingness to work on identifying the situations in which a given difference is pertinent, and those in which it is irrelevant

- A recognition that every person is a member of multiple groups, and that no one can be defined by her membership in just one

- A commitment to stepping in when one of your staff members behaves in ways that make other coworkers uncomfortable (e.g., if they are harassing fellow employees, making racial comments, or acting otherwise destructively)

- An understanding that homogeneity can be unhealthy for an organization and a commitment to incorporating diverse perspectives

The same openness and flexibility that serve you well throughout your library career are key to effectively managing diversity in your institution.

Managing Across Generations

When we think about diversity issues in the workplace, generational topics sometimes tend to receive short shrift. As a library manager, however, you will almost inevitably end up with responsibilities for staff members significantly older or younger than you, and you will get better results if you honestly acknowledge the potential gaps in communication and perspective that may get you in trouble. While generational issues cannot absolutely define a person's outlook, they create sometimes quite distinct backgrounds, perspectives, attitudes, and expectations that it behooves you to be aware of. People's shared experiences with their generational cohort tend to lead to a shared perspective on certain issues and shared expectations about managerial behaviors and communication styles.

Watch out, though, for the temptation to draw sweeping generalizations like: "All twentysomethings are job-hoppers and won't commit to staying at my library," or: "All fiftysomethings are technophobes who will have trouble with our automation system." During the hiring process—or at any other time—it is unfair and discriminatory to preemptively judge someone's abilities based solely on their age.

Whether you step right out of library school as a fresh-faced 26 year old into the directorship of a small rural library, are promoted from within after a couple of years on the job and now manage a group of paraprofessionals who have been at an institution for their entire working lives, or find yourself at age 50 in charge of a group of teenage pages and clerks, you will need to modify your managerial approach to fit the work and communication styles of your staff. Beyond communication styles and gaps, generational issues can also affect attitudes toward technology, change, and employer loyalty—or lack thereof.

As hierarchical lines are blurring and a number of long-term library managers are retiring, many librarians are becoming managers at a younger age. Younger managers can face the problem of being taken less seriously by administrators, other managers, and library boards—as well as by library clients!—or of having their ideas dismissed merely because of their age. (See more on dealing with those above you in Chapter 10.) Those manager survey respondents who assumed management responsibilities at a relatively young age share their impressions:

- "I was fairly young when I became a library manager, and often felt as though my older colleagues discounted my opinions and input."

- "The five FTE (full-time employees) here had been without a department head for almost a year, and didn't welcome someone fresh out of school coming in to 'tell them what to do.'"

- "I was the youngest person on the staff and I didn't know how to confront my older colleagues who had more work experience than I did."

- "[My biggest challenge was] supervision of a staff who are all almost twice my age. We work well together (now), but there was initial shock and dismay for them, and an 'oh-my-goodness-what-did-I-get-myself-into' feeling for me."

- "I was the youngest person on the staff. Even the pages who shelved the books were older than I was! I had a bumpy beginning. It was difficult to curb my enthusiasm of finally working in a library. I had tons of ideas, being right out of library school. Trying to convince the older paraprofessionals with all their experience to listen to my ideas was a challenge."

- "The entire workgroup either had, or could have had, children or grandchildren my age. How was I to challenge and motivate them?"

- "My age when accepting the position was probably the biggest issue for everyone around me. When I started this job there was only one person, out of a staff of 18, that was younger than I was. Gaining their trust and confidence in my abilities was a long effort—it actually took the better part of the first year for that to happen."

- "Long-time staff didn't take well to answering to someone much younger than them. I was in my late 20s, they were in their early 60s."

Successfully managing across generations requires respecting the talents and contributions of every individual. Although as a manager fresh out of school—or fresh into library management— you may be brimming with ideas and enthusiasm, you can benefit by tempering this energy with the acquired wisdom of longtime staff. As one younger manager learned: "When you have much more experienced librarians and staff who report to you, respect their experience, ensure that they have the tools, resources, and job satisfaction to get their jobs done, and then get out of their way and let them do their jobs as they know best. This will win you respect and their support for when you present your initiatives for them to contribute to and work on." Value the institutional memory represented by the knowledge and experience of long-time staff.

Managers with responsibilities for staff members significantly younger than themselves also face generational gaps in communication and outlook. The graying of the library profession, as well as an emphasis in many institutions on experience and paying one's dues above all else, means that management responsibilities in many libraries are currently concentrated in baby boomer (those born between 1945–1964) and older librarians. Whether you were promoted into management after a number of years of working in libraries or made a mid-career change into the field, you may be asked to take on responsibility for younger recent grads, high school pages, or others young enough to embody a different outlook and priorities than your own.

Generation X (those born in the mid 1960s to late 1970s) and younger library employees have come of working age into a world where they have watched as a changing economy downsized their elders, and many as a result have less loyalty to their employer, or to any institution, than previous generations. (Although the dot.com bust may have tempered this somewhat.) They have grown up with technology, and can experience impatience with older coworkers who may have a longer learning curve. As opposed to some of the older library workers who entered the field when it had more of an aura of stability about it, many younger library workers have lately entered librarianship precisely because of its current sense of change and possibility.

You may also have difficulty with younger library workers who do not want to put in the same time "paying their dues" as their older colleagues needed to—especially in a traditional library setting, where your younger employees might think they can easily move out of the profession and utilize their library skills to make more money and advance more quickly in a nontraditional setting. Work on emphasizing the intangible benefits of working in your institution and on providing room for staff to grow in their positions and bring in ideas for new programs and services. The flattening of library hierarchies and the choice of the profession as one where people can make a difference can also help retention and motivation.

Younger staff who are new to the field or to your institution may also bring unique perspectives and a fresh pair of eyes to their jobs. After you have spent years in the field, in one position, or in a particular institution, it can be difficult to step back and look objectively at its processes and practices. Younger and newer staff who lack these preconceptions can challenge you by asking why things are done a particular way. Pay attention to their perceptions, and take the opportunity to think about the real reasons behind the way things are done and whether existing practices could be changed to better serve patrons or improve efficiency. This type of flexibility can be useful to libraries in a changing environment. Studies have shown that people who age well are those who keep learning, adapting, and growing—and who better to challenge you to do so than your younger library workers, for whom change is a constant?

Harness the energy of younger workers and new graduates, who bring the excitement of tackling library challenges for the first time. Managing younger workers also gives you the opportunity to mentor your staff and help them grow in their positions. (See more on mentoring in Chapter 3.)

Managing Diversity

One manager survey respondent notes that: "Diversity's one of these things that you have to work on, but nobody wants to talk about. This isn't because people don't have any interest in the issue, but rather because it can be an awkward subject even to approach." The concept of managing diversity covers a range of groups, from persons with disabilities to cultural or ethnic minorities. Managing diverse groups often means managing people who do not share your background or values, which can lead to gaps in communication and difficulty in creating a sense of workplace community. Openness in communication and a willingness to confront these gaps in outlook will serve you well.

A number of legal requirements and regulations govern the way in which you handle diversity issues in your institution. These requirements range from the Americans with Disabilities Act to the Civil Rights Act. Avoid, however, falling into the trap of honoring diversity only insofar as the law and your institution's policies make you comply. Try to move beyond mere tolerance to a true empathy for others' points of view. Understand that maintaining our relevance and the strength of both our organizations and our profession requires incorporating diverse backgrounds and points of view. Homogeneous workforces are at a disadvantage because it is more difficult for them to break out of established patterns of thinking or to challenge the status quo. Studies even point to events like the space shuttle Challenger disaster as occurring in part because of a homogeneity on project teams that led to a "group-think" atmosphere; leading to a culture where the shuttle's defects were not resolved prior to launch. This is another argument for allowing all levels of staff input into library decision making.

Chapter 5 also includes a section on conflict resolution that discusses further how people's perspectives and backgrounds affect both their points of view and their actions. Diversity demands respect for a variety of backgrounds and viewpoints, within the framework of what is best for your organization and its patrons. Work on identifying your own assumptions. Also realize that diversity is the norm in today's libraries, just as it is in the general population; a homogeneous workplace today is neither desirable nor likely. As Christine Watkins points out, "It's also true that not only librarians of color can serve patrons of color, but institutions that reflect their communities are generally more effective, responsive, and accountable to those communities."[3]

Because of the need to serve a diverse community and get along with colleagues from a variety of backgrounds, you may wish to take the opportunity to include instruction on diversity issues when creating your training programs or in-service days (see Chapter 3). There are a number of workshops and models intended to teach library employees respect for other backgrounds, points of view, and so on, which can benefit both library staff and library patrons. Choosing and using such training can be difficult; many library employees are predisposed to mock such efforts as "cheesy," and a less-than-well-done workshop will just confirm their belief that diversity programs are less than useful. In many cases, however, some sort of diversity training may be necessary to help library staff identify their own stereotypes and assumptions and to see instances in which their language or behavior could be hurtful to other staff members or patrons. Pay particular attention to cultural differences among the major ethnic and cultural groups represented in your community and among your staff. See an example of one diversity training program at http://www.lib.utk.edu/~training/diversity.

Librarianship as a whole suffers from a "middle-aged white spinster" stereotype. This image obviously does not reflect all—or even most—librarians, but our image problem means that we often need to battle to attract a younger and more diverse workforce. Associations such as ALA have established scholarships and programs like the Spectrum Initiative to help attract a diverse pool of MLS students, but these are not always successful. The dismantling of LIS programs at historically black schools such as Clark Atlanta University will only exacerbate the difficulties in recruiting, educating, and retaining a diverse librarian population. As a library manager, you can do your part to recruit new members of the profession, to encourage people in your own institution to enter library school, and to model the profession to others.

Be aware also of the various role models that are available—or not available—to different groups within your own institution. If your library's leadership is relatively homogeneous, you might make an effort to encourage a diverse staff to take advantage of mentoring opportunities and to join relevant organizations outside your institution. For various groups, these range from REFORMA (http://www.reforma.org) to ALA's Black Caucus (http://www.bcala.org) to SLA's Gay and Lesbian Issues Caucus (http://www.sla.org/caucus/kglic). Your state association or system might have smaller local groups, caucuses, or chapters that provide additional targeted in-person networking and mentoring opportunities.

Realize that cultural differences can affect a number of everyday interactions between you and your staff members, both verbal and nonverbal. A gesture as simple as a tap on the shoulder, direct eye contact, or differing ideas of an appropriate amount of personal space, can lead to feelings of discomfort or an assumption of disrespect. In any situation, cultivating respect for other individuals and retaining a willingness to modify your own behavior to create a comfortable working environment for your staff will go far.

Managing diversity also includes managing people with varying types of disabilities. The library literature gives much press to accommodating patrons with disabilities, but less attention has been paid to hiring and managing disabled staff. Managers who are uncomfortable, consciously or otherwise, with the idea of managing staff members with disabilities can be more reluctant to hire them, even if they would never straight out say so. These managers are needlessly depriving themselves of potentially impressive employees because of their own issues.

The Americans with Disabilities Act (ADA) requires that you make "reasonable accommodations" so that disabled workers can carry out their job duties. These accommodations can encompass a number of options, from adaptive software to an elevator key, depending on the type and degree of disability. Once you have experienced working with one disabled individual, you will see first-hand how your library is able to accommodate workers with differing needs and become more able to look past a disability to work with a person. As with anything else, experience makes the unfamiliar seem commonplace.

Resources for librarians managing diversity within their institutions include ALA's Office for Library Personnel Resources (OLPR) and Committee On Diversity. ALA's Office for Diversity offers training and workshops on diversity issues, ideas on recruiting a diverse workforce, and other resources; it also publishes five times a year a bulletin called *Versed* that addresses diversity issues in libraries. Check the ALA Web site at http://www.ala.org/diversity for more information. ACRL, Southeastern Library Network (SOLINET), and the Historically Black Colleges and Universities (HBCU) also cosponsor an annual National Diversity in Libraries conference, with the goal of increasing diversity among library staff and collections and improving service to diverse users. See http://www.librarydiversity.org.

Understand that you will also have legal and ethical require-ments governing the way in which you interact with your library's diverse clientele. A diverse staff and an overall comfort level with diversity issues should serve you equally well here.

Managing Different Groups

All libraries, except for the smallest one-person operations, are comprised of people working at different tasks and with differing levels of responsibility. Each group requires a somewhat different managerial approach. In any approach you take, however, adher-ence to the principle that all staff members have the same right to fair treatment and the opportunity to learn and grow in their posi-tions is an excellent starting point.

Managing Professionals

Managing a group of professional librarians carries potential pitfalls. Managing professionals has been likened to "herding cats," as each may have his own idea on how the department, the institution, or at least his own small part of the organization should be run. Joan Giesecke suggests that: "Managing profession-als is a form of managing managers. While many professional libraries may not think of themselves as managers, as profession-als they manage their time, manage the delivery of services, and manage resources."[4] Managing professionals who themselves have some "management" responsibilities requires that you mod-ify your approach to include more staff input and to allow more autonomy. Librarians can be especially difficult to manage in teams due to a professional value of individuality.

Managing a group of colleagues with a shared professional background, however, can also be quite rewarding. Librarians bring their professional expertise and perspective to bear on the running of departments, programs, and services, and you will all benefit by working together to incorporate this group's various ideas and talents.

Managing Paraprofessionals

The chance to manage paraprofessionals (support staff, or non-MLS personnel) creates myriad opportunities for the perspicacious library manager. Many paraprofessionals possess a wealth of knowledge about a particular institution, its customers, and its procedures, built up from years of experience. In most institutions, turnover has generally been lower among nondegreed staff. As a new manager, you may find that when you enlist the assistance of your paraprofessionals you will receive the most help in assimilating into the institutional environment, getting to know library patrons, or seeing how procedures and programs are carried out.

Nip any condescension toward non-MLS staff by your degreed librarians firmly in the bud. As Susan K. Martin writes: "Separating out any group of people as less than qualified, or less than capable of participating in the complicated world and work of librarianship is unfair to that group of people, undercuts the mission and goals of the organization, and reflects poorly upon the profession of librarianship itself."[5]

Rhonda Hankins, Communications Coordinator, The Jamail Center for Legal Research, University of Texas at Austin puts it even more bluntly in her response to the staff survey, saying:

> One of the poor traits library managers can fall victim to is strictly dividing "professional" and "nonprofessional" duties. While there may be valid institutional reasons for hiring staff members with the master's in library science degree or equivalent, favoring the "professional" staff with advance notice of library news (say, pending budget cuts or policy changes) damages morale and creates a divided workforce. Resentment breeds, hostility simmers, and the library suffers. What

your mother taught you is true, managers—treat people how you want to be treated. Lousy library managers who cannot respect nonprofessionals create a nasty work atmosphere.

Find more on clear communication to all staff in Chapter 5, but realize your responsibility to avoid fostering divisiveness among library staff members. A number of respondents to the staff survey mentioned a frustration with perceived management favoritism toward MLS staff.

Managing paraprofessionals also allows you the opportunity to provide the education and training necessary for your staff to move up within the organization. Encourage your parapros to investigate certification, library technician, or MLS programs; the profession and your institution can only grow stronger by the infusion of new blood and new ideas. Encourage your institution to provide financial support for MLS education, if possible. Encourage your staff to join paraprofessional organizations and roundtables, such as Council on Library/Media Technicians (COLT; http://colt.ucr.edu) or ALA's Library Support Staff Interests Round Table (SSIRT; http://www.ala.org/ssirt), as well as local organizations. Invite them to participate freely on e-mail discussion lists for nondegreed library workers, such as LIBSUP-L (http://listserv.delta.edu/archives/libsup-l.html). Networking is as important for paraprofessionals as for MLS-librarians and library managers. Like the roles of librarians, the roles of support staff are constantly evolving, and in many libraries nondegreed staff have great levels of responsibility—or even manage the whole place.

Managing Students, Volunteers, Temps, Contractors, and Interns

Managing any group of "nonregular" employees presents unique challenges. Those who come to work in your library as volunteers, students, interns, or other nontraditional employees may bring very different values or ideas about what library service (or their particular job) should entail. They may lack loyalty to your institution, or may require extra training to bring them up to speed. Your management of these individuals thus requires modification to meet their specific needs. Union rules may also govern the way in which you can hire and deploy these different groups.

Managing students can be particularly challenging, because work-study employees or high school pages may lack the same commitment to the goals of your institution as regular staff members. (See also the discussion of managing across generations earlier in this chapter.) While some student workers are dedicated, part of your mission with others may be merely to train them how to have a job, impressing on them the importance of such basic issues as arriving on time and the concept of proper work attire.

Volunteers work out of a somewhat different motivation than many of your other staff members. You will need to have specific policies in place in order to identify volunteers' skills and to deploy, train, and use them most effectively. Also realize that volunteers may have multiple commitments and competing priorities, and that some cannot be relied upon to keep regular schedules. Again, this will vary person by person and library by library. In some libraries, union rules may prohibit the use of volunteers in many areas, on the assumption that unpaid labor could be used to replace the work of paid staff members. In others, you will need to address staff concerns that their jobs are in jeopardy because of your use of unpaid workers, or rebut your board's (or other community members') suggestion that volunteers can effectively replace paid staff entirely.

Along the same lines, you need to decide on the tasks volunteers can be relied upon to carry out. You may want to be careful, for example, of deploying volunteers in any capacity where patrons' privacy could be compromised, or of using untrained volunteers to complete tasks normally taken on by degreed librarians. Look for special projects or for supplementary tasks that could benefit from volunteers' efforts. Examples include homework centers, book sales, library tours, and book buddy programs. Take the opportunity to recognize your volunteers for their efforts, however, especially if you are using teenagers completing community service hours or others who would likely appreciate the attention. Realize that volunteers who donate their time to the library can be a great base of support to draw upon in other areas as well; treat them with care!

Decide how extensive a volunteer program you are willing to manage and how useful volunteers may be at your institution, and then recruit accordingly. Treat your volunteers seriously: Have them fill out applications stating their skills, interview them, and train them for the tasks at hand. Some libraries have even begun conducting background checks on all volunteers, or at least on those who will be working directly with children. To find additional volunteers, you can approach organizations such as high schools, which often have a community service requirement, senior organizations, and so on. Also examine your library's insurance policy to be sure that volunteers are covered—the last thing you need is an uncovered on-the-job injury.

Library and information temporary/employment agencies are a growing business, and temps (from agencies or otherwise) who have already learned your library's culture and procedures can be a great resource to draw upon when the time comes to hire someone for a permanent position. (See more on outsourcing and contracting in Chapter 7.) Libraries may choose to hire temporary employees to work on a fixed project, such as adding RFID (radio frequency identification) tags to collections, doing retrospective conversion, or cataloging a batch of foreign-language materials. They may also hire on a contract basis for a grant-funded or other position of fixed duration, to provide training, or to set up a special program. These temporary employees need management and supervision, just as permanent staff members do.

You may also be responsible for managing the work of an intern from an MLS or LTA program. Interns often are quite self-motivated, as their time in your library provides them with invaluable skills and experience that will help them move into a permanent library-related position in the future. Using interns in your library also provides you with additional opportunities to mentor younger library workers and identify potential future employees.

Managing Mixed Groups

Usually there are not such clear-cut lines around the groups of people for whom you are responsible, and you will concurrently manage people from a variety of different groups. Managing a mixed group (or groups) of people with various backgrounds and educational, responsibility, and age levels can be difficult. Staff members may notice any variation in the way you treat people, and will inevitably assume that these variations point toward a favoritism toward someone other than themselves. You need to be sure to give all of your staff members an equal opportunity to excel and to grow in their positions.

Different individuals, departments, and projects, due to their different function and personalities, however, may truly require different handling. The key here lies in making sure that your expectations of and respect for your employees are similar, and that you encourage each to work up to his or her potential and to meet organizational goals by carrying out their duties. You do not need to treat everyone the same way; you do need to treat everyone—and everyone's work—as equally important. You are there to help motivate, guide, and support your employees. Make use of people's individual strengths, which might also require a reexamination of job descriptions or duties. Too many libraries neglect to take a regular look at their existing job descriptions in light of changing circumstances and community needs; doing so can serve the dual purpose of better meeting the needs of your community while also better utilizing the skills of your staff members.

Managing Customers

It may seem strange to think about managing your customers, but, because librarianship ultimately comes down to our relationships with our patrons, you will need to manage these as carefully as your relationships with your staff. Whether your library just calls this customer service, or plays the "invert the organization chart" game that shows graphically your commitment to putting patrons first, your library's purpose and activities always boil down to service to its constituency.

Managing customers is in some ways similar to managing staff. You want to influence behavior by encouraging patrons to attend programs, use services, and support the institution, for example. Convey your excitement about the library to patrons, and encourage your staff to do the same. (See much more on marketing your library and interacting with your community in Chapter 10.) Developing your library's relationship with your customers lets them feel a vested interest in your library's success. Satisfied clients can be your biggest advocates, and you need always to keep in mind that your users provide the very reason for your institution's existence.

In the same way you provide your staff with the tools they need to do their jobs, gauge whether the tools you provide your patrons enable them to do their own work. Is your OPAC user-friendly? Is your staff? Do your collections match the needs of your community?

Librarians are best able to manage multiple and different groups by drawing on their ability to multitask and to see things from various perspectives. Library managers who make a habit of reading and learning widely can transfer this same openness to managing diversity in their institutions, incorporating multiple perspectives and backgrounds into their libraries.

Notes

1. Lucile Wilson, *People Skills for Library Managers: A Common Sense Guide for Beginners* (Englewood: Libraries Unlimited, 1996) vii.

2. Ron Zemke, Claire Raines, and Bob Filipczak, *Generations at Work: Managing the Clash of Veterans, Boomers, Xers, and Nexters in Your Workplace* (New York: AMACOM, 2000) 154.

3. Christine Watkins, "A Community Mirror: Reflections on the Color of Librarianship," *American Libraries*, Nov. 1999: 64.

4. Joan Giesecke, *Practical Strategies for Library Managers* (Chicago: ALA Editions, 2001) 2.

5. Susan K. Martin, "Clinging to 'Status:' The Attitude of Librarians to the Non-MLS Staff," *The Journal of Academic Librarianship* 23:3 (May 1997): 222.

Recommended Reading

Adkins, Denice and Isabel Espinal. "The Diversity Mandate." *Library Journal*, April 15, 2004: 52–54.

Balderrama, Sandra Ríos. "This Trend Called Diversity." *Library Trends* 49:1 (Summer 2000): 194–214.

Barlow, Cara. "Don't Just Serve People With Disabilities—Hire Them." *American Libraries*, Sept. 1995: 772–773.

Beck, Mary Ellen. "The ABCs of Gen X for Librarians." *Information Outlook*, Feb. 1, 2001: 16–20.

Bennis, Warren G. and Robert J. Thomas. *Geeks and Geezers: How Era, Values, and Defining Moments Shape Leaders*. Boston: Harvard Business School Press, 2002.

Berger, Marshall A. "Technology Brings Challenges and Opportunities for Support Staff." *American Libraries*, March 1997: 30–31.

Block, Marylaine. "Preserving Institutional Memory." *Ex Libris*, May 23, 2003. <http://marylaine.com/exlibris/xlib77.html> 23 August 2003.

Chervinko, James S. "Temporary Employees in Academic and Research Libraries." *The Journal of Academic Librarianship* 12:4 (1986): 217–220.

Connelly, Julie. "Youthful Attitudes, Sobering Realities: A Tough Labor Market Hasn't Shaken Priorities of Younger Workers." *The New York Times*, Oct. 28, 2003: E1, E6.

Jones, Marie. "Strategies for Managing an Aging Workforce." *The Southeastern Librarian* 50:4 (Winter 2003): 10–15.

McCarthy, Cheryl Ann. "Volunteers and Technology: The New Reality." *American Libraries*, June/July 1996: 67–71.

McCook, Kathleen de la Peña. "Diversity Deferred: Where Are the Minority Librarians?" *Library Journal*, Nov. 1, 1993: 35–38.

McKenna, Patrick J. and David H. Maister. *First Among Equals: How to Manage a Group of Professionals*. New York: The Free Press, 2002.

Riggs, Donald E. and Patricia A. Tarin, eds. *Cultural Diversity in Libraries*. New York: Neal-Schuman, 1994.

Thiederman, Sondra. *Making Diversity Work: 7 Steps for Defeating Bias in the Workplace*. Chicago: Dearborn, 2003.

Urgo, Marisa. *Developing Information Leaders: Harnessing the Talents of Generation X*. London: Bowker-Sauer, 2000.

Watkins, Christine. "A Community Mirror: Reflections on the Color of Librarianship." *American Libraries*, Nov. 1999: 64–66.

Winston, Mark, ed. *Managing Multiculturalism and Diversity in the Library: Principles and Issues for Administrators*. New York: Haworth, 1999.

Zemke, Ron, Claire Raines, and Bob Filipczak. *Generations at Work: Managing the Clash of Veterans, Boomers, Xers, and Nexters in Your Workplace*. New York: AMACOM, 2000.

Chapter 5

Managing People: Communication and Leadership

> *While average leaders tend to be invisible, the best leaders frequently walk around and strike up conversations with their staff, asking about their families and other personal matters. They also let it be known that they want to be informed, creating an atmosphere of openness that makes it easier for communication to take place.*
> Daniel Goleman[1]

Any list of the qualities of a good manager highlights communication and leadership skills, and reams of literature are devoted to helping those in management positions develop, or at least display, these qualities. Librarian managers have an edge in the communication department; much library-related training and background involves learning how to impart information to others. Now, use these skills with your staff, board, patrons, and other groups. Realize also that communication skills can be learned, and make the effort to turn yourself into a great communicator.

Leadership skills go hand-in-hand with communication because an integral part of being a leader involves the ability to communicate with others. You will need to be able to clarify your goals and to communicate those goals to your staff in a way that makes them want to help achieve them. Good communication skills will also help you have productive interactions with your larger community, your own boss, and your colleagues. (Interaction with these groups is addressed in Chapter 10.)

Communication

Libraries that fail to recognize the importance of freely flowing communication are failed organizations. You will need to hone your own communication skills in order to share effectively what you want from your staff, what your upper management or larger institution requires from them, the goals of the organization, information on upcoming changes, and so on. You will also need to encourage your staff members to communicate freely with one another—and with you—as well as to communicate effectively with patrons. Good communication on all sides and at all levels is essential to accomplishing organizational goals; top-down communication is important, but is only one piece of the puzzle. Try to avoid falling into the bureaucratic "need-to-know" trap; libraries and librarians thrive on the free flow of information in all directions. As one respondent to the staff survey emphasizes: "I am always appalled that a profession that is so concerned with the dissemination of information is full of managers that are so poor at communicating information to their under people. Sometimes, I feel like it isn't always the case that the managers are just personally poor communicators, I think library managers too often think that their under people don't need to know things or shouldn't know things ... this is wrong and detrimental to the organization."

Follow some simple guidelines to communicate more effectively as a library manager. First, never pretend to have knowledge or capabilities that you do not have. If you do not have the answer to an employee's immediate problem, promise to find out and get back to him within a set amount of time, then do so. If you try to save face or sidestep an issue by lying, your employee will be angrier when he finds out the truth than if you had been honest from the beginning. Always be truthful with your staff. When employees learn things through unofficial channels of communication—and they will!—rather than from you, your lack of communication will begin eroding the foundation of trust you need for productive working relationships. Having the "official" word, further, will help stop often-inaccurate rumors from spreading throughout the institution.

This is another reason never to hoard information. Libraries, devoted to the free flow of information, should understand more than other organizations the importance of keeping the lines of communication clear and of giving people the information they need to do their jobs and to create innovative solutions. While keeping your staff informed, take the time to explain the reasoning behind your decisions and to elicit reactions and feedback from others, who may have fresh ideas or perspectives to contribute.

In addition to being willing and able to provide information to your staff, be open to the information that they can provide you, and ready to act on what they tell you. Always be eager to listen; never dismiss an idea merely because someone is a paraprofessional, is new, is young, or is otherwise apart from the normal decision-making hierarchy. Encourage communication at all levels. As one manager survey respondent puts it: "While many decisions are left solely to the manager, always take time to consult with others, particularly those you supervise. Their ideas and suggestions, as well as their knowledge of their job, will help you more than you know!" Listen to your staff and act on their suggestions as appropriate; you'll show your employees that you value them, their contributions, and their knowledge of the library.

Work together with your staff to implement new programs and services and incorporate new ideas, keeping your library relevant and attuned to your patrons' changing needs. Another manager survey respondent explains: "Listen to your staff. They have great ideas! Many times a staff member comes to me with a great idea and I tell her to 'run with it' and see what she comes up with. Some of our best programs and projects are because my staff all work together, sharing suggestions and brainstorming." Listening to and learning from your staff can also help you feel less alone in your position, especially in a smaller library. Understand that you are part of an entire group of people, both staff and management, who care about the success of your organization; work with them to ensure that success.

If a staff member brings a situation to your attention, do what you can to resolve it in a timely fashion, and provide progress reports. Have a realistic "open-door" policy, so that staff know you are approachable, and give employees your full attention when they are speaking. Let staff bring even bad news or complaints—although no one welcomes bad news, you will never be able to resolve situations of which you are unaware. The chance to air grievances may help in and of itself. Consultant and writer Cliff Farides notes of his management success: "I understood that people wanted to be listened to and sometimes just being a 'ventee' would resolve many problems." When you listen, really do try to hear what staff are saying. One respondent to the staff survey expresses her frustration with a previous manager, saying that she "didn't and couldn't really listen, though she appeared to be listening—frequently seemed to be hearing (and responding to) something going on in her own head instead of what the other person was saying."

When talking to your staff, remember to listen to what is behind their words. People are sometimes understandably reluctant to speak bluntly to managers who have power over their jobs, work life, or raises. Emphasize your preference for respectful honesty, and be alert to the times when staff may be circling around their true concerns. Again, this will become easier as you get to know your staff members and where they are coming from, as well as the feelings and background that may affect what they actually say. Watch for nonverbal cues as well as listen to people's specific words. Use artful pauses in conversation to give them a chance to think about and expand on their statements or to gain the confidence to be more specific, and refrain from interrupting your staff. Ask clarifying, open-ended questions to get them to open up further. Demonstrate that you understand their feelings and position by reflecting these back in your own words. ("So, I hear you saying that you feel … ")

Give credit where credit is due. As Edward Lawler bluntly points out: "Employees want managers who are focused on human capital, not their own egos. The manager who is always front and center, monopolizing the credit for all good things that happen, is not valued by the employees who work for him or her. To be effective leaders, managers need to share the successes and the limelight in many ways."[2] Be very careful always to credit those responsible for ideas, projects, and successes in your library. If you make a habit of claiming all the recognition for their good work, they are unlikely to be motivated to repeat their efforts and their relationship with you as a manager will be strained. Recognition can be a powerful motivator; those who are credited for their good work will be inclined to try to duplicate their success.

When emphasizing the importance of good work, make your priorities clear. Make sure your staff knows what tasks are most important, when rules can be slightly bent, how the workflow is organized, and what to do first. You cannot fault them for not acting on your priorities if you have never communicated your wishes. You might also wish to create a procedure manual to guide staff through resolving common situations; review its contents regularly in light of changing circumstances.

When talking to library employees, watch both your own language and your nonverbal communication patterns. The way you express yourself and the way you come across to your staff can have a big impact. Many managers fall into negative patterns of speaking and responding, with no real awareness of how others perceive them. This awareness needs to extend to your body language and other nonverbal cues as well. (Are you standing too close when you talk? Are you crossing your arms on your chest, tapping your fingers, looking at something else while the other person is talking? Do you allow phone calls or e-mail to interrupt you while others are speaking?) Watch for any tendency to be sarcastic or to put others down. It is easy to fall into patterns where you automatically communicate this way, but sarcasm from a supervisor can be wounding, and detrimental to your relationships with your staff. Their inability to deal with sarcasm or other belittling behavior on your part is not their problem, but yours— you are the manager, and it is your responsibility to modify your own way of communicating.

View things from your staff's perspective. Peter F. Drucker puts it succinctly: "Empathy is a practical competence."[3] This includes not overwhelming staff with irrelevant information, while still providing them with that which is necessary to do their jobs and function inside the institution. It also includes addressing issues and problems from their point of view, emphasizing the points in which your staff is likely to be most interested. Pay attention to diversity issues in your library and to the ways in which staff members' backgrounds affect the way they communicate with you and with each other; you need to be alert to the potential for diverse backgrounds to cause unfortunate errors in communication.

Strive for clarity and conciseness in all of your communications, whether verbal, written, or electronic. One manager survey respondent explains: "Always be as specific about what you want as you possibly can. Communication is a major stumbling block. Statements always are open to interpretation, so the more specific your requests, the better off everyone is." Being clear extends to speaking clearly and distinctly; mumbling managers may find that staff are too nervous to ask them to clarify their statements and that their important communications are therefore lost in translation. Learn the difference between assertive and aggressive communication; display confidence through your words and tone, while never using your position to intimidate others.

For important communications, allow various methods to back each other up. After an oral performance review, for example, provide an employee with a written copy of your comments for her future reference. Follow up an e-mail discussion with an in-person chat. Learn here where redundancy is helpful and where it is unnecessary so that you can also avoid the trap of unnecessary communication—do not leave someone a voice-mail message merely to tell them that you have just sent them an e-mail. Use common sense to guide you in deciding what matters are important enough to use various channels of communication.

These ideas all of course boil down to the importance of staying in touch with and approachable by your staff. If you direct a library, be sure to visit each department often and to schedule regular department head and staff meetings. If you manage a department, spend some regular time one-on-one with each employee, hold regular department meetings, and make a point of keeping your hand in when it comes to the day-to-day work. Realize the importance of ongoing communication, and of communication that is not strictly work-related. Say hello, ask how someone's weekend went, see how their kids did at their last soccer game. Get to know your employees as individuals and make them feel comfortable in all of their conversations with you. Fostering a culture of communication leads to an empowered and happy staff, which in turn leads to better-served and happy customers.

Technology

Computer technology has opened up a number of new avenues for communication, from the ubiquitous e-mail message to instant messaging, blogs, and intranets. Part of your job as a manager may involve getting your staff accustomed to using these various methods, clarifying when each is appropriate, and balancing "face time" with electronic communication. If you make a habit of issuing important memos via e-mail, for example, you need to be sure that your staff makes a habit of checking their in-boxes on a regular basis. If you make a habit of issuing lengthy memos via e-mail, realize that many people will not take the time to scroll through the whole message. If you implement an internal Weblog to post library issues, new reference materials, or items of note, ensure that staff are trained on its use and that it is easily (one click) accessible.

Also recognize the interaction of technological and generational issues (which of course does not fall along strict age lines). Staff who have been accustomed for years to bringing their proposals to their supervisors in person may not feel comfortable with now presenting their ideas via e-mail, for example. As you add e-mail and other electronic technologies to the communications mix, realize that it is very difficult to manage effectively in a completely virtual format, which lacks the verbal and other cues of in-person interaction. Face-to-face communication with employees may often feel more personal, and allows them to feel a greater connection to you and your words. One manager survey respondent says that library managers need to: "... know when to use e-mail to communicate, when to use the telephone to communicate, when to use group discussions to communicate, when to use one-on-one and face-to-face communications methods. E-mail is often a last resort."

Resist the temptation to use technology for technology's sake; use the appropriate method of communication for what you are trying to convey. When presenting information that people might want to keep handy, such as instructions for logging into the network or numbers they need to call in an emergency, a printed memo that staff can tack to a bulletin board or file might be most appropriate. E-mail can be inaccessible in times of technological crisis. Match your communication method to the formality and urgency of the situation, as well as to the specific audience. For important communications, use multiple methods to reinforce your point. Follow up e-mail with a meeting, a phone call with a memo.

Think also about the tendency of technology to make you always available. You may need to begin to set limits; some managers set aside specific times of the day to read and respond to e-mail, while others let voice mail handle their calls at busy times. Find a balance that allows technology to work for you, rather than you being at its beck and call.

Meetings

One of the most derided of all workplace activities, meetings nevertheless serve an important function in allowing library employees and managers a set aside time and space to communicate, brainstorm, and collaborate. Meetings are also essential in getting people to turn their group efforts toward organizational goals. Since most people have had horrendous meeting experiences, if you learn to facilitate useful ones, your staff will be impressed by your abilities—and eternally grateful. One staff survey respondent, for example, shares: "We have these meetings that are really frustrating. They basically consist of relaying information from memos or previous meetings that we haven't been invited to, then involve lengthy complaints that are outside of the scope of the agenda and never lead to any solutions. A more effective manager would allow room for comment, but keep everything on track, and either invite us to the original meetings or send us an e-mail recap." Ask what your staff finds most frustrating about your institution's current meetings, and work on those issues first. When people realize that meetings are no longer wasting their time, they will feel more inclined to contribute—or even to attend. Items often covered in library meetings include new policies, problem patrons, reports from working groups on large projects, problem-solving and brainstorming sessions, ideas for new services or expansion of existing services, and coverage of new material or programs.

The number one rule of chairing meetings? Keep them short, productive, and on schedule. When meetings take up so much of your or your staff's time that you are unable to get to the day-to-day work of running your library, take a hard look at your priorities. Meet only as necessary, not just for the sake of meeting; have a concise and descriptive agenda as well as set objectives. Do not over-schedule either the topics for discussion in any one meeting or meetings themselves. You will get a feel for this over time, but group discussion, once it gets rolling, often takes longer than anticipated. Avoid the trap of rushing through the last half of every meeting or regularly going over your scheduled time. Make it clear at the outset whether a particular meeting is intended to impart information, solicit input, share ideas, or make decisions. Make your agenda and your introduction reflect the meeting's goals; part of your job as facilitator is to define the purpose of the meeting and keep it moving toward its goal or goals.

Think about the necessity and timeframe of any meeting you call—if monthly staff meetings, for example, seem to drag, try shortening the allotted timeslot and see if you can tighten them up. As Robert Kriegel and David Brandt point out: "Meetings are a lot like the hot air they produce: They'll expand or contract to fill the space available. If you're scheduled for an hour and a half, people will fill up that time. Shorten the meeting and generally the same amount of work gets done."[4] If you need just to share a straightforward piece of information, consider writing an e-mail or a memo rather than calling a meeting.

Also keep unplanned meetings to a minimum and stick to a regular schedule if possible. While the odd emergency situation may call for an unannounced meeting, in most cases people will appreciate being able to plan their schedule—and their comments! Turn your organization of information skills toward planning and organizing meetings. When meetings are planned in advance, you or your staff have time to prepare. You can provide background material for people to read beforehand, and/or particular ideas for them to think about and to bring comments. You do not want to make a habit of meeting only in an emergency. If you get in the habit of conducting regular and productive meetings, your staff will be accustomed to meeting, discussing, and working together to resolve less pressing issues, and then can transfer those skills to resolving crisis situations as well.

Keep your meetings focused and on target. You may have a staff member who continually digresses from the topic at hand and returns to a pet subject, or have a few who are easily sidetracked by tangential issues. Be willing and able to cut these off-topic conversations short in order to concentrate on the business at hand. Most attendees will thank you for it, and you will find that your meetings become much more productive and shorter. Use agendas, and make sure everyone attending receives one ahead of time. Agendas ensure that attendees are not blindsided, that they are prepared to stay on track, and that they can be prepared to discuss the various agenda items.

Keep meetings on time. Start at the announced time, even if some people have not yet arrived. Keep on schedule, and finish at the announced time, even if people would like to keep talking. Again, this allows people to schedule their time productively, and, after they become used to the system, will encourage them to keep their comments during the meeting brief and topical. You can always use the trick of scheduling a meeting an hour before most people are scheduled to leave for the day; this ensures that they have a personal stake in ending on time.

Make sure everyone gets a say. Working with a mix of different personalities, you know already that some have a tendency to dominate discussion, while others prefer to keep a low profile and may feel more comfortable voicing their opinion privately. While you can respect this to some extent, the function of meetings as a place for group discussion and problem solving is lost if some people do not feel comfortable speaking up or if the same voices are always heard. Create a space for quieter staff members to have their say by addressing them directly; try tactics such as: "What do you think of his proposal?" or "I'd like to hear your ideas on how this will affect your workflow." Use open-ended questions here, to avoid getting back just a "yes" or "no" answer. Never allow more vocal staff members to silence or disparage the ideas of others. Develop methods for shifting the conversation away from those who tend to monopolize the meeting, and never let attendees put each other down. Ask quieter participants to help contribute by presenting a specific agenda item at the next meeting, giving them a preset topic to talk about.

Share your enthusiasm for the topic(s) being discussed. Enthusiasm is infectious, and your interest in the subject will help other people to feel comfortable with sharing theirs. As meeting chair or facilitator, your attitude goes a long way toward setting the tone for the meeting as a whole. When thinking about comfort levels, pay attention also to the physical environment. Just as a cheerful, well-organized, and comfortable library welcomes patrons and in itself increases their positive feelings toward your institution, a meeting room that is well lighted, laid out so that people can comfortably converse, and not subject to extremes in temperature enhances positive feelings among staff.

Meetings in libraries may be more or less formal, depending on the size and type of your institution and the type and size of group that is meeting. A team meeting of people who have been working together for years will have a different feeling than a meeting you facilitate between department heads and board members, or one you hold for all staff, but each requires the same attention to detail and basic skills to stay on target.

Conflict Resolution

Most library managers hate dealing with conflict. This is natural! Still, you cannot afford to let interpersonal conflicts fester. If left unaddressed, these conflicts will eventually undermine the effectiveness of your department, or even of your entire library. Make a commitment to stand firm when faced with difficult situations or personalities; when you agreed to become a library manager, you assumed responsibility for dealing with conflict. One manager survey respondent emphasizes: "Don't put off facing difficult personnel problems. They will only get worse with time. The sooner you deal with the problem, the sooner it will be resolved. Procrastination is the enemy of management."

Have confidence in your own ability to resolve an unpleasant situation. Try never to make decisions or to react, however, in the heat of the moment. If a conflict flares up between two of your employees, for example, in most cases it will help to give them (and yourself!) some time to cool off before sitting down to talk to them about the problem. If you must react immediately, try to remove the person or people from the situation first, adjourning to your office or to another private and/or neutral location. Recognize the grievances of both parties, trying to empathize with each, even if your own sympathies lie largely on one side or the other.

Many conflicts largely boil down to differences in personality and outlook. Realizing that you are here dealing with adults and are unlikely to be able to change their personalities, you need instead to provide your conflicting employees with the tools they need to get along. Your job as manager is to ensure that their conflict does not interfere with institutional or departmental goals, that it does not poison the work environment for others, and that they are able to do their jobs. Realize also that workplace conflict is inevitable and natural; differing points of view, priorities, and personalities often lead to disagreements.

Learn also the difference between one-time conflicts and a pattern of destructive behavior. Conflicts between colleagues are inevitable, but ongoing or repetitive issues create a bigger problem. Occasional conflicts can be useful in drawing out ideas and hammering out resolutions; these clashes reflect creative tension and differences of opinion rather than a pattern of destructive interaction. Ongoing arguments that lack resolution, or conflicts that degenerate into personal attacks, are something else entirely. More than one observer has likened workplace and family dynamics; try not to let yours become dysfunctional. Look at the underlying issues that may be affecting participants' reactions—conflicts generally take some time to build, and rarely appear out of the blue. If you have entered a managerial position at an institution where conflicts have been allowed to brew for some time, a seemingly new situation may just be another manifestation of a long-running argument.

When managing your own conflicts with employees or peers, recognize that you bring your own background and point of view to every interaction, just as your staff members do. Your job as a library manager is to think about your own patterns and to assess their effectiveness in managing the interpersonal dynamics in your library. Sometimes, modifying your own behavior slightly is enough to ameliorate the situation, or to prompt the other party to modify hers. Try to empathize with the other person's point of view, which can also give you an effective starting point for making an argument that their behavior needs to change. Try to really listen to the other person; avoid, for example, arguing your side in your head while they are talking. It is even more important that you nurture your own ability to minimize conflict with others than that you work to manage conflict among your staff members. You serve as an example for staff who will (consciously or unconsciously) often model their behavior on yours.

The willingness to deal with conflict needs to extend to the ability to say "no." Supervisors who give in to every request quickly gain reputations as pushovers. Make your decisions based on the best course of action for the library, not on what seems the most comfortable or convenient or popular choice. This can be especially difficult for librarians, whose training and background have taught them to want to say "yes." ("Yes, we can get that material; yes, I'd be happy to help you with that.") Library managers, however, need to learn to set limits and to moderate their responses accordingly. Saying "no" is at times essential, to avoid over-committing either yourself or your staff. Set limits for your staff, in the same way you sometimes need to set limits for your patrons. ("No, you cannot use those book covers to make a collage for your school report; no, you cannot run screaming through the stacks.")

Building Relationships

Managers who have worked their way up through the library ranks may find they have an edge over those managers new to librarianship, being able to empathize personally with the situations faced by their subordinates. Those new to the library world will need to build that empathy over time. Never make the mistake of only working on your relationships with senior staff or other managers; if nothing else, understand that your newer and younger librarians will someday be in those ranks, and it can then be too late to start. Realize also that ideas can come from many sources.

One of the most important steps in building successful relationships with your staff is never being afraid to admit that you were wrong. Your staff knows no one is infallible; what will put them off is a boss who pretends to be perfect or one who fails to learn from her mistakes—or, especially, one who makes a habit of blaming others! Take responsibility for your own actions before expecting your staff to do the same. Honestly owning up to any miscalculations in judgment can go a long way toward building a foundation of trust, and can help staff feel more comfortable and less likely to try and hide their own inevitable errors. As one manager survey respondent emphasizes: "Don't worry about admitting you do not know everything. Staff will learn not to fear mistakes when they see that you are willing to admit to yours." See more on building relationships with various groups in Chapter 10.

Leadership

While leaders are not necessarily managers, the best managers are leaders, when it comes to their own department, division, or library. As an accidental library manager, it may take some time for you to feel fully confident in your own abilities. Like anything else, effective leadership is a learned set of skills. You will continually learn and grow throughout your career. Be careful, however, to project an aura of confidence in your own abilities from the outset. You can of course admit you have learning to do, but you do not want to give staff the impression they can walk all over you. Unfortunately, there are always those who will try to take advantage of your good nature or inexperience. It is harder to recover from a situation in which staff have developed disrespect for you than it is to begin as you mean to continue.

Dip into one, or several, of the never-ending streams of guides to effective leadership to find theories or lists of characteristics. Basically, the most effective leaders are those who encourage and guide their employees to learn, grow, and help the organization achieve its goals. Yes, what we have been talking about all along!

Your best and simplest method of being a leader is to become a manager that others will want to follow and to emulate—to lead by example, never falling into the "do as I say, not as I do" trap. Library managers overall do not fit well into the model of heroic leadership, or of leadership by authoritative directives. Libraries work better under the model where you as leader serve as a catalyst, encouraging others to do their best work in pursuit of commonly shared goals, and getting them to want to follow your plans and ideas. Energize and enthuse your staff! Leadership in libraries best succeeds when your employees become committed to their work and your library's success, rather than merely doing their jobs. Communicate your vision for your library and/or department and get others to share in that vision, so that you can work toward it together.

Those who are new to library management can think about the opportunities they have had in the past to lead others—whether in a volunteer organization, a club, a committee, or even a group project in school. Diane Rosen, Library Technician and Manager of Circulation at Nellis Air Force Base Library, Nevada, claims that: "Being a mother of three prepared me to be a manager more than any schooling or training I have ever had."

Delegation

Part of your role as a leader will be to help build confidence in others. Part of building that confidence is learning when to delegate responsibility. This may be difficult. After all, you are ultimately responsible for the quality of your staff's work. However, you do your staff no favors by making a habit of doing work that others are capable of doing. Failure to delegate hinders your staff from growing in their positions, encourages under-challenged staff to under-perform, and takes time away from your own managerial responsibilities. You waste your library's money when you draw a higher salary to do tasks your staff members can handle;

this is not the best use of your time. Be prepared for the fact that in many libraries, especially in larger and/or more hierarchical institutions, managers' work may largely take place away from the day-to-day activities of librarianship. One manager survey respondent even mentions that her biggest management surprise was "... how much you are removed from actual, traditional library work." Meredith Goins, Librarian, National Limb Loss Information Center, Knoxville, Tennessee, explains of her previous experiences as a small-town director: "I had to learn to give up things I enjoyed to others so I could get done what I needed to do."

No library manager should confuse the need to delegate tasks, though, with the "I didn't go to library school to do this" syndrome. This attitude quickly devolves into an excuse to get out of unpleasant duties, and unnecessarily pits MLS against non-MLS personnel. Especially in smaller libraries, be prepared to fill multiple roles and to do what you need to do to keep your institution humming along.

Leadership involves allowing and helping your staff members to grow. Even if you now find it quicker and easier to do an easily delegated task yourself, in the long run you merely add to your own workload and deprive the library of your efforts in other areas. Part of successful delegation involves training, teaching your staff member(s) how to do a job and overcome the slowness that may drive you crazy in your initial attempts at delegation. One staff survey respondent observes: "Too often managers don't want to take the time to train employees to do tasks they can do themselves, but also complain of being overworked. If managers do pass on work that is interesting to employees, however, they can enrich the work experience of those employees and lessen their loads."

Recognize when your reluctance to delegate stems from a reluctance to give up the tasks you are familiar with, that you enjoy, or that distract you from some of your less-than-pleasant managerial responsibilities. You may have been promoted to management, for example, precisely because you were so efficient in your previous position as a cataloger or as a reference librarian. You may retain a fondness for your old duties. You cannot, however, expect your staff to accept change if you yourself stick entirely with what is comfortable.

Implement delegation as a tool, carefully matching the items you need to delegate with the staff members whose abilities and interests match what needs doing. This will become easier the longer you are in your position, as you will begin to form a realistic picture of people's strengths and abilities. Successful delegation lets you provide people with responsibility and autonomy, allowing them to grow and be challenged by their positions. You can use similar strategies to help reevaluate the abilities and tasks of the professional staff that report to you. Librarians tend to take on duties easily carried out by clerical or other less-trained personnel, either because they enjoy these duties or because "that is the way we have always done things." Deploy staff effectively to make best use of your library's resources. Effective leadership includes leading others to develop some of the same communication skills described earlier in this chapter. Employee motivation requires an environment in which employees support each other, as people's colleagues can be just as capable of undermining confidence, morale, and performance as can their managers.

Motivation

Becoming a leader in libraries means becoming the kind of manager that inspires others. Think back to the various bosses you have had and about the qualities shared by those who inspired you to do your best work. Now, how can you best epitomize those qualities? Model the behavior you want your staff to engage in. Positive motivation is often a better strategy than reprimanding—motivated employees want to do well, rather than just acting out of fear.

It may be comforting for library managers working under strict budget constraints or union rules governing raises to realize that studies show that salary is rarely the biggest motivating factor for employees. However, some employees can be easily demotivated by the impression that they are being compensated less-than-fairly, especially when compared to their coworkers. Think about what motivates your employees as individuals; every staff member is different. Katharine Salzmann, Archivist/Curator of Manuscripts, Special Collections Research Center, Morris Library, Southern Illinois University, Carbondale, Illinois, says: "You have to realize how truly different people are, and how one person's motivation can vary so much from another's. You cannot apply one management style across the board. While it is important to be consistent and fair, it is also important to really know those who report to you, and to understand what type of leadership you need to provide them so that they can do their best."

Some general rules, though, apply in motivating most library staff members. Again, common sense here is borne out by research showing that:

- Employees appreciate and are motivated by recognition of their work. Make a point of rewarding good work publicly. People need to know that their efforts are noticed and appreciated, and others will then strive to achieve some recognition of their own. Positive reinforcement goes a long way. One manager survey respondent suggests: "Give credit where credit is due. It may be one of the only bright spots a staff member may possess, in knowing 'they own' a piece of their efforts and are acknowledged for it. If you are secure in yourself and in your abilities, then share this confidence with others." Another says: "Praise your staff! You should be able to find at least one thing your staff members have done each day to praise, or give a 'well done' comment, or even an opportunity to say thank you for a good day's work. Praise and appreciation go a long way!"

- Employees are more motivated and are happier in their working environments when the lines of communication are kept open. (See more on communication earlier in this chapter.) Secrecy and inadequate information breed resentment.

- Employees are motivated by finding meaning in their work. Again, good news for many library environments, in which it is natural to focus on the meaning of the day-to-day work in terms of the institution's mission of service to its constituents. As Guy St. Clair and Martina J. Reich write: "In fact, scratch the most hardened knowledge services employee and you'll discover that the reason he or she is in this line of work is because, as a knowledge service professional, he or she can make a difference. Without question, that is what drives most knowledge professionals to do the work they do (emphasis in original)."[5] This is especially true of professional librarians who have made a deliberate commitment to the field, but the "make a difference" factor applies to many library staff members. Help motivate them by showing and noting how they can make a positive impact and how they are making a difference.

- Employees are motivated to strive when their supervisors trust them to do a good job and trust them with responsibilities that let them take on new challenges—or to move up to new positions. "Empowerment," although a horribly overused term, nevertheless is necessary in creating a culture in which staff can thrive and work to create a thriving organization.

- Employees are motivated by being challenged in their work and having the opportunity to learn and grow.

Empathize with your employees here. If you were satisfied to remain stagnant, would you have accepted or agreed to move up into your management position? While people need different levels and types of challenges, most appreciate the opportunity to stretch themselves.

- Employees are more motivated when they perceive that they are treated fairly and with respect. Never play favorites; never belittle an employee for any reason; show that you take them, their work, and their ideas seriously.

- Employees are motivated when they know they can count on the support of their supervisors. If they are fearful of being called on the carpet for minor mistakes, they will be reluctant to go beyond. If they know that their manager will undermine their decisions or fail to back them up in front of patrons when they follow library policy, they will become resentful.

Your ideal employee will be largely self-motivated, which makes her in some senses self-managing! Your role here then will be that of a guide or of a coach (see next section) to help her realize her potential and to help provide the framework and the set of values—the library culture—within which people can contribute to the good of the organization.

Different employees will also be more or less motivated by different factors. Again, you will begin to understand these differences as you get to know the people that you manage. For some, public recognition of a job well done may be all the motivation they need to continue to do well. Others may need the opportunity to continually challenge themselves by taking on new responsibilities, while others may be motivated by the opportunity to earn merit increases. Some may be motivated to continue their education and become more valuable assets to the library, if they will receive a new job title and/or increased compensation for their efforts.

Think about the different types of rewards you can offer your staff, and about tailoring the reward to the level of accomplishment and the specific person. Can you reward people with a small but symbolic cash bonus or a gift certificate to an area business— say $25 or $50— for suggesting a successful new program or service? Can you institute an employee-of-the-month program, with a visible but perhaps nonmonetary reward, such as a prized parking spot? Can you provide flexible scheduling or partial telecommuting options for highly self-motivated staff members who are seeking this kind of flexibility, and whose work can be done off-site or at odd hours? Can you provide highly productive and motivated employees with additional responsibilities or the flexibility to institute their own programs? Can you encourage your director to write a personal thank-you note to an employee who has done a particularly good job, or to pick an employee to praise during each staff meeting? Can you encourage staff to nominate their coworkers for employee of the month? Can you provide interested staff members with the opportunity to attend meetings of their state or national library associations? Discuss options with your administration.

One staff survey respondent, Rhonda Hankins, Communications Coordinator, The Jamail Center for Legal Research, University of Texas at Austin, notes: "I also think library managers should be aware that staff salaries are relatively low. Supposed merit raises of 3 percent a year are typical. Therefore, it is incumbent on library managers to provide perks however they can. Create opportunities for staff members to attend conferences, take classes, go to special events. Be flexible with schedules, and always be complimentary when you can be. People who work in libraries generally don't get tremendous fiscal rewards, so it is important for library managers to find some way to reward excellence."

Above all, avoid the temptation to micromanage, which inherently demotivates your staff. (See Chapter 6 for a glimpse of staff's hatred for micromanagement.) Librarians and other professional-level staff can be especially sensitive to micromanagement; let them get on with their work and avoid interfering without cause. As Michelle Caulk, Electronic Services Librarian, St. Charles Public Library, Illinois, says: "Relax and let people do their jobs! It's the opposite of micromanaging. The tighter you rein people in the more they're going to resent you. Train them well, provide useful feedback, correct them gently when necessary, and let them do their jobs." Employees will best be motivated when morale is high overall, and morale withers in a micromanaged environment.

Goal Setting

Your job as a manager involves getting people to do their best work and reinforcing their commitment to both institutional and personal goals and objectives. Goals are generally fairly broad; objectives are specific and measurable steps toward one of these general goals. Both go along with motivation, in that when people have a goal to strive toward, especially a self-defined goal or one that they personally value, they are motivated to do good work in pursuit of that goal. Any goal and its associated objectives must be clear, realistic, achievable, and possible within the library's current environment. Work on getting people to define goals for themselves, and then work out together how they can achieve these goals, and how you can help.

Some managers use the "SMART" approach to help think about setting achievable and useful objectives that are: Specific, Measurable, Attainable, Realistic, and Time-bound. Objectives must be specific: clearly stated and understandable; measurable: you are able to see easily whether the objective has been achieved; attainable: the objective can be achieved; realistic: achievable with the available time, resources, and energy; and time-bound: achieved within a certain specified timeframe. Each of these SMART objectives must pertain to a particular goal. (You may see slightly different words making up the SMART acronym in various management literature; the aim, however, is the same.)

Managers in public and school libraries may have an easier sell in getting their people to commit to institutional goals. People often enter such institutions because their personal philosophies and values are in line with institutional priorities. Your staff members will be less motivated to work toward institutional goals when they are unable to see the clear benefits deriving from these goals, and part of your job as a library leader will be to clarify an institutional vision for your employees. Be sure, therefore, that you are able to define and easily summarize the goal and mission of your institution, as well as those for individual departments or sections you may manage. Once your goals are in place, desired actions should then follow.

Coaching

Coaches may either be permanent managers, or temporary coaches that come in to provide help with a specific task or problem. (More about the coaching theory of management can be found in Chapter 11.) The term "coaching" of course originates in sports, but you do not have to be a fan to see its potential in the workplace. Just as sports coaches do, workplace coaches help their team or individuals reach their potential and improve their performance. Effective coaching therefore depends heavily on goal setting, as outlined in the previous section; managerial coaches help their employees picture what success looks like, so that they can also envision the road they need to follow to get there. Coaching focuses on helping an employee realize his own problems and envision his own solutions, increasing his commitment to resolving them.

Coaching is necessarily somewhat labor-intensive on your part, as you need to be involved with your employees and spend time with them working through issues—rather than just reacting to events. Coaching requires you to be involved in their professional development, work performance, and interpersonal issues. It requires you to care about them as people and about their accomplishments; it requires you to build a relationship with your employees as individuals. Coaching is not a substitute for other types of management, but is a supplementary strategy that can be useful in certain situations.

Although there are similarities, coaching differs from performance appraisals in that it is intended to help strengthen a very specific area of performance. It is also ongoing when need and opportunity arise, rather than occurring at structured intervals.

Team Building and Collaboration

Teams have been the hot organizational structure in many libraries for some time now, in recognition of the fact that we are more effective when we learn to use our strengths together. (See more on the teams theory of management in Chapter 11.) Teams can be either short-term or permanent structures. Even without creating formal teams, any library employing more than one person can benefit from an effort to get disparate personalities to work together effectively in groups and from the realization that combining different perspectives can actually make for a more effective team. A climate that encourages cooperation, collaboration, and communication, as opposed to group-think, allows people to use their individual strengths together in pursuit of common library goals.

Part of your work as a manager will be to build, lead, and motivate teams—which can be within your department or comprised of people throughout the institution, at different levels and with different backgrounds and skills, working together toward a clearly defined common goal or project. Teams are intended to achieve specific outcomes, and need a shared purpose in order to be successful. Each member must know why the team was established and what it is intended to accomplish, and must throughout the entire process receive the information necessary to carry out the team's mission. This is yet another instance where the free flow of information is essential.

The power of teamwork lies in the fact that working with others has the potential to elicit our own best efforts. People on teams can play ideas off each other, balance each other's strengths, and produce results stronger than those available from any single individual. Your responsibility for motivating your employees also therefore includes motivating people to work together. Strong employees may fear that, in any group work, they will end up carrying the load for other staff members, or that they will be penalized for others' failures—the college group project syndrome. When people with these fears are placed on teams, they may still tend to work primarily as individuals and refuse to collaborate. This situation cries out for your assistance in blending the team's talents and functions and in focusing their attention on the project at hand. Perfectly effective workers might still need your guidance to gel together as a group, to define their roles within the team, or to feel comfortable participating fully in group discussions and decisions. They might also need your assistance in demonstrating the joy of teamwork; the sense of possibility that occurs when a group sees what can be achieved by working together.

Although teams do need to be evaluated on their work toward set goals, never let the use of teams eclipse individual accomplishments; people still need to be evaluated as individuals and for their contributions to their organizations. Recognize their work both individually and as it contributes to the team's success. Also be sure to provide teams (or to let them define for themselves) a clearly delineated project to work on. The completion of a set project allows each team member to feel a real sense of accomplishment.

Teams will be most effective if you build personal relationships with each member, getting to know their strengths and priorities.

One manager survey respondent advises: "Make time to spend with each member of your team. ... Learn how they feel about their job, their strengths and weaknesses, and ask their opinions frequently. Keeping the team members 'in the loop' is critical to building an efficient team." Build successful teams, and you help build a feeling of ownership and personal stake in the success of your library. When each person has a part in working toward a goal, each has a reason to see it accomplished.

Some libraries have moved toward a largely team-based management structure, in which traditional department heads have been replaced by teams of people. Each team member holds responsibility for a different area of the department, decisions are made collaboratively, and evaluations are carried out by peers. In such an environment, you may also carry out some management responsibilities without a formal management title. See the section on "co-managers" in Chapter 2 for more on this structure.

Other libraries emphasize the value of "self-directed teams," in which people voluntarily come together to form teams to complete certain tasks when they see that a job can be completed better and more easily with a group effort. These teams are more fluid and can form and dissolve, add and subtract members as people feel necessary. Self-directed teams leave less of a direct role for managers, aside from providing the tools and support necessary to get the job done. You can always support any type of team by offering its members some relief from their usual duties for the duration of a big project, and by providing the tools and funding necessary for them to achieve their mission.

Decision Making

Decisions to be made in libraries range from hiring decisions, to those about strategy, to those governing day-to-day operations. The types and weight of the decisions for which you are personally responsible will of course vary depending on the level of your position and your type of library. In the end, however, any manager is responsible for making decisions, and is accountable for the consequences of those decisions. Decision making in libraries involves considering the different available options, gathering input, and choosing the best option for your institution. Your decisions do have to be connected to your and your library's goals in order to be meaningful.

All of your efforts to establish freely flowing communication will be useful here in gathering input on important decisions. Both your library's administration and your employees will need to rely on you to have the final word when needed, though. This is sometimes difficult for librarians, who tend to bog down in the information-gathering part of decision making. Finding information and gathering input is what librarians are trained for and comfortable with. Reference coursework, for example, teaches us to collect data, but then to hand it over to patrons to interpret rather than doing our own analysis and making our own decisions on its use.

Try to avoid agonizing over less-crucial decisions, which can paralyze you and make you a less-than-effective manager. Learn to make the day-to-day decisions reasonably quickly and without second-guessing yourself. As Elizabeth Fraser, Head of Reference Services, Kanawha County Public Library, Charleston, West Virginia, puts it: "Sometimes the fear of making mistakes can be paralyzing. You will make mistakes. That's okay. You will probably learn more from them than some of your successes." Your staff will gain respect for you as you make the tough decisions, even if they do not agree with all of your conclusions. Indecisive managers risk losing the respect of their staff, who will see them as wishy-washy or weak.

Your entire career as a librarian has helped you develop communication and leadership skills. Every interaction with a patron, every memo, every discussion with a supervisor, every newsletter blurb, every idea about your library's future, every successful project, every report and abstract—each of these builds up your foundation as a library leader. Make effective communication and leadership a natural part of your library life, developing a set of skills that merely needs extending to your managerial relationships.

Notes

1. Daniel Goleman, *Working With Emotional Intelligence* (New York: Bantam, 1998) 189.

2. Edward E. Lawler III, *Treat People Right! How Organizations and Individuals Can Propel Each Other Into a Virtuous Spiral of Success* (San Francisco: Jossey-Bass, 2003) 206.

3. Peter F. Drucker, *Managing In a Time of Great Change* (New York: Penguin, 1995) 7.

4. Robert Kriegel and David Brandt, *Sacred Cows Make the Best Burgers: Paradigm-Busting Strategies for Developing Change-Ready People and Organizations* (New York: Warner, 1996) 23.

5. Guy St. Clair and Martina J. Reich, "Knowledge Services: Financial Strategies and Budgeting," *Information Outlook* 6:6 (June 2002): 27, 29.

Recommended Reading

Ballard, Thomas H. "Delegating Away the Peter Principle." *American Libraries,* Dec. 1983: 734–736.

Bennis, Warren and Patricia Ward Biederman. *Organizing Genius: The Secrets of Creative Collaboration.* Reading, MA: Addison-Wesley, 1997.

Euster, Joanne R. "Teaming U." *Wilson Library Bulletin,* Jan. 1995: 57–59.

—. "Think Hard, Play Hard." *Wilson Library Bulletin*, March 1994: 58–61.

Katzenbach, Jon R. and Douglas K. Smith. *The Wisdom of Teams: Creating the High-Performance Organization*. New York: HarperCollins, 1993, 1999, 2003.

Knecht, Mike. "Virtual Teams in Libraries." *Library Administration & Management* 18:1 (Winter 2004): 24–29.

Kouzes, Jim and Barry Posner. *The Leadership Challenge, 3rd ed*. San Francisco: Jossey-Bass, 2002.

Metz, Ruth F. *Coaching in the Library: A Management Strategy for Achieving Excellence*. Chicago: ALA Editions, 2001.

Nichols, C. Allen. "Leaders: Born or Bred: Confessions From a Leadership Training Junkie." *Library Journal*, August 2002: 38–40.

Rogers, Michael. "The Money Tradeoff." *Library Journal*, Nov. 1, 2003: 40–41.

Ross, Catherine Sheldrick and Patricia Dewdney. *Communicating Professionally: A How-To-Do-It Manual for Library Applications, 2nd ed*. New York: Neal-Schuman, 2002.

Soete, George. *The Library Meeting Survival Manual*. San Diego: Tulane Street Publications, 2000.

Stine, Philip C. "Invisible Management, Visible Results: A Personal Story." *Strategic Leadership* 28:6 (2000): 23–27.

Tennant, Roy. "Building Agile Organizations." *Library Journal*, April 15, 2001: 30.

Wilson, Lucile. *People Skills for Library Managers: A Common Sense Guide for Beginners*. Englewood, CO: Libraries Unlimited, 1996.

Chapter 6

What Library Staff Want

Toxic managers are a reality in organizational life.
Your ability to deal with such managers will have
a significant impact on your career.

Roy H. Lubit[1]

Chapter 1 talked about learning by example, looking at your experiences with your own previous managers to find examples to emulate—or to avoid. Some of the 343 respondents to the staff survey here provide their own examples and points of view on a variety of ineffective, counterproductive, and just plain scary managerial actions, tactics, and personalities. (Survey questions are reproduced in Appendix A.) These respondents also provide insight from the perspective of working library staff into the factors that make a productive and effective manager. Out of these 343 respondents, 71 percent, or 242, possessed an MLS or equivalent. Seventy-eight percent, or 269, work in a "professional" position. (Percentages have been rounded to the nearest percent.) Job titles range from secretary to department head.

Most management books focus entirely on the managerial perspective; few give a voice to those who are actually being managed. Frontline staff, however, have an unparalleled perspective both into what works and what fails in the management of their institutions. By truly listening to what these library staff members have to say, many anonymously (57 percent, or 197 respondents, requested anonymity), you can consciously work to avoid many of the pitfalls that have befallen your fellow managers and to assimilate the qualities and behaviors of an effective library manager.

Learning from these examples, you can begin to manage your own staff well and help to counteract some possible negative experiences in their pasts.

Potential Pitfalls

Some of library staff members' main concerns about their managers are expressed below, and a number of direct quotes from the survey explain specific behaviors to avoid under each area. In many library environments, your main managerial duties directly involve managing staff. Staff members who are disgruntled with their managers can create an unpleasant environment for other staff members and for patrons, and may take out their frustrations in ways that harm the institution as a whole. You wish to cultivate positive personal relationships with your employees, to limit staff turnover, and to create a supportive work environment for all. You also wish to prevent your library from becoming the focus of complaints on forums like the Contrarian Librarian (http://groups. yahoo.com/group/contrarianlibrarian), or for your library's managers, director, or board to become the target of an angry site such as AFPL (Atlanta-Fulton Public Library) Watch (http://www. afplwatch.com). View the following comments as cautionary tales, and honestly examine your own managerial tendencies to see if you exhibit any of these behaviors.

Library staff, reflecting the independent environment of most libraries, were quite critical of managers who tended to nitpick or to micromanage their behavior. Of the 343 survey respondents, a full 25 percent (87) mentioned some variation of the term "micromanagement" when discussing either their own worst managers or the qualities managers should avoid. A number of additional respondents also mentioned the need to avoid micromanagerial type tendencies, without using the word itself. Respondents shared experiences like:

- "They tend to make OTHERS wrong, rather than attempt to understand and value people who do not act or see things the way they do. They rule by intimidation, micromanaging, encouraging conformity and lack of assertiveness, 'do what I say—not what I do,' etc."

- "This man controls all of the work we do, doling it out by the thimbleful, such that I never know what I'll be doing the next day. I have very little autonomy in my work. At the age of 45, I am treated like a teenager who cannot be trusted."

- "She could not let go of any project and had to second-guess me every step of the way. She was indecisive about what she wanted and how to go about getting it. She did not trust her employees to do anything but the most mundane tasks without her direct supervision."

- "He was a despot. He would time your breaks to the minute. He was a bureaucrat through-and-through, and cared more for rules than humans."

- "He spent large chunks of the year on travel, but he was also a micromanager. He'd say: 'Don't do any more until I get a chance to look at this,' then go out of town for three months. It was maddening!"

- "She was a micromanager. She stifled any creativity I had and made it impossible for me to like my job."

- "She was a micromanager promoted beyond her ability, dedicated to absolute control of her subordinates, and easily angered by even a perceived challenge to her authority or expertise."

- "He wanted to do it all his way, so it would be the 'right' way, and get all the credit. He hardly ever delegated. He was a micromanager. He squashed people's ideas until nobody wanted to risk taking any initiative."

- "Micromanager—I would get my e-mails back on paper with red ink all over them. He wanted perfection from me, was always criticizing what I did, yet rarely completed his own work."

Realize that, while you have an understandable impulse to help your employees succeed and enjoy a personal stake in their success, most library staff do their best work when allowed reasonable autonomy. Micromanagers often create the very problems they are trying to avoid, damaging morale and productivity by their constant interference.

Library managers, though, need to recognize the difference between avoiding micromanagement and avoiding giving guidance. While library staff appreciate the independence to do their work unfettered, they also appreciate a certain amount of communication from their managers. Another common concern among survey respondents was their managers' lack of clear communication of both library and personal goals, as well as a lack of encouragement or recognition of a job well done. They expressed frustration with this unclear communication or direction on their day-to-day jobs, sharing thoughts like:

- "While her attitude was one of displeasure, I was never sure what I was doing wrong."

- "She was uncommunicative and offered me no feedback or constructive criticism, yet gave me a terrible annual review. When I told her that I was completely unaware there were any problems with my performance, she replied that: 'That was the problem—you didn't know there was a problem.' Huh?"

- "There was no planning (in the almost two years I worked for her we had zero meetings), no objectives laid out and then followed-up on and no clearly outlined responsibilities or hierarchy."

- "The worst library manager I ever had was a very poor communicator. This always made my job and life in general difficult. I never understood where she was coming from and often didn't have the information I needed to do my job well or at all. I often just couldn't plain understand her. There were many misunderstandings between us and I often wasn't sure what she expected of me."

- "He lived behind a shut door. He lived on another level … he appeared to be almost unreachable. It was clear that he did not like to interact with staff and that he would prefer it if we did not talk to him or ask his opinion about anything. He managed from above … like a god! You never knew what he was going to do next because his staff did not always know what was going to happen. He was unpredictable … staff meetings were an enigma."

- "The worst manager was the worst because he did absolutely nothing, either for me or with me. He essentially just said: 'Here's your office,' and then literally left me alone to figure out everything else, and he knew it was my very first professional library position."

- "She does not communicate clearly. She will organize some event in the library and not tell us anything about it except for what is on the fliers and that is usually not clear. We end up looking bad when we don't know the answers and she doesn't share them with us."

- "When first promoted would ask for input from the staff, but seemed to seldom pay attention to it. Eventually didn't even pretend to ask for input, things just happened without any discussion or warning."

- "She would make knee-jerk decisions without getting any input from staff members, even though she had many smart, professional people on her staff. … She would keep things secret from the staff, then drop announcements on us like bombs, and everyone would worry and fret about why things were happening. She banned departmental meetings."

(See more on the importance of communication in Chapter 5.)

While a lack of communication was frustrating, others were even more concerned about their experiences working for overtly abusive or angry library managers. Respondents shared such unfortunate experiences such as:

- "Every decision was second-guessed and verbal insults were made in the public spaces in front of other staff and customers."

- "The worst manager I have had was unpredictable, moody, and always had a scapegoat—at one time or another each of us in the office. She actually screamed at her staff members when she was upset, and she upset the patrons (we often had to clean up after her in that sense)."

- "She bullied her staff with verbal and psychological abuse. Very much like the queen in Alice in Wonderland."

- "The worst library manager I ever worked for had many flaws as a manager: She was condescending, hostile, sarcastic and extremely moody with the staff. She made rude comments about patrons behind their backs and was disliked by many in the community."

- "Lost temper frequently, yelled. Condescending, did not respect others. Nicey-nicey to the powerful."

- "I have very little respect for my director. His work record is abysmal; he lacks respect for his female staff, and is extremely overbearing and controlling. He is very slow to institute new ideas, and has a tendency to pit the staff against one another."

- "My manager, chosen I'm sure because she fit someone's political agenda, was rude, nitpicking, and moody. She apparently thought that being demanding and nasty would increase productivity."

- "This manager had a tendency to like to joke about me and put me down. For example, the manager would say: 'I can't believe you have an English writing degree and just wrote that! Haven't you ever written in the business world?' or 'Don't you have anything better to wear?'"

- "The manager was very moody and took it out on the staff. You had to judge the mood of the manager each day in order to decide whether or not you could approach them with a question or a problem. The manager made some hurtful remarks in a staff meeting in regards to another staff member. While the remarks could have been taken as a joke, they were not."

- "This person routinely treated staff as if they were idiots, ignoring staff opinions and sometimes actually yelling at staff in front of others."

- "Daily, she brought her countless home problems to work with her, frequently ranting, raving, and swearing at family members on the phone without ever even closing her office door."

There is of course no excuse for verbal abuse or taking out your personal problems or anger on staff members. The lesson for all library managers is to realize that their words and behavior have a real impact on staff and on the way they react to you as a manager. Pay attention to the ways in which you communicate and to the effects of your communication style on others.

Other types of directly divisive managers include those who decide to show favoritism to a certain subset of staff or to pit one group of staff members against another. This comes into play fairly often among managers who favor MLS-degreed staff members over those without the master's, but can take a number of forms:

- "The worst library manager I ever had did not respect my years of service and my capabilities because I did not have a master's degree. She did not include me in discussions and in a way ostracized me from my youth services team."

- "Over a two-year period she contributed greatly to high staff turnover. She treated men and 'superiors' and peers more carefully than the professional women she supervised."

- "Extreme favoritism to one employee being groomed for next-in-line (perceived, or otherwise) top position. The attitude is bad enough to frustrate other professionals."

- "I hate it when librarians play class wars because they have an MLS and the support staff person does not. Just because someone doesn't have your degree doesn't mean that they are not a valuable player in the library team and that you can't learn from them. Also, they are real people with feelings. If you are not a good example then you shouldn't be all high and mighty with your power."

- "Those who enjoy 'teacher's pet' status are excused from pulling their share of the workload, while those less favored are continually having more and more dumped on them."

- "This manager gossiped about employees with other employees, played favorites, and had to be pampered and flattered daily in order to survive."

- "He openly favored particular library departments, which led staff to try to raise their stock even more by attacking/maligning others in those departments he did not favor."

- "He was stupid. Also was anti-Semitic. I felt he was always trying to catch me at something in order to berate me."

- "The worst library manager I have had was my supervisor during my graduate assistantship while working on my MLS. She was constantly 'putting me in my place,' reminding me that she was a librarian and I was a lowly grad assistant, not a librarian."

- "She was unfair in allocating the workload. Those she liked got the easy jobs. Those who were not her favorites got far more work and the less appealing work. She remained aloof from the 'peons' under her and would not consider socializing with us."

No tendency to favor one group or individual staff member over others will go unnoticed. Each of your staff members deserves attention and professionalism from you, as well as the opportunity to succeed.

Milder forms of toxic managers included those who failed to support their staff in front of patrons or in pursuit of library goals. Library staff praised flexibility and a willingness to listen in their managers, and were quite critical of those who fell short in these areas. Comments here included:

- "She did not listen to all sides of a story before passing judgments, a bit like 'Simon' on American Idol."

- "Legalistic—relied on the rules of the profession and workplace rather than to adapt to situational variables. Very controlling."

- "The manager would not back me up, always gave in to the patron's demands, even if it was against policy. It seemed to me that it was not about the 'customer is always right,' but that my manager didn't want to have to deal with anything unpleasant."

- " ... he was prepared to let students and faculty flout library policies at will, and take advantage of (and in the most egregious cases, verbally and even physically abuse) library staff without sticking up for them or encouraging them to stick up for themselves. This created an atmosphere that made me uncomfortable, as I knew that in any case where a situation might come down to my word versus a student's (or worse yet, a professor's) about how a certain interaction had taken place, that the director as a matter of course would just not support me."

This is another reason to create clear policies and to make it clear when staff can be flexible in their enforcement. You need all to be on the same page, and you need to support your staff.

Another variation on the theme of not sticking up for library staff is that of managers who tried to avoid conflict altogether. Part of any manager's responsibilities involves conflict management, and survey respondents have experienced first-hand the destructive effects when managers refuse to fulfill that role:

- "Avoided confrontation to the point of destruction of teamwork and morale, staff fell apart."

- "He was oblivious (and deliberately so) to personnel issues and staff conflicts. By the time these issues came to his attention, they were so out of control that solving them involved the campus affirmative action officer and the local faculty union. Library staff members were forced to take sides in the resulting controversy. It shouldn't have been permitted to escalate that far."

- "She was one of the shyest people I have ever met. She always whispered and would never correct anyone, no matter what they did."

- "She will not take responsibility for day-to-day operations of the department, discipline of problem employees being the main issue. ... When you are told of a problem in the department, deal with it. Please don't pretend that you are sympathetic, promise you will handle it, and then leave for the day to do personal errands."

- "Laissez faire attitude toward problems. (They ignored problems and made themselves unavailable for administrative support in times of need.)"

Conflict avoidance is perhaps one of the most common problems among library managers who were promoted due to their technical skills rather than their people skills. Think about the long-term impact of being unwilling to take action to resolve problem situations rather than just the short-term ease of avoiding them.

Lastly, a number of respondents expressed frustration with managers who had the habit of taking credit for others' work, accomplishments, and ideas. While managers do hold the responsibility for steering the efforts of those in their department or institution, good managers give credit to their staff and recognize individual accomplishments. Bad managers tend only to assign responsibility when things go wrong, and to hog the limelight when things go right.

- "I was a pawn to be worked. Everything I did, she took credit for."

- "She attempted to get coworkers to have bad feelings against one another, took credit for other people's work when it was successful, blamed others when something went wrong."

- "I do not enjoy working for passive-aggressive people who when talking to you accept your ideas but then do nothing with them—or take the credit themselves."

- "Took credit for things that underlings did—didn't honor us."

- "Before you even opened your mouth, her answer was 'no.' And then two days later this was 'her' idea and it was implemented."

- "She lied. She took credit for others' work (mine and other people's) and blamed us if there was anything wrong."

Part of supporting your staff involves recognizing their accomplishments, supporting their efforts, and talking them up to higher management.

The previous comments of course express the patterns that were most common and most frustrating to respondents. Others mentioned varied other concerns, from frustration with managers who are unable to deal with change ("*Move forward*. It is a new day, and you can't manage a library today like you did ten years ago") to annoyance with those who appear uninterested in staff members' or the library's success ("I would really appreciate it if she seemed to take more interest in the library and didn't seem to be biding her time till retirement").

Preferred Patterns

What people would prefer is not in all cases what is best for them. In the case of library management, however, staff's preferred managerial patterns make a great deal of sense. Respondents showed a true appreciation of managers who treated them well and helped them do their best work, who fostered clear lines of communication, and who enabled library staff to work together in pursuit of library goals. The preferred qualities outlined below will help you chart a path toward being more effective with your staff. While the previous sections explained behaviors to avoid, survey respondents also shared experiences with a number of outstanding managers and ideas about the qualities they would like to see in their own managers.

Library staff preferred managers who work with them to set goals and who encourage them to grow and to move forward in their positions. Comments included:

- "If you value excellence, be a boss who makes it OK for staff to make mistakes. It's the greatest gift in the workplace to know that your manager wants you to set goals, try new things, and learn."

- "One of the best things about her was that she was constantly looking for opportunities for me to gain experience and move ahead, even when it ultimately meant that I moved up to a better job in another library."

- "I am encouraged to think outside the box and am always given the benefit of her guidance when I need it, her advice when I want it, and her support when the best-laid plans go awry. I grow every day under her tutelage."

- "Support for my growth as a professional that includes honest appraisals of needed areas of growth and assistance in developing strategies to meet those needs."

- "The thing that made him special was that he was so willing to teach me new things, bring things to me that he thought I'd be interested in, and to share what he knew."

- "A library manager needs to create an environment that enables and encourages all of his or her team members to work to the height of their capabilities, and to extend those capabilities. This can bring about enthusiastic staff members who enjoy their work. That enjoyment shows in the quality of service provided to your patrons, and the quality of the work done."

- "The director was sensitive, empathetic, and always ready to help with skill development of each staff member. We were encouraged to attend workshops and conferences to achieve this."

- "I want someone who gives credit where it's due, and allows and encourages people to grow in their careers."

- "The best manager I ever had placed an emphasis on staff development. She scheduled regular performance checkup meetings with her staff so everyone would have a chance to maximize their potential."

- "This manager took a personal interest in teaching me multiple approaches to librarianship, valued and considered my opinions when my opinions were asked for, and encouraged me to pursue an MLIS and make librarianship my career."

As in any interpersonal situation, library staff warm to those managers who express an interest in them, their careers, and their professional growth. (See more on fostering professional development in Chapter 3.)

In line with their dislike of managers with a tendency toward micromanagement, staff clearly and repeatedly expressed a desire for autonomy and their appreciation for supervisors who refrained from excessive interference in their jobs:

- "He gave me instruction and directions, was available when I needed to ask a question and let me do the assigned job without breathing down my neck. He gave me responsibility and trusted me to get the job done and to ask when I needed help."

- "The best manager I had trusted my judgment. The manager let the staff assist with making decisions on procedures. The manager did not stand over our shoulders while we did our work."

- "Let people do their jobs!!!"

- "I most appreciate a manager who treats employees like adults—assumes that we're all professionals, and we will get the job done, although some of us have different styles."

- "What makes my current boss special is that she does not micromanage her staff. She hired competent, capable people and she is not threatened by them. She is available and approachable, but does not hover or rework something once you've finished."

- "Trusted, empowered employees provide better service (and otherwise do better) than those that are required to report to their manager before making the smallest of decisions."

- "I appreciate managers who provide direction while they allow autonomy."

- "Actually, I've had three good managers. They were and are good because they let me do my job, without micromanaging, yet were and are always available at any time if I have a question about performing my job."

While these comments may have been expected, given respondents' vehement opposition to micromanagement, they also show the real value that library staff tend to place on a more participatory and relaxed style of management.

Other staff valued bosses who seem to be on their side, who fight for salary increases, promotions, and good working conditions, who back them up in front of patrons, and so on. While staff certainly noticed if managers fail in any of these areas, they showed equal appreciation for those who excel:

- "Show respect for staff by creating reasonable work schedules, and advocating for good work conditions, pay and benefits."

- "He looked out for us as his number one priority. He always defended us and our workload/workflow with the administration. He realized that we are who make him look good or bad, so he took very good care of us; not by coddling or by flattery, but by respect."

- "She was very supportive of professional development. When the administration refused my petition to have the tuition for a second master's degree that I wished to pursue paid for under the institution's tuition reimbursement plan, my manager went to her manager and lobbied successfully to have my salary raised to compensate for the tuition."

These types of supportive managers were often mentioned in the "best manager" section of the survey; realize that you need to fight for your staff's needs as well as for those of your customers, because a satisfied staff are better able to provide customer service.

Support of library staff includes showing that their contributions to the institution are significant and that their work is noted and appreciated. An understanding of the importance of each individual's work and of its place in the proper functioning of the library encourages morale:

- "I don't feel that we are on a lower level than the librarian or that the work we do is insignificant. I feel respected for what I do and feel my contributions are appreciated."

- "Even though I am a part-time paraprofessional, she makes sure I feel like part of the team and encourages me to voice my opinion in all matters. This is a sure sign of a good manager—making sure all your employees know they are valued and important to the organization."

- "They were fair, honest, direct, and respecting. They sought opportunities to praise on work well done—often."

- "I especially like it when managers try to catch their employees doing something right, instead of only talking to them when improvements need to be made. And I really appreciate it when a manager treats me as a valued member of the team, no matter what my position may be."

- "Finally, what made her so extraordinary was her fundamental appreciation for every individual and his and her unique attributes. She could find strengths and highlight the positive in everyone, while getting their buy-in to work on their weaker points."

- "Keep giving feedback ... appreciation for specific actions, not an infrequent 'you're the greatest,' which you cannot live up to. Believe and let it be known that everyone's job is important to the organization, not only yours."

- "They should most definitely praise good work when they see it, as this helps to motivate the team. Lack of appreciation can be very demoralizing."

Beyond not taking credit for others' accomplishments, go out of your way to note when your staff members have performed well.

Hard-working library staff members also appreciate seeing that their managers work at least as hard as they do, and respect those that keep up their "front-line" skills. They also understand that managers who keep their hand in understand daily library issues more personally than those who limit themselves solely to administrative duties. Library managers also were asked to become familiar with the tasks of those they supervised, as well as the workings of the institution as a whole:

- "She led by example. She worked just as hard if not harder than anyone else in our department."

- "Even though she was management, she still worked the desk right alongside us and helped out when staff was short. She was a great reference librarian and kept up her research skills."

- "Too many administrators (directors, assistant directors, and others on that level) have forgotten what it's like to serve the public. ... Whenever possible, administrators should work at a public service point during the busiest time of day to get a feeling for what their staff actually does. This is particularly true when an administrator is hired from outside the system; the best way for them to understand the staff culture is to participate in it."

- "This manager could also work anywhere in the library. She took over in all areas if staff were ill or suddenly called away from work."

- "He was active and about in all departments of the library. Talked with staff and faculty informally, not just in meetings. He did such outrageous things as actually working the reference desk on occasion. As a result he really understood the day-to-day aspects of keeping the place going."

- "Work alongside staff so you know what is happening in the library."

- "Take time to learn the functions or basic tasks of all workers or departments being managed."

- "She put all of us at her level and was not afraid to get her hands 'dirty.' She would pitch in when we needed help at crunch times (i.e., numerous books to be reshelved at the end of a semester, reserves waiting to be processed at the beginning of a semester)."

While you do need to learn to delegate, refrain from delegating away all of your responsibilities or avoiding keeping your hand in on the front lines.

Staff members also encourage their managers to understand the importance of communication. This includes clear communication from managers to employees, approachability, and the willingness to listen to and learn from staff:

- "Managers need to share enough information with employees so that everyone understands what is happening and their place in the overall scheme of things. When employees understand the why and how of something, they are more apt to do things correctly, and to take ownership, responsibility for and satisfaction from the job."

- "I can't stress strongly enough: Listen to your people!!! If you must assume something, let it be that your folks know what they're talking about. They know the nitty-gritty of how patrons use the library and its resources. They hear on a daily basis comments, compliments, and complaints that patrons would never bring to you."

- "I could talk to this manager at any time about staff, programming, and my personal goals without any confidences being breached. I could discuss staff problems and receive advice or a direction to go to get ideas."

- "She always kept the staff and on-call staff 'in the loop,' as well as always listening to our ideas and concerns, taking us seriously. I also really liked how she explained her reasoning for various policies; it is easier to explain to patrons when you understand."

- "Listen. Listen to your employees when they offer suggestions and listen to your patrons when they offer feedback or make requests."

- "One manager I had at a large university acquisitions department had Friday morning meetings, and usually someone (if not her) brought bagels and other light snacks. We'd hash out workflow, plans for the fiscal year and interdepartmental issues while enjoying a good nosh. I looked forward to these meetings, not only because of the food, but because of the open, approachable nature of the management style. It wasn't "you're doing this,' it was, 'how do we do this and could you please pass the lox?' It was more like a coffee klatch with friends, except we were actually productive and felt energized and motivated to do a successful job afterward."

- "Openness is perhaps the one most important responsibility. This can apply to being willing to listen to a question or suggestion from a staff member as well as the public."

- "She sought input for decisions at all levels, understanding that the frontline employees often see issues more clearly or in a perspective administrators are unable to see."

- "The best manager that I worked for allowed for open communication, even of difficult issues. She was open and honest and made herself available to employees to discuss whatever might come up in the workplace."

Library managers need to foster the free flow of information inside their institution in order that their libraries can fulfill their mission of fostering the free flow of information to patrons.

Staff also do understand the need for managers to set overall goals for the library and to steer the institution or department in a direction that serves the needs of patrons. They looked for managers who are also leaders:

- "The need for a leader with clear articulated goals is so vital. The ability to make the vision a reality and make staff excited to be a part of it."

- "The tone of an organization, it seems to me, is usually set by the person at the top. One of the keys to successful library management is the ability of those in charge both to manage and to lead. Managers ought to provide a positive vision for the future and to encourage everyone to embrace the effort required to attain the realization of that vision."

- "I think library managers need to have their finger on the needs of the community they serve and be creative in finding ways to meet those needs. I see library managers as being the ones for setting the direction the library goes in and seeing that the staff have the appropriate training to move in that direction."

- "Having vision, and having comprehension of the day-to-day workflow in order to see how to implement vision without compromising basic necessities of service."

- "The library manager's primary goal should be for her library or department to provide the best service or otherwise do the best job it can. Everything the manager does should be focused on that goal, not on making the manager's life easier."

Part of becoming a leader in your library is the ability to set the overall vision for your library or department, and to communicate that vision to others. (See more on leadership in Chapter 5.)

Many respondents also mentioned the need for a sense of humor and for managers to be willing to learn from their own mistakes ("Develop and keep a sense of humor. If you don't have one, find another field;" "someone who can be self-deprecating and who can laugh at themselves"). They also looked to their managers to create a climate of trust ("I think the most important role for a library manager is to build a climate of rapport and trust among the library staff"), and to have the ability to make decisions ("If you want authority, you *must* accept responsibility").

A number of respondents expressed parenthetical thanks at being asked their opinions in this survey, which serves to reinforce the importance of listening to and learning from your staff. Give them the opportunity to share their opinions and experiences; encourage innovation and the free exchange of ideas.

Notes

1. Roy H. Lubit, *Coping With Toxic Managers, Subordinates...and Other Difficult People: Using Emotional Intelligence to Survive and Prosper* (Upper Saddle River, NJ: Prentice-Hall, 2004) 1.

Recommended Reading

Lubans, John Jr. "She Took Everything But the Blame: The Bad Boss is Back." *Library Administration & Management* 16:3 (Summer 2002): 156–158.

Lubit, Roy H. *Coping With Toxic Managers, Subordinates...and Other Difficult People: Using Emotional Intelligence to Survive and Prosper.* Upper Saddle River, NJ: Prentice-Hall, 2004.

White, Herbert S. "Tough Times Make Bad Managers Worse." *Library Journal,* Feb. 15 1994: 132–133.

Chapter 7

Managing Facilities and Technology

Library systems face incessant, rapid changes in technology and mounting demands or new services. That's why it is essential to view any new library facility as a living, growing organism.

Peter Booth Wiley[1]

After you have experienced the stresses involved in managing people, the prospect of managing library facilities and technology may at first seem almost relaxing. "Things" rarely talk back! (Although, the more you work with computers, the more likely you may be to suspect otherwise ...) Unfortunately, managing people vs. managing things is not usually an either/or proposition; as a library manager, you will in most cases find yourself in charge of both. Furthermore, just a few days spent personally bailing water off of a leaky roof, chasing down vendors, or fielding frantic calls when your computer network is down may change your perspective.

Several manager survey respondents mentioned building and facilities issues as among their biggest managerial challenges. One even said that her biggest surprise upon entering library management was "how many things can go wrong with the facility." Julie Farnsworth, Library Director, Pleasanton City Library, California, similarly noted that her biggest surprise was: "How much time you spend on the building itself. Coming into the job, I expected politics, staff issues, collection concerns, technology—but plumbing? Yep, that and roofing and HVAC and carpet wear and building design and much more." Amanda E. Standerfer, Library Director, Helen Matthes Library, Illinois, concurs: "Managing an old building (when there is no money for a new one or even to fix the old one) is also very challenging. ... I'm a librarian, not a construction worker!" Building management is not often among the skills taught in library school, and little in librarians' previous experience may seem at first glance to match up with the required skills for keeping library facilities and technology humming along.

Since the bulk of your management responsibilities, though, will likely revolve around people, the following sections only highlight some major areas of systems and facilities management that you may be involved with. Should your management role require you to assume increased responsibilities in these areas, a number of resources to help you prepare are listed at the end of the chapter and interspersed in appropriate sections.

Systems Management

Managing technology in libraries also often involves managing techies or others with technological responsibilities—yes, back to people again, just that quickly! Managing techies is an art unto itself, but most will thrive under the same autonomy and respect you provide to librarians and other staff. Techies will also appreciate your effort in communicating clearly and effectively with them. Make an effort to familiarize yourself with enough technical jargon and background to serve as an effective liaison to technical staff. You may also need these communication skills to serve as the technical liaison to tech support, to your larger institution or consortium, and to vendors, especially in smaller institutions with no formal systems staff. If you do not directly manage technical staff, you still will need to rely on the more technologically astute individuals among your staff and colleagues to help keep you up-to-date and to recommend technological upgrades and implementations for your library.

Also make an effort to keep yourself educated about the technology you manage. While you may not need to know specific details, a broad understanding of technology trends plus a background in what types of technology you use, how they are deployed, and what they can do will serve you well as a systems manager. Any librarian today needs to become comfortable with and proficient in using the basic technologies in her institutional environment; managers have additional responsibilities and must lead the rest of their staff in accepting and working with technological change.

Managing systems and technology also includes the ability to assess realistically the technological needs of your patrons and to implement technology (and staff) to meet those needs. Your tasks here can range anywhere from ensuring the currency and sufficiency of library technology, to maintaining your ILS, to scheduling and evaluating technology trainers. Here, you retain traditional duties for ensuring that library programs, facilities, and services meet the needs of your patrons; only the nature of these programs, facilities, and services differs. Library managers may also be involved in writing a technology plan for their institution, either as part of a larger strategic plan or as a stand-alone plan. Technology plans are often required by state agencies or by the terms of grant or other funding opportunities. For help on technology plans and to view a number of examples, see http://www.ilsr.com/tech.htm. To make use of a free technology planning tool, check out TechAtlas, available via WebJunction.org: http://webjunction.org/do/Display?contentPage=/static/NPower_tools.html. (This page also provides access to another free tool called TechSurveyor, which enables you to inventory your library's hardware and software and to garner a picture of your staff's technological skills.)

Facilities and Collections Management

Management of your facility and collections can also include the responsibility for the physical security and stability of the building and its contents (including the safety of library staff and patrons). Duties involved in fulfilling this responsibility range anywhere from hiring and managing security guards, to maintaining the physical integrity of electronic equipment, to minimizing theft and destruction of library materials, to dealing with alarm vendors. You may also be responsible for managing the staff who maintain the physical plant of your building, from custodial workers to contractors. (Find more on managing a variety of groups in Chapter 4.) Have policies and procedures in place for hiring and evaluating security and maintenance personnel, just as with librarians and paraprofessionals—as well as policies and procedures for them to follow.

Realize that these staff members also represent your institution to your patrons, and provide them with the training and background they need to present the united front you want. Dealing with the staff members that maintain your facility can add to your managerial responsibilities. You will need, for example, to be sure that all staff members can communicate with security when a problem arises, and to make it clear what issues security guards will or will not be responsible for. You will need to clarify the types of situations in which maintenance should be called, and what issues maintenance staff will or will not be responsible for. As with all staff, you will need to delineate roles and responsibilities and to evaluate based on set goals and objectives.

Many library managers will also need to engage in disaster planning, which has moved higher on our professional radar since the events of 9/11 and recent weather-related library catastrophes. This is often more formalized in larger libraries, but any library needs to have at least a simple disaster and emergency plan in place—as well as a plan for how to continue library service (however basic) in the event of a disaster. Look at your own plan; if it has not been revised in years, dig it out and see if it needs updating. As a department or other middle manager, you can contribute to the disaster plan as regards your own section of the library.

In the smallest libraries, some very basic steps can be useful in recovering from an emergency: Have a list of emergency procedures; keep phone numbers of managers and emergency services handily accessible; keep first aid kits, blankets, and other basic supplies handy; have a basic outline on restoring and salvaging various library items available. Also check your library's insurance policy to see where you might wish to beef up coverage. SOLINET provides a collection of resources on preservation and access, including succinct leaflets that list the contents of a basic disaster plan, discuss the disaster-planning process, provide an emergency services checklist, and so on. See: http://www.solinet.net/preservation.

Facilities Management

Your library, whatever its type, depends largely on the physical facility it is housed in and on that facility's amenities to provide usable service to its community. There are few purely virtual libraries; each needs somewhere to house its books, to put its terminals, to teach classes, hold programs, seat staff, run network cabling, and so on. Your institution's environment impacts your staff's work environment and your patrons' ability to use your services. Managing a facility, therefore, is equally as important as managing staff or as any of the other factors involved maintaining in a smoothly running institution.

Some library managers will find themselves managing facilities as part of a number of other duties, others may have facilities management as a primary duty (or find it expanding to take more and more of their time). In other institutions, managing the physical facility will be assumed by the larger company or organization of which the library is a part. Many different managers can have overlapping and complementary responsibilities for different aspects of facilities management; a systems manager, for example, may be responsible for tasks such as wiring network cable and planning the layout of a new computer lab, but lack responsibility for any other physical aspects of the library; a publicity manager may have sole responsibility for signage and displays; and an assistant director the responsibility for building maintenance, security, and upkeep. Each will need to work together with other managers in keeping the facilities as a whole humming along.

If it comes time for your library to expand, renovate, or construct a new building, your job can for some time entail activities as diverse as campaigning for a referendum; planning for future space needs; ensuring compliance with ADA and other federal, state, and local laws and regulations; choosing an architect; and working with a consultant. Administrators or heads of building committees will need to begin by creating a building plan that outlines what you intend to offer in the new facility and how you will use its space. This allows your architect and/or consultant to offer plans that meet your projected needs and priorities. You can find a bibliography on planning and building libraries at http://www.slais.ubc.ca/resources/architecture/readingsright.htm; consult its listings and other resources as you begin the process.

When planning your new space, try to project as far ahead as possible, building not only for current needs but for future expansion. Think about incorporating factors such as environmentally friendly ("green") design, maximum accessibility, room for additional wiring, and so on into your new facility, in order to help it serve your existing and future needs. Middle managers will be required to provide input on their departmental needs in the new facility. This input can range from estimating the feet of shelving needed for their collections, to the selection of furnishings for their area, to showing the need for study rooms, to suggestions about the size and layout of break room facilities. Middle managers also need to comment on the building plans as they emerge, seeing if the space seems well organized and sufficient for both staff and patrons, and suggesting modifications as necessary.

Public library planners can make use of tools such as the Libris DESIGN software (http://www.librisdesign.org) to help with their planning process. (The software is free to California libraries and to others who have taken a training class on its use, for which there is a charge.) This Microsoft Access database application allows you to create a building program and cost estimate. Such self-planning tools are especially useful for smaller libraries that cannot afford a consultant. Any manager beginning a building project can talk to library architects at conference exhibits, and you may also wish to tour other similarly sized libraries in your area that have recently completed their own projects. For inspiration, look at the photos and descriptions in the annual article describing the *Library Journal* building of the year winners and in the annual *American Libraries* showcase of new and renovated facilities (however much you may need to scale these back for your own purposes). You may also be responsible for writing or contributing to a Request for Proposal (RFP) that will go out to potential architects, and/or for evaluating and choosing among competing architects.

Library directors or assistant directors are often involved in raising all or part of the funding for a new building project. You will need first to clarify the library's goals (including space needs, technology needs, and so on) and then market your plan to decision makers (to your community when a referendum is in order, to deans, or to vice presidents). Target your campaign specifically to the priorities of those who have the decision-making power over your funding. (See more on this in Chapter 10.)

Post-construction, you will also be responsible for evaluating how well your new building or addition or remodel is functioning to serve the needs of your community. Given your new traffic flows, do staff or materials need to be relocated or reorganized? Is signage sufficient and well placed? Does your expanded space require a higher level of staffing than originally anticipated, in order to meet expanded patron demand for services and run library operations efficiently?

Most library managers will have inherited their facility as-is, and be limited both monetarily and structurally as to what they can do with it. In this case, part of your job will be to do what you can within such constraints to improve your facility and make it more useful and amenable to patrons and library staff. A building that was constructed 25 years ago, for example, will not have been built with current technology in mind and will need some creative thinking to accommodate an ever-expanding network of PCs and cabling. (Can you convert your internal network to wireless to alleviate the need for additional Ethernet?) An aesthetically lovely Carnegie library designed pre-ADA may have many stairs, narrow doorways and aisles, and other factors that may require substantial remodeling to bring it into ADA compliance. A library constructed in an older community may not have the space or materials to effectively serve a new influx of children and teens without some major rearranging, reallocation of funds, and purchase of new display shelving, furniture, and signage. Old staff desks and other furniture will not have been built with PCs in mind, and their layouts may be less-than-ergonomic. Think about ergonomic, efficiency, and ADA issues when planning—minor modifications now can save you costly problems later.

If you work for a public institution, your major facilities purchases and repairs—such as a new roof or building rewiring—may be required to go through a bidding process that can greatly slow down your purchases. Some institutions even have a low bid requirement that can tie your hands when it comes to choosing a contractor. Other institutions may be more political than you initially realize. Is the mayor's son, for example, an electrician? Guess who may have the contract for your building's wiring. Political goodwill and precedent weigh particularly heavily in some public libraries. If you manage a facility in a corporate setting, you may encounter similar political or territorial issues; your space may, for example, be coveted by people who argue against the need for a physical library now that "everything is online."

You will best be able to navigate political waters and manage these fights if you cultivate a clear-eyed awareness of your own political situation. Too many librarians tiptoe around political topics, when they in fact affect nearly all of our activities. Political savvy is necessary for all librarians, but is especially necessary for library managers. (Read more about dealing with politics in Chapter 10.) You will also need to ensure that your facility is in compliance with local codes and regulations. Your local fire inspector, for example, will be less-than-pleased if your hallways are blocked with stacks of boxes or if emergency exits are not labeled prominently.

Managing facilities includes ensuring that they are welcoming and inviting environments for your patrons and that they serve your customers' needs. Remember that your job as a manager is to direct the library's people and resources to serve institutional goals, the main one of which is always to serve your customer. See whether your physical library serves the customer. Look at factors from signage to seating, from handicapped accessibility to lighting, from the cleanliness of the facility to its security. In stand-alone buildings, think about exterior items as well—is the library clearly marked? Is the outside kept free of litter; are the bushes trimmed; is the grass mowed in a timely fashion? Often the assistant director will be in charge of ensuring these things are taken care of.

Ensuring that your facilities are welcoming is also important in maintaining continuing community support for your library. You do not want community members to think: "Why should I throw more resources into that money pit?" You do not want your corporate colleagues to dread going into a dank, dark basement to pore through musty files. You do not want a patron to slip on ice in an unsalted parking lot and decide that his fall warrants a lawsuit. Think about how the physical environment affects the usability of library resources and about how environment affects both staff and patrons.

Collection Management

Many library managers will assume some collection management responsibilities, whether you serve as a manager of collection development, or whether collection development is one facet of your or your staff's responsibilities. There are a number of factors to consider in developing and maintaining an effective library collection. (See more on serving as a collection development manager in Chapter 2.) First, you will need to set new policies to effectively govern your collection development activities, or to use your management role to evaluate and revise your institution's current policies. Having policies in place now can save you time and trouble later. Be sure also to have clear policies that govern the process by which patrons can request that materials be added to or removed from the collection.

Part of collection management involves making room for new materials and keeping your collection current by weeding out old or underused items. As with many library issues, bad handling can make this a political hot potato. When engaging in large-scale weeding projects, for example, remember the 2001 Chicago Public Library political debacle in which local publications treated readers to photos of thousands of items being disposed of in dumpsters, allegations that staff were gutting the collections of a certain branch, and information on a Friends lawsuit seeking to halt the "deep weeding" of these items. This is one reason why collection policies and guidelines—and political savvy and goodwill—are so important.

Ensure that your collections are up-to-date and that their contents meet patrons' needs. In a school, this includes purchasing material more heavily in areas that directly support the curriculum. In a public library, this can include allocating additional funding to purchasing non-English-language materials for a growing non-English-speaking segment of your community, or purchasing more materials on DVD and CD to meet growing demand. In a corporation, it can include keeping current with company goals in order to provide the materials that support current corporate objectives. Collection management here requires balancing funding for collections with funding for other library needs, as well as balancing funding among competing areas of the collection. It may take some political savvy to reallocate funds to meet changing community needs; you may run into opposition from groups who oppose any modifications to your traditional purchasing patterns or who believe that the library should not be spending money on certain types of materials.

While maintaining a balanced collection that serves the needs of your library's various constituencies has always been tricky, collection management and development in an electronic era can be even more interesting. Current licensing agreements emphasize access over ownership, which requires you as a collection manager to think about future issues of access to needed materials when your existing contracts expire. Collection management encompasses all resources—print, digital, any media—and the way in which your patrons' access to each interrelates to meet the informational (and possibly entertainment) needs of the community you serve. Your job as a collections manager parallels any other managerial position in libraries, in that it boils down to meeting the needs of your patrons while achieving the goals of your institution.

You will need to collect data that show how your collections are actually being used, in order to base your purchasing, weeding, and other decisions on community needs. In a rapidly changing environment with multiple formats, you cannot merely rely upon assumptions or preconceptions about how people should use your collections.

Outsourcing

Some libraries have begun outsourcing specific functions to vendors or outside workers; others have outsourced the entire management of their institution. Outsourcing can include anything from using workers from a temporary agency to complete a short-term project, to using contractors to conduct specific projects or programs, to employing a consultant during a referendum drive or new building project, to outsourcing nighttime virtual reference services, to contracting out the overall management of the library to a company such as Library Systems and Services, LLC (LSSI). Some libraries choose to outsource the services that are furthest from the defined "core mission" of their institution; others see outsourcing as primarily a cost-cutting measure, choosing to outsource those functions that can be done more cheaply and efficiently by people or companies outside the library.

Larger outsourcing decisions are likely made above your head by the library board or other governing body, so your duties here boil down to how well you work and manage in an outsourced environment—or how well you make the argument against outsourcing and work to prove your own and your staff's value and professionalism in tough budget times. This essentially involves showing your decision makers a return on their investment and making the case for your library's needs. (See Chapters 9 and 10 for more information.)

More minor decisions, such as the use of temporary personnel for short-term projects in your department, may be entirely up to you. Considerations here range from the cost (including benefits) of full-time regular employees vs. temps, to acquired knowledge of the institution (or of the field), to minimizing turnover. Before making outsourcing decisions, you should also look at other institutions that have outsourced similar services or operations and learn from their experiences. Hawaii's negative experience with outsourcing all public library book purchasing, for example, should be a wakeup call to libraries contemplating similar arrangements. Hawaii became burdened with a number of impractical and duplicate items, at a higher than anticipated cost, and was unable to stock specific items to meet local needs. The state had to back out of its contract.

A major concern in managing and using outsourced services will be maintaining the quality of service your users deserve and expect. Contractors and outsourcers may not hold the same values or commitment to library service as those who have made a conscious commitment to the library profession, and their contracts may not allow or inspire them to change services to meet a community's changing needs. Patricia Glass Schuman writes: "What worries me are those services that, if privatized, might have the potential to violate the public trust. We must draw a line between the simple purchase of products and the privatization of intangible core activities like service, selection, policy setting, and management. Do we really want our libraries held hostage to the whimsy of the marketplace?"[2]

You will also need to allay your staff members' concerns that they will be downsized or replaced by temporary or contract workers. ALA's Office of Intellectual Freedom offers a number of resources to help managers make outsourcing decisions for their institutions, including an outsourcing checklist and guidelines. See for example: http://www.ala.org/ala/oif/iftoolkits/outsourcing/Default2446.htm.

The time you have spent working in various library facilities and with library technology is your best preparation for managing these services. Your work with patrons and as a librarian gives you a picture of the needs of your institution, and your interactions and discussions with your colleagues give you ideas about ways to improve your own technology, systems, and facilities. As always, use your library background and your common sense to create a usable and useful environment for both staff and patrons.

Notes

1. Peter Booth Wiley, "Beyond the Blueprint." *Library Journal,* Feb. 15 1997: 113.

2. Patricia Glass Schuman, "The Selling of the Public Library," *Library Journal,* Aug. 1998: 52.

Recommended Reading

"ALA Library Fact Sheet 10: Disaster Response: A Selected Annotated Bibliography." *American Library Association.* 2003. April 4, 2004 <http://www.ala.org/ala/alalibrary/libraryfactsheet/alalibrary factsheet10.htm>.

Alire, Camila, ed. *Library Disaster and Recovery Handbook.* New York: Neal-Schuman, 2000.

Brown, Bill. "The New Green Standard." *Library Journal,* Dec. 2003: 61–63.

Campbell, Anne L. "Magical Models." *Library Journal,* Feb. 15, 2003: 38–40.

Cravey, Pamela. *Protecting Library Staff, Users, Collections, and Facilities.* New York: Neal-Schuman, 2001.

Ebbinghouse, Carol. "Library Outsourcing: A New Look." *Searcher,* April 2002: 63–68.

Gordon, Rachel Singer. *The Accidental Systems Librarian*. Medford, NJ: Information Today, 2003.

Kahn, Miriam B. *Disaster Response and Planning for Libraries, 2nd ed.* Chicago: ALA Editions, 2003.

—. "Managing Disaster: Emergency Planning for Libraries." *Library Journal*, Dec. 15, 1993: 73–75.

Mayo, Diane and Sandra Nelson. *Wired for the Future: Developing Your Library Technology Plan*. Chicago: American Library Association, 1999.

Rizzo, Joseph P. "Get with the Program! Building a Vision of Place." *Library Journal*, Dec. 2002: 66–68.

Schuman, Patricia Glass. "The Selling of the Public Library." *Library Journal*, Aug. 1998: 50–52.

Stover, Mark. *Leading the Wired Organization: The Information Professional's Guide to Managing Technological Change*. New York: Neal-Schuman, 1999.

Tucker, Dennis C. *Library Relocations and Collection Shifts*. Medford, NJ: Information Today, Inc., 1999.

White, Herbert S. "Library Outsourcing and Contracting: Cost-Effectiveness or Shell Game?" *Library Journal*, June 15, 1998: 56–57.

—. "Why Outsourcing Happens, and What To Do About It." *American Libraries*, Jan. 2000: 66–71.

Wiley, Peter Booth. "Beyond the Blueprint." *Library Journal*, Feb. 15, 1997: 110–113.

Chapter 8

Managing Change

People are the gatekeepers of change. They have the power to breathe life into a new program or kill it. If they're excited and positive; it's open sesame. If they're not—and that's most of the time—it's clang! The gate's slammed shut in your face.
Robert Kriegel and David Brandt[1]

Most people are inherently uncomfortable with change. Change moves us out of our comfort zone, makes us think, disturbs our routine. Change in people's work environments especially discomfits those who have built identities based around their jobs. Change, however, is the norm in today's libraries; most are no longer comfortable places for those accustomed to routine. This may be difficult for some of your staff members to accept, particularly those who have been in their positions for some time and/or who entered the field when it had a seeming sense of stability about it. Despite the transformations that have swept the field in recent years, some library staff refuse to acknowledge the inevitability of change—or to acknowledge that change in libraries (as well as in our larger society) is nothing new.

As a library manager, you will need to accept change as a constant. Your role is to anticipate and implement effective change, and to help your staff members participate, innovate, and cope. You will need to build an attitude of excitement about the possibilities of change and about your library's future, working to create a change-ready organization. You may need to challenge ongoing, longstanding practices, some so entrenched that no one remembers their original purpose. Understand that change is a way of life in today's libraries; some changes are merely more dramatic than others and will require more overt preparation on your part.

Managing change effectively requires understanding the ways in which people react differently to different types of changes. In libraries, these changes can range from an adjustment in the procedures for accomplishing a common task, to a change to a different automation system, to responding to a changing community with changes in programs, services, or collections, to a change in managers. Each type brings unique challenges. Different staff members may be able to take one alteration to their work environment in stride, yet display a certain inflexibility about others. Once you get to know the people in your library, you will have a better idea of what different types of change may mean to each person, and how best to get them to accept those that seem less natural.

If possible, take some time to settle in and familiarize yourself with the workplace environment, organizational culture, and various personalities before proceeding with major changes. (The definition of "major" may here vary, depending on whom you ask.) Also, even if you were promoted from within, you will need to get to know your staff members from a different perspective and to give them time to adjust. Your presence as a new manager is a change in itself.

Your Change Options

Be wary of making a lot of changes, especially dramatic changes, at the outset of your new management position. Your plans stand a better chance of success once you get to know the day-to-day workings of your department and/or institution, as well as the strengths, weaknesses, and skills of your staff members as individuals. You need to accept that major change takes time. As Sandra Nelson, Ellen Altman, and Diane Mayo note: "Change doesn't happen because managers want it to. Change occurs when staff on all levels understand the reasons for the change and the benefits that are expected to result from the change and then incorporate the change into the way they do their jobs."[2] One respondent to the staff survey suggests: "Don't rush in and try to change everything overnight. Take some time to see what is already in place and use the strengths that you see there to build upon."

This is not to say that you should avoid making your necessary daily decisions and implementing smaller changes; do not let the fear of change keep you from proceeding with the ongoing management of your library or department. Recognize the difference between major and minor changes, and realize that people are much more likely to get on board when they know why changes are occurring. Look at why and how things are done before moving ahead; sometimes there are valid reasons that you as a new manager may not be aware of.

Internal vs. External Changes

Internal change is deliberately created by your library. You have more control over the type and pace of such changes, while external change, from without, is inherently out of your control. External changes can create the need to rethink your library's strategy and direction. Your institution may face a sudden and dramatic drop in funding; its community may be changing; its building may be crumbling—all of these are changes that come from without. All library managers must deal with external changes, no matter how hard these are to anticipate or to plan for.

External change can also be imposed by your administration or larger institution, and you as a department head or supervisor need to lead your people. Here, use what power you have to empower your staff. Can you bring their suggestions to higher management? Can you implement training, ideas, practices that will ease the transition? Planning for change involves planning for its people-related aspects as well.

Ongoing Change vs. Crisis Management

If your work life devolves into a constant series of putting out fires, it may be time to step back, look at the overall picture, and strategize a new way of managing change in your organization. The occasional crisis is, of course, inevitable. When crises begin to take over and replace your regular work, though, this is a sign that you and/or your institution need to modify the ways in which you are managing. Focusing entirely on crises diverts your attention from achieving your own and the library's long-term goals.

Gradual change is often more effective. Incremental, ongoing changes are easier for most people to accept, because the rest of their work life remains stable and provides them with a reassuring continuity. This gives them a chance to adjust more easily and to see changes as less threatening. Small and successful changes build a pattern of success that allow people to feel confident in their ability to process change in general. Over time, these gradual changes can also build, step by step, to have an amazing impact on your institution. As one manager survey respondent notes: "I view management as an ongoing process of refinement. Change doesn't happen quickly—and by this I mean changes in staff attitudes, changes in procedures, etc. 'Selling' change as a process of refinement goes a long way toward gaining buy-in from staff."

Gradual changes are often easier for your patrons to accept—as anyone who has lived through the switch from a traditional card catalog to an online system can tell you. Dramatic change is of course sometimes inevitable, but you will in this event need to lay as much groundwork as possible. Change seems most dramatic when it comes as a surprise or when people are not prepared. Building on small successes can also help you get used to managing change. Once you have successfully managed minor and incremental changes, you can build on these to make more difficult or major adjustments.

Overcoming Resistance to Change

Change is doomed to fail if library staff are not on board. People display their resistance to change in a number of ways. Some staff members will choose passive resistance, merely continuing to do things the old way, pretending that change is not coming (or has not arrived), or dragging their feet in going along. Others will actively work to sabotage your change efforts, or continuously complain, point out every minor snag, and undermine others' excitement and morale. In a union environment, change resisters may file a grievance, effectively stopping or slowing down the process until their complaint is resolved. Even those who believe in the overall value of a given change may resist it when it comes to their own work life or department. The first rule of change, therefore, is to get your staff excited first, rather than to institute changes from the top down and expect them to fall in line later. As staff members get on board, they will encourage their peers to do the same: a kind of grown-up version of peer pressure.

When you have been working and worrying for weeks, months, or even years to plan for and implement a given change, it can be hard to fathom that the process can be even more difficult for your employees. But your staff members are, after all, the ones who will need to live with the daily impact of a changed environment. Whether or not management realizes this, employees do.

The first step, then, in overcoming resistance to change—especially dramatic change—is to address people's worries. People naturally become concerned that proposed changes will put them out of a job, that they will be unable to adjust or to learn how to use new technology, that they will lose personal or professional power in a new environment, or that a proposed plan will not work in your particular institution. Talk to your employees to find out their true worries, addressing them realistically and reassuringly. Be sure to talk to change-resistant individuals one-on-one, as people's reasons can be varied and personal. Part of alleviating staff's concerns, especially when an upcoming change is technological, is to provide people with the training they need. Never let changes in technology or in other library operations make your people's skills obsolete; give them the background and training to succeed in their changing environment. Also make it clear that these changes are not intended to denigrate the value of the way things have been done in the past; rather, they are to meet changing demands and circumstances.

Another part of alleviating people's concerns requires that you address the very real issue of resource allocation, as the library's environment, priorities, and activities change. In most libraries, adding new programs or facilities, services, or technologies requires a concomitant examination of existing programs and services, with an eye to what might be cut or shifted. No one wants to see her pet project lose funding, even if a particular activity is no longer serving your library's patrons. Here, you will need to get people involved with and excited about new projects, redirecting their attention and interest while you reallocate library funds.

Make it perfectly clear that change is coming. Some libraries have gone through so many workplace changes that their staff automatically assume that any new ones will be quickly passing fads. They therefore plan to ride them out, and then go back to the way things were before. Watch out for people who give mere lip service to change but fail actually to modify their activities. Inertia is powerful; you need to become the irresistible force overcoming the seemingly immovable object.

The major rule of successful change? Communication, communication, communication. Communicate every step of the way. People have an inherent and dramatic resistance to change that seems randomly imposed. As Peter F. Drucker points out: "Balancing change and continuity requires continuous work on information. Nothing disrupts continuity and corrupts relationships more than poor or unreliable information (except, perhaps, deliberate misinformation). It has to become routine for any enterprise to ask at any change, even the most minor one: 'Who needs to be informed of this?'"[3] Lack of communication also contributes to rumors and gossip about upcoming changes, creating an underlying atmosphere of fear and misconceptions.

While keeping the lines of communication open on your end, also give other people a say. Invite input, comments, and ideas, and implement those that will be helpful to the transition. If your staff feels as if their ideas are taken seriously and that they have a hand in creating change, they will be more likely to support it. Invite ideas throughout the entire transition, not just during the immediately preceding period. Buy-in grows out of real involvement.

Give people a clear and positive picture of what their changed environment will look like. Build up the pluses! People are less nervous about change when they have a realistic picture of what to expect, and an idea of what they should be excited about. Here, give concrete examples of how a proposed change will directly and positively affect a department or an individual. If you are switching to a new automation system, for example, demonstrate to circulation staff that they will now be able to produce their own reports at the touch of a button rather than having to send a request to your library system and wait for printouts to arrive a week later. Show reader's advisory staff how they can use the integrated best-seller lists and reviews built into a new OPAC to provide personalized patron service. Also continue to demonstrate these positives after the change has been implemented, reinforcing your message and excitement during the transitional period. Show people why change is necessary, what it is intended to accomplish, and how it improves the service they are able to offer your customers.

If you hire a consultant, or work with vendors and other outside individuals to help facilitate a particular change process, be sure that they also contribute to this open communication and positive emphasis. Consistency in presenting and promoting change is essential. Outside agents who lack familiarity with the personalities in and practices of your institution can have difficulty working with and training library staff.

Be sure throughout the process to foster a foundation of stability that people can draw upon in preparing for any change. Again, if at all possible, implement change incrementally. This makes the process seem less drastic, and people can draw comfort from the rest of their environment. Incremental steps also allow you to make change and innovation an ongoing process in your library, rather than a series of dramatic events. Try to implement one major change at a time; do not require people to adjust in multiple areas at once.

Think also about the way in which changes in one department, section, program, or service of the library will affect other departments, sections, programs, or services. Will establishing a new service use funding currently allocated elsewhere, requiring cutbacks? Will starting a new program take staff time currently being spent on other tasks, requiring others in their department to fill in or to take on new roles? Will implementing a new idea overlap current services, making an existing program redundant? Will adding new shelving take up space currently being used for displays? Try to anticipate these side effects and to plan for the consequences of your actions.

Encouraging Innovation

Especially in larger organizations, staff must have a stake in and input into effective change. You need to create a library culture that welcomes change and innovation. Any innovation, however, has to be managed and looked at in terms of how it will help your library (or your part of the library) fulfill its mission. Particularly when it comes to library technology, glowing articles and pushy vendors can tempt you to implement interesting-looking new programs, and services—without taking the true needs of your patrons and staff into consideration.

With that in mind, realize that change is most effective when it is at least partially instigated by the people affected by it. Your job as a manager is to create a culture in which your staff is comfortable expressing their ideas and suggestions for ways in which to do things differently, where they can help create change rather than just reacting to it. In order for this to be successful, your staff has to know that their suggestions are taken seriously. As they see their ideas implemented, they will be more willing to give additional suggestions and to share the benefits of their experience and knowledge. They will also feel empowered by having had a hand in creating change; this feeling of empowerment leads to more motivated employees.

When people come up with creative solutions, be cognizant of your own possible tendencies to look first for the negative, why something cannot be done. Realize that change can be hard for you, too, but that fostering innovation requires openness to new ideas and possibilities. As you think these solutions through and make concrete plans, ideas can be modified or discarded in order to match your needs, budget, and so on. At the outset, though, remain open to a variety of possibilities. Contemporary libraries need constantly to be looking for new solutions and ideas. If people question existing practices, take an honest look at why things are done that way, and at whether you are just acting out of habit. Look at whether particular activities truly serve the goals of the library. As Tara Alcock, City Librarian, Petersburg Public Library, Alaska, suggests: "Don't be afraid to challenge conventional library wisdom. As a manager you have a wonderful opportunity to be innovative—seize that!"

Mark R. Willis notes that: "One of the most dangerous phrases in the English language is: 'We've always done it that way.' Change is part of daily life for all of us, and that includes the library."[4] Examine even seemingly innocuous activities for the "we have always done it that way" mentality. Even small actions that are duplicative and/or unnecessary can over time add up to extraordinary amounts of wasted time and effort. Tami Farmer, Adult Public Services Lead, Clermont County Public Library, Batavia, Ohio, explains: "Just because it is traditional, doesn't make it right for today's customers or staff."

Chapter 3 talked about the need to hire adaptable, flexible people to fill positions in today's libraries. This is partially because of the ongoing need for change leaders and innovators. Nonmanagerial staff, who are more intimately involved in dealing with patrons, technology, and/or the day-to-day workings of the library, will also often be in a better position to see where innovation is necessary—especially larger and/or more hierarchical institutions in which managers focus entirely on their management responsibilities and are largely divorced from hands-on practice.

Technostress

Technology brings such changes that the difficulties people encounter in dealing with technology-induced stresses have been given their own name—technostress. Combat technostress by helping library staff become comfortable with technology and integrate it naturally into their daily work life. For many, technostress often grows out of a distrust of and discomfort with technology. Inadequate training contributes to these fears.

Ongoing training and support is necessary to help staff develop a solid familiarity with the technology they need to use in their

work each day. When people have a stable foundation of understanding and can see concrete ways in which technology helps
them do their jobs, technological change or setbacks become more
annoying than daunting. Annoying is much easier to live with.

Resources to consult in creating a technology training program
for staff include:

- ALA's Continuing Library Education Network and
  Exchange Round Table (CLENERT): http://www.ala.org/
  clenert. Addresses all aspects of continuing education for
  library staff; includes a discussion list, quarterly newsletter, and programs at ALA meetings.

- Gordon, Rachel Singer. *The Accidental Systems Librarian.*
  Medford, NJ: Information Today, 2003. Includes chapters
  on technology instruction techniques and lifelong
  learning.

- New Jersey Library Association's technical competencies
  for librarians: http://www.njla.org/resources/
  techcompetencies.html. Look at their guidelines when
  establishing your own (more specific) set of technical
  competencies, so that you know where to focus your
  training efforts.

- WebJunction.org: http://www.webjunction.org. Provides
  a number of free online workshops on various aspects of
  library technology, sample training materials, and online
  discussion forums.

Think about what staff members need to know to do their jobs
effectively.

Remember also to pay attention to the ways technostress
impacts you as a manager, especially if you are in charge of planning for and implementing technology in your library. Take the
time to build your own foundation of knowledge and your comfort
level with various types of technology.

Strategic Planning

At its core, strategic planning involves effectively planning, creating, and managing forthcoming changes in the way your organization functions. A formal strategic plan may regularly be required (generally every three to five years) by your board, your larger institution, or your state, or may be required as a condition of grant funding. In addition, strategic planning as a strategy for influencing the direction of your library should be interwoven throughout all of your management activities. Always have your broader plan in mind when making daily decisions. If you fail to plan and to work toward specific goals, then your management career can easily devolve into putting out one fire after another, never looking at how your actions fit into the bigger picture.

Strategic plans tend to grow from a much more nebulous and shorter mission statement. Mission statements lay out the overall purpose of your institution in one or two paragraphs, but never specifically address how this purpose is to be achieved. Keep your institution's mission in mind when creating a strategic plan, defining goals that support your stated institutional purpose, and outlining how best to meet those goals. If your library lacks a mission statement, look at creating one as your first step. (See Linda K. Wallace's *Libraries, Mission and Marketing* [Chicago: ALA Editions, 2004] for examples and discussion of creating an effective mission statement.)

Strategic planning involves a number of steps:

- Prepare to plan. Get your group, organization, employees, and anyone else involved in the planning process prepared to move forward. This includes establishing a planning group and clarifying what will be involved in the planning process.

- Perform a needs assessment. This involves looking at your current environment and activities and seeing whether you are meeting the needs of your customers.

- Create goals for your library or department or section. Think here in terms of long-term goals: where do you want your organization to be in five years? What do you want your department to have achieved?

- Create specific objectives that support each of these goals. What needs to change in order that these goals can be achieved? What steps do you need to take to achieve each goal? What specific programs or activities will you be implementing?

- Identify the resources necessary to accomplish each of these objectives. What funding, staff, or equipment will you need? What type of training will staff need to carry out new activities? Who will be responsible for carrying out each of these steps?

- Outline how you will communicate your plan and your objectives to staff, decision makers, and your community. Different types of communication and different levels of comprehensiveness will be necessary for each audience.

- Implement the plan. Carry out the steps you have outlined in the planning process.

- Create and use a mechanism for evaluating how well you have accomplished the objectives outlined in your plan.

Strategic planning in most libraries takes place by committee; group members can be drawn internally and from the library's broader institution and/or community. If at all possible, try to keep control over the composition of your planning group, while being careful to allow all interested parties a voice.

Strategic thinking in today's libraries works from the assumption that change is a constant, and involves trying as much as possible to anticipate changes. This is easier in shorter-term strategic plans. Although no one can predict the future, you can use the information at your disposal about the library's environment and about trends in your organization and community to envision possible scenarios. You can think of strategic planning as preemptive problem solving—allowing you to prepare yourself, your institution, and your staff to tackle future issues, face future challenges, and find solutions.

Public libraries and other nonprofit library organizations need to engage in strategic planning—and define a strategy!—just as much as corporate entities do. Part of your strategy involves continually defining how your institution, or your part of it, can best carry out its mission in terms of your changing environment. The choices, goals, objectives and activities you outline in your strategic plan all follow from this definition. After defining your broad goals, you will need to convert these into more specific and definable objectives. These need to be realistically achievable in the timeframe and with the funding available. Be sure to make the separation between the mission of your institution, which remains constant, and your strategy, which concretely outlines how best to accomplish this mission in light of changing circumstances.

It can be tempting to pursue interesting yet possibly tangential ideas—should your library install wi-fi and open up free Internet access to the general public (or at least those of the general public with wireless-enabled laptops, PDAs, and other devices)? Should it partner with a local community center in establishing a joint literacy program? Should it begin offering more in-depth research to local businesses for a charge? As always, these questions have to be looked at in terms of whether they will help you accomplish your mission, of how well these ideas are related to your core goals, and of whether implementing new programs means that attention and resources will be taken away from your core activities.

Strategic planning also includes looking at your existing activities, products, and services and determining whether these are still necessary, whether they will continue to be necessary in the near future, and whether they need to be somehow transformed to reflect the changing needs of your patrons. "Because we've always done it that way" is an unacceptable attitude in today's library; part of strategic planning means mastering the art of letting go— and passing these decisions on to your staff. While welcoming innovation initiated by staff, library managers also need to become change leaders within their libraries. While planning, work with staff and with other managers to consider multiple points of view and to integrate their various expertise. Again, staff need to be involved in planning for change, rather than receiving a finished plan from "on high." Discuss the fact that the library is engaged in strategic planning and invite staff to be involved or to provide their input to designated committee members or managers. The level of formality of staff's involvement depends on your type and size of library and on your organizational culture.

You need to use all of the information currently at your disposal about your core constituency and how it is likely to change over the next few years, about how your services have been received and what new services people are looking for, about how your funding patterns seem likely to change, about how pricing for some of the services and materials you provide is likely to rise out of reach. Do not make the mistake of relying entirely on old assumptions about what your patrons need and where your funding is coming from. Gather new information by examining demographic data about your community or company, by surveying library users (and nonusers), and by collecting current statistics on usage. You will also need to examine technological trends and shifts to see how these might transform the way your library operates.

However much information you put together, it will never seem to be enough when you are thinking about the future of your library, or even of your small part of it. Unfortunately, you will still need to create your strategic plan and make the tough decisions. Using the information you do have, you will need to create a picture of your library in one, three, or five years. Working backward from this image, you will need to outline the steps you took to get there, and show how each builds on another. You will need a stated plan in order to work proactively toward your goals, rather than drifting aimlessly, reacting blindly to events, or relying on past processes and procedures to see you through.

Many strategic planners in libraries use the SWOT formula as a tool. SWOT stands for: **S**trengths, **W**eaknesses, **O**pportunities, and **T**hreats. Strengths and Weaknesses refer to those existing library conditions that allow the institution to provide quality service or that negatively impact its ability to do so, while Opportunities and Threats discuss external factors creating both positive and negative scenarios that are likely to occur in the future (such as a referendum or property tax freeze). Analyze the group of library needs reflected in the combination of these four areas together, and work from your list to create a plan of how your library can meet these needs.

In addition to looking at how your library will evolve, set goals for library staff. You may wish to outline plans for training, for example; without development and growth, your staff will be unable to support the other goals you outline. Also, build into your strategic plan steps for evaluating its success in terms of the goals you have laid out for your department or institution. List specific activities and steps that support the goals you have outlined, ensuring that each of them directly supports one or more goals. Then, monitor these activities as you implement them and be willing to modify as needed. Be flexible: Part of dealing with change in libraries includes the willingness to examine all of your plans in light of changing circumstances. No one is able to predict every variable affecting your services, varying demand, or technological changes. While many underlying values may remain constant, the concrete steps you take to support these may be different than you and your coplanners originally envisioned.

Always take the time you need to plan. While it may seem unnecessarily time-consuming now, it will save you from making costly mistakes and from wasting time, energy, and money in the future. Your strategic plan allows you to harness innovation to serve your institution's goals and mission. Ensure that your finished plan stays clear, concise, and readable, realizing that it may need to be comprehensible to groups as varied as your governing body or authority, grant-awarding body, board, or other group less versed in library jargon than yourself. Strategic plans need to be straightforward, simple, and understandable by various groups in order to succeed.

Take the time to go back and reflect on the progress you have made. Look at what has been accomplished since your last one- or three- or five-year plan. Get people excited about the goals they have already achieved, which will translate into excitement for setting new challenges. If you neglect to follow through on or evaluate your plans as an ongoing process, people will realize that you take your planning less than seriously. Think about providing some formal recognition or celebration when a particular goal has been reached or program successfully implemented. Transitioned to a new circulation system? Have a staff appreciation day and buy pizza for everyone. Established a new homework center and reached your targeted daily attendance? Reward volunteers with T-shirts. Small celebrations can have a large impact.

Implementing and following through on your plan will require all of the strategies for managing change previously outlined. The best preparation for managing change in a contemporary library, though, is your experience as a twenty-first-century librarian. Librarians that lack the ability to cope with change rarely are promoted into a management position—now, help impart your own coping skills to others. Use the foundation you have built through effective communication, effective personnel management, and effective decision making to build upon in implementing necessary changes in your institution. Use your sense of the profession and where it is headed, coupled with your knowledge of your own institution and community, to develop a vision that you and your staff can work toward.

Notes

1. Robert Kriegel and David Brandt, *Sacred Cows Make the Best Burgers: Developing Change-Ready People and Organizations* (New York: Warner Books, 1996) 5.

2. Sandra Nelson, Ellen Altman, and Diane Mayo, *Managing for Results: Effective Resource Allocation for Public Libraries* (Chicago: ALA, 2000) 14.

3. Peter F. Drucker, *Management Challenges for the 21st Century* (New York: HarperCollins Publishers, Inc., 1999) 91.

4. Mark R. Willis, *Dealing With Difficult People in the Library* (Chicago: ALA Editions, 1999) 22.

Recommended Reading

Bull, Jennifer. "Managing the Emotional Side of Change." *Library Mosaics,* March/April 2002: 11–12.

Cargill, Jennifer and Gisela M. Webb. *Managing Libraries in Transition.* Phoenix: Oryx Press, 1988.

Curzon, Susan C. *Managing Change: A How-To-Do-It Manual for Planning, Implementing, and Evaluating Change in Libraries.* New York: Neal-Schuman, 1989.

Dougherty, Richard M. "Planning for New Library Futures." *Library Journal,* May 15, 2002: 38–41.

Drucker, Peter F. *Management Challenges for the 21st Century.* New York: HarperCollins Publishers, Inc., 1999.

—. *Managing In a Time of Great Change.* New York: Penguin, 1995.

Feinman, Valerie Jackson. "Five Steps Toward Planning for Tomorrow's Needs." *Computers in Libraries,* Jan. 1999: 18–21.

Kriegel, Robert and David Brandt. *Sacred Cows Make the Best Burgers: Developing Change-Ready People and Organizations.* New York: Warner Books, 1996.

Kupersmith, John. "Technostress in the Bionic Library." Originally published in Cheryl LaGuardia, ed. *Recreating the Academic Library: Breaking Virtual Ground.* New York: Neal-Schuman, 1998: pp. 23–47. 2003 rev. ed. < http://www.jkup.net/bionic.html> 2 May 2004.

Lubans, John Jr. "Leaving the Comfort Zone." *Library Administration & Management,* 17:4 (Fall 2003): 196–197.

Nelson, Sandra. *The New Planning for Results: A Streamlined Approach.* Chicago, American Library Association: 2001.

Sull, Donald. "Why Good Companies Go Bad." *Harvard Business Review* Feb 1, 2000. This is an enhanced edition of HBR article 99410, originally published in July/August 1999. <http://harvardbusinessonline.hbsp. harvard.edu/b01/en/common/item_detail.jhtml?id=4320> 2 May 2004.

Chapter 9

Managing Money

For knowledge services, financial strategy and budgeting are two sides of the same coin. Those with management responsibility for knowledge services must first identify what their work will provide—the products, services and consultations that will emanate from the knowledge services function. At the same time, they must identify advocates and champions with whom they can share their enthusiasm for the work they do.

Guy St. Clair and Martina J. Reich[1]

Many accidental (or potential) managers who despair of managing their personal budgets effectively on a librarian's salary try to avoid even thinking about being responsible for an entire institution's—or even one department's—budget. A certain mystique has grown up around accounting and budgeting. Recent high-profile business scandals may concern library managers, given that even the "experts" seem to have lost control of the numbers. In addition, while librarianship is attracting an ever-more-diverse pool of practitioners, it still appeals to a preponderance of liberal arts majors who lack formal training or background in mathematical and budgeting concepts. Librarianship is associated in many people's minds with books and research rather than with numerical literacy.

Any library manager, though, can master the mathematics and numerical understanding needed in her organization. Managing money requires common sense and a willingness to look at numbers in the context of what they really mean for your institution. Find meaning in the figures by relating the numbers to your own institution, department, services, or people. Unless you accept a management position as a library budget officer, you do not need to master accounting, but you do need to be able to read and make sense of the reports your accountant (and/or auditor) creates for you. You need to learn the priorities of the decision makers that hold power over your institution's budget, and to think about how to make yourself one of their priorities. You need to learn to work within budgetary constraints, and how to loosen those constraints to provide the services your customers need and deserve. You need to understand how your budget compares to those of similar-sized institutions, and how this affects the services you are able to provide.

The following sections will broadly discuss some of the money issues you may need to deal with in your library. In-depth explanations of financial statements, budgets, and cost-benefit analysis are beyond the scope of this book, but are covered quite thoroughly elsewhere. See "recommended reading" at the end of this chapter for ideas on where to start. Has math always scared you? Pick up one of the many books aimed at math phobics and work on your basic numerical literacy and your mathematical comfort level. Start with John Allen Paulos' classic *Innumeracy* for a useful and example-filled overview of probability and of what numbers mean in various contexts (New York: Hill and Wang, 1988), or with any of a number of basic business math titles, such as *Business Math for the Numerically Challenged* (Franklin Lakes, NJ: Career Press, 1998). Once you have the basics down, the rest involves understanding what the numbers mean and taking action based on what the numbers tell you. The longer you serve in your management position, the more sense numbers will make to you in relation to those from previous years.

The following discussions are not intended to make you a library accountant, budget whiz, or financial expert, but merely to provide a broad overview of some money-related areas you may need to deal with during your career as a library manager. As Lisl Zach notes: "In order to compete effectively for resources, it is important for librarians and information professionals to incorporate the underlying notions of financial management into their day-to-day operations and become comfortable with the vocabulary and techniques of budgeting."[2] Learn some of the jargon involved in budgeting and accounting so that you can carry on a coherent conversation with your library's financial officer or accountant. Then, work with your accountant, your board, and/or your auditor to assimilate the specific knowledge you need for your own management situation.

Accounting

Public libraries and other governmental institutions must comply with mandated accounting standards, the latest of which is GASB Statement 34. (GASB stands for Governmental Accounting Standards Board, a nonprofit independent agency that issues standards for governmental financial reporting. More on GASB and its role can be found at http://haplr-index.com/gasb34faq.htm and at http://www.accounting.rutgers.edu/raw/gasb/index.html.)

Current discussions of accounting often talk about "activity-based" accounting, which measures the costs of not doing something as well as the costs of each task required to complete an activity. Reducing costs therefore requires analyzing your library's activities and defining the tasks that can be streamlined or eliminated, especially those that are less central to helping your library meet its goals. Costs are defined as direct (those that can be identified specifically as belonging to a particular project or department or activity) or indirect (those that are necessary to run the institution as a whole but cannot specifically be identified as pertaining to one project, department, or activity). Indirect costs can include items such as heating and lighting, direct costs can include items such as materials purchased for a particular program. In library terms, you can think about cost not only monetarily but in terms of community goodwill and the continued relevance of your organization. You therefore need to consider the long-term costs of *not* performing an activity in addition to any potential short-term savings.

Traditionally, institutions use one of two accounting methods, cash- or accrual-based. Accrual-based accounting records expenses when items or services are purchased (no matter when the bills are paid), and revenue when it is billed (no matter when it is received). Cash-based accounting records expenses when actually paid out, and revenue when actually received. Accrual-based accounting also spreads the value of capital assets across the useful life of those assets, rather than just reporting the value of their purchase in the year of purchase as in cash-based accounting. The method that your library uses may be dictated by your larger institution or by governmental regulations; GASB 34 demands the use of accrual accounting, for example, and you will need to be prepared to think about how your library's capital assets depreciate, or lose value over time. (This includes books and other materials— see http://www.lla.state.la.us/gasb34/Libcoll.pdf for a rough guide.)

Most libraries employ an outside accountant to prepare and/or audit their financial statements. As a manager, you will be less likely to have to do much "hands-on" accounting (although this can differ for directors of very small libraries), but you will need to know how to interpret these and other reports. General financial statements may be too broad to help you make effective departmental decisions, so be aware of the need to collect additional and more specific data.

Libraries also face the dilemma of funds that are encumbered (committed) but not yet spent. For example, you may order 20 copies of the latest John Grisham novel from a jobber in April, but the book is not actually published and received until July. The funds for those 20 copies are already encumbered, but you will not receive an invoice from the jobber until the items are actually shipped to you. These bookkeeping issues are especially challenging when they straddle the change of your library's fiscal year. You will need to keep track of encumbered funds, especially as a director or as head of an acquisitions department.

Budgeting

Basically, a budget estimates the costs of various library activities over a given period (usually a year). Budgets allocate library resources toward library objectives, laying out your spending plan for the next year. Once a budget is set, you will be responsible for staying within its guidelines.

Large portions of your library's operating budget may already be "locked in." Salaries, for example, will remain relatively constant or rise consistently until staff members leave (or are downsized), and costs such as heating and cooling are determined largely by your facility's construction and local weather patterns. You may also be constrained by union rules, endowment stipulations, or by town or institutional spending requirements. However, this still leaves a great deal of resources that you will need to allocate as fairly as possible, ensuring that the library serves all its constituents effectively. (This does include library staff!) Relate your budget to your library's strategic plan (see Chapter 8), as the goals and objectives outlined need to be funded. Strategic planning also allows you to modify your budget to meet changing circumstances, rather than building only on what your library has done in the past.

Larger libraries may employ budget officers who assume the main responsibility for an institution's overall budget. Part of your duties as any type of library manager, though, will likely include working with a budget—which includes making the purchasing decisions that best fit available funds and library needs. This will also include budgeting for new programs, services, and equipment, based on available funding. If you lack the funds to initiate a new service, your duties include looking at where funding can be found, cutting from elsewhere, or reallocating. It will include ensuring that your library or any of its individual departments manage their money, and that they do not expend all of their funds early in the fiscal year.

Directors will have responsibility over the budget as a whole, while department heads or other middle managers may oversee particular funds, or budget categories. A collection development manager, for instance, will have responsibility for the acquisitions fund, a children's manager responsibility for the children's programming fund, etc. This also gives middle managers practice in managing a budget, should they eventually move into an upper management position.

Types of budgets used by libraries include:

- Lump sum. In a lump-sum budget, you receive a single lump amount with little specific indication as to how it should be spent; there is often little relation to the actual goals of your library or department. This gives you great leeway in spending, but little guidance on doing so.

- Formula. A formula budget allocates resources according to predetermined standards. A college's formula budget, for example, might allocate 10 percent of the school's total budget to the library. A large library's formula budget might allocate a certain number of public services staff members per each 1,000 community members served.

- Line-item (sometimes called "expenditure"). The most common budgetary method used in libraries, line-item breaks a budget down into multiple categories and assigns a dollar amount to each of those categories. (Expenditure lines can include salaries, print materials, computer equipment, and so on, while income lines can include taxes, fines, copying fees, and so on.) The line-item method makes it easy to compare expenditures in a given category from year to year, but you have to take care to ensure that lines reflect actual uses of funding as circumstances change.

- Performance. Performance budgets break down by department, and focus on the actual costs of staff time and materials that are spent in carrying out each departmental function.

- Program (sometimes called "function"). Program budgets are based on organizational objectives. They link the money spent on a particular service or program directly to an organizational goal, showing the resources needed to meet each of these goals. This includes the staff time, materials, and so on spent in carrying out each program. Program budgets break down library service into essential programs, break each of those down further into more specific activities, then define services that fall under each activity. For example, a library's technical services department might break down into the broad activities of cataloging and acquisitions, then break cataloging into original and copy cataloging, then break original cataloging down into books, periodicals, videos, CD-ROMs, and so on. Activities and services are ranked by importance, and costs are established for each, to help in assigning their budgets. This lets you more precisely see how money is expended for particular programs and services. You can also look at alternative methods for carrying out each goal, and decide which will be the most cost-effective alternative.

- Zero-based. Zero-based budgets, instead of starting from how much money the library has, start from the programs and services the library wishes to offer and estimates costs and benefits for each. Then, each proposed activity is analyzed in terms of what will be needed to carry it out and whether it is necessary to meet the goals of the institution, requiring that each be justified. Programs are then prioritized, and funding allocated in ranked order until the money runs out. Zero-based budgeting is not always a yearly process, but can be useful on a regular basis in determining the core services of your institution and allowing you to weed out those that no longer meet community needs. It is an especially useful tool when library funding has been cut, helping you define where to make necessary cuts in programs and services.

These budgets can overlap; a library might, for example, use line-item budgeting and then do a zero-based exercise on occasion. A library might receive a lump-sum budget, and you as director are then responsible for transforming this into a line-item budget you can present to your board for approval. Budgets can follow the calendar year, or your library might have an otherwise-defined fiscal year (from July 1 to June 30, for example).

Library managers will generally find that staff salaries and benefits take up the majority of expenditures, often going as high as 60 percent. You will need to balance the need to compensate staff fairly with the need to balance budgets and cut costs.

Most libraries use some form of line-item budget. Examples of the broad items that may be included in a line-item budget include staff, materials, facilities, electronic resources, technology, materials and supplies, and programming. Each of these can be further subcategorized, depending on your institution's size and needs. The budget lines for staff, for example, can include salaries, benefits, and training. The staff line can be broken down into professional staff, clerical staff, and maintenance staff, or into various other categories, depending on the organization and needs of your institution.

Budgets can be further subdivided by department, which allows supervisors of various library sections to have more knowledge of and control over their budgets and gives the administration a more accurate picture of expenditures. A line-item budget will be broken down into a number of specific items that fit into these broader categories. If your budget is not officially broken down further, you can create a spreadsheet for your own use that further subdivides categories. If certain categories consistently exceed their budgeted funding, it may be time either to revisit the budget as a whole in order to reallocate funds, or to rein in spending in those specific areas. Realize also that, should circumstances change mid-year, you may need to go before your board or other funding body to move money from one main category of the budget to another.

As a new manager, you might be surprised by just how much of your budget is already locked in—or by how little money you really have left to work with. Money that is already locked in is known as nondiscretionary funding: that is, you lack the discretion to choose what to do with these funds. The electric bill has to be paid, salaries must be paid, your consortium dues must be paid. Your nondiscretionary funds are generally spent on fixed-cost items, those for which spending patterns remain relatively constant. You (and/or other management members) will be making the spending decisions regarding the library's discretionary funds: that is, you have the discretion to choose where to spend these funds among various programs, services, and materials. These are variable-cost items, for which you have more control over spending. You can try to balance your budget by cutting back or changing the library's spending patterns, for example, by purchasing fewer books than last year or by switching jobbers to get a better discount.

As a new director, you might be in the uncomfortable position of needing to resolve a budgetary mess left by your predecessor. One manager survey respondent was taken aback by her initial budget surprises, sharing: "I had a lot to 'clean up' when I first got here. It took almost two years (and counting) to get things in order with the budget, the board, the personnel, the collection, the building, etc. The board was rather uninformed about the budget, so my biggest surprise was that they told me they had money during the interview, and then my first day I had to cut about $30,000 out of the budget!" You may also be in a situation where serials pricing, health insurance premiums, or other specific items are rising much faster than the cost of inflation, requiring you to find ways to raise additional revenue or to make cuts in these or other areas.

State standards might also affect the way in which you can allocate your budget in a public or school library. Libraries that fail to comply with standards risk losing state funding and eligibility for grants, so be careful to comply with those that apply to your institution.

In some special libraries, the costs of specific library services may be charged back to the requesting department or project, effectively coming out of multiple budgets. You may be involved in setting these charge-back rates, in which case, you need to establish the variety of costs involved in any transaction. These costs can include anything from the time spent by staff members working on a specific request, to the direct costs of interlibrary loan, photocopy, and/or database fees, to the indirect costs of the space the library occupies. In some situations, charge-back fees are then passed on to specific clients; in others, fees are absorbed by an internal department, section, or project.

When preparing each year's budget, you need to balance anticipated revenue with projected needs. As a director, discuss your library's changing needs with your department heads and use their input when working out your overall budget. Look at whether your overall income is projected to increase or decrease, and by what percentages. Prepare a preliminary budget based on last year's (and earlier years') numbers as well as on this year's plan, and then gather input from department heads and other interested parties to help the final version reflect your library's funding and needs as accurately as possible. Depending on your library's structure, the final budget may need board approval or that of another higher authority. Part of your responsibility as a director, then, will be to present the budget to your board, to be able to clearly explain its components, and to justify specific requested allocations. You will need to be able to do this both in writing and in person.

Leave yourself sufficient time for the budget process, including time needed to gather input, get statistics, and gain approval. Create a budget timeline to guide yourself through the process. This will become easier each year, as you get a better handle on what is involved.

Doing More With Less

Shrinking state budgets, a backlash against rising property taxes, corporate belt-tightening, and a faltering economy all mean that libraries and information centers in the new millennium tend to face the challenge of meeting an increased demand for services—from access to costly electronic databases and academic journals, to non-English materials, to homework centers and after-school programs, to public-access Internet terminals and training—at the same time that their funding is being slashed. Academic libraries compete for funding with other institutional departments; public libraries compete for theirs with other local services; corporate libraries compete with other company departments and the perception that needed information is now available online at every desktop. Even if your yearly budget remains the same, rising salaries, materials costs, and other inevitable increases mean that even a consistent level of funding will fail to keep pace with expenses without cutbacks somewhere. Chapter 10 talks more about marketing your institution, and the following sections about ideas on getting more funding for your library. In some cases, we can also take a page from corporate belt-tightening measures and work at streamlining some of our own programs and services. Look at where staff might be duplicating one another's efforts, or where services, programs, or collections are receiving less use.

Some library managers balk at implementing a "doing more with less philosophy." Managers note that, if they continue to provide the same services with reduced funding, or make cuts only in the places that are least visible to their customers, they are in some ways supporting the argument that the original level of funding was never really necessary. Further, providing the same services with fewer staff or resources stretches your employees and does little for morale. An alternative strategy is to target cuts where they will affect those who have control over your library's funding, or those who are likely to complain the loudest. The theory here is that reduced service will inspire people to increase funding; the counterargument is that people will be disinclined to increase their support of an institution that fails to meet their needs.

Be careful in where you choose to cut, and be sure to look long-term. If you decide to buy cheaper computer equipment to save money that can be used for current programming, for example, will it break down sooner or require more ongoing maintenance, driving repair and upkeep costs up in the future? If you follow Seattle Public Library's lead of closing its doors for a couple of weeks each year, will your patrons lose heart or look for alternatives? Think about costs in terms of the entire life of an item or a program.

Your job as a library manager involves balancing and funding competing priorities. In tough budgetary times, someone has to decide where to cut, how to continue providing the best possible service, and how to find ways to provide that service more efficiently. Doing more with less can mean that you personally have to make the hard choices about reallocating scarce resources and prioritizing library programs and services. Sometimes, you will just have to reconcile yourself to doing less with less. You will also need to be able to analyze the actual savings from proposed cuts and to compare these to your funding gaps.

You will better be able to adjust to shifts in library funding if you become versed in projecting your institution's likely revenue. Cuts should rarely come as a surprise. This is one reason to foster political and community connections, so that you are kept in the loop on your community's, institution's, or larger organization's funding and its projected shortfalls. Know who makes the funding decisions about your library.

Getting More

In an environment where libraries are seen as competing for funding against a number of other essential agencies and departments, it can be difficult to argue for our fair share. There are a number of strategies, however, to help you get a bigger piece of the funding pie. Garnering support for increased funding is an ongoing process. You are sure to be rebuffed if you only come out to make your arguments at budget time; lay the groundwork for library support on a continual basis. You can help your cause by gathering appropriate statistics and numbers about your community and your institution (described in a later section). Think about ways to show the true costs and benefits of your library's services.

In some cases, you can turn to outside sources of funding, such as grants, donations, and fundraising. ALA has a number of resources that help libraries apply for grants and perform other fundraising activities. Start by examining ALA's own list of association-sponsored or cosponsored grants, which can be found at http://www.ala.org/work/awards. ALA's Library Administration & Management Association (LAMA) also maintains a fundraising and financial development section with an associated moderated discussion list; find more information on this section at http://www.ala.org/ala/lama/lamacommunity/lamacommittees/fundraisingb/fundraisingfinancial.htm. One of the biggest advocates for building alternative funding structures for libraries, Steve Coffman, makes regular presentations on the issue. View the PowerPoint for one panel discussion at http://www.infotoday.com/il2003/presentations (under Tuesday Evening Session). View others at WebJunction.org by doing a search for "alternative funding."

Fundraising

For guidance on and ideas about fundraising, join LAMA's fundraising and development section's e-mail list. Some libraries have looked into new and innovative ways of raising funds. The Alliance Library System (Illinois) and the mid-Illinois Talking Book Center, for instance, comaintain an online shopping directory ("The Shoppes of Library Lane," at http://www.mitbc.org/librarylane), with proceeds supporting improved service and MLS scholarships. Always be ready to compare the costs of running any fundraising activity with what you stand to make. For example, if you sell a holiday calendar featuring historical photographs of your town from the library's collection, you will need to figure the cost per unit of producing, reproducing, and selling these calendars (including staff time). Figure out your break-even cost, estimate how many units you will be able to sell, and then price your calendars appropriately.

Friends of the Library groups raise money for public libraries in various ways, from in-house activities such as gift shops, coffee bars, and book sales, to events like walk-a-thons and calling campaigns. If your public library lacks a Friends group, consider starting one; if the group is small and moribund, consider how you can help reenergize it. Look for Friends members among vocal library supporters, regular library users, regular library groups, and so on. Visit http://www.folusa.org for more information. As a director or manager, you can serve as the library's liaison to the Friends group. Harnessing the energy of library supporters in constructive ways can benefit the library monetarily. In addition, supporters can elicit community support for your institution by advocating to both politicians and the general public. Your Friends group can register as a 501(c)(3) tax-exempt organization, which creates special requirements for campaigning and fundraising; your library's lawyer should be able to provide guidance here.

Referenda

Public libraries face the almost-inevitable prospect of campaigning for a referendum at some point, as funding needs or communities change or when a new building project is pressing. Campaigning for a referendum involves much more than ensuring that your measure appears on the ballot at election time. Your ongoing publicity and marketing efforts—and culture of good customer service—work to build a foundation for success long before a referendum is ever needed.

As a library manager or director, you may be involved directly in coordinating a referendum campaign, or responsible for dealing with a consultant or for providing Friends and/or board members assistance in their campaign efforts. These major one-time projects also require you to develop a capital budget that supports your specific activity. You must show the need for a major capital outlay, estimate its costs, and work on obtaining funding. Then, you will be responsible for using these funds in approved ways; building grants and approved funding often come with strings.

Grants

When looking into securing grant funding for your library, realize that granting bodies often provide matching grants, which still require your library to supply a portion (usually half) of the funding for a given project. As additional evidence of your commitment, some will also want to see how your institution will continue funding a program or service after the grant period ends. These caveats, plus the lack of assurance of future funding, make grants a less-than-perfect replacement for ongoing funding. Grants are often a good supplement to your ongoing funding. Granting bodies include state libraries, ALA, IMLS, individuals, private foundations, state and local humanities councils, large companies, and local organizations.

Realize that acquiring successful and significant grants can give your regular funding bodies the impression that their support is less necessary than in the past. This is less of an issue if you use grants for one-time projects that need extra funding, such as equipment replacement or building projects, rather than for ongoing expenses such as general operating funds or salaries. Make it clear that grant money is funding supplemental programs and that it does not replace the ongoing support of your traditional funding bodies. Understand that you will need to factor in staff time and other hidden costs. For example, if you receive a grant to purchase books on a certain subject, you will need to factor in the staff time needed to process and catalog these extra items. If you receive a grant for computer equipment, you will need to factor in the staff time needed to install and maintain that equipment.

Large libraries may employ a development professional responsible for all grant-seeking activities. In smaller institutions, however, directors or managers often take on grant-writing in addition to their other duties. When writing a grant application, you need to call on all of your communication skills to paint a very clear picture of your institution, community, needs, and the intended use for the grant funds. You will need to be able to define the amount of funding you want, what it will be spent on, and the specific benefits this program, service, or equipment will bring to your institution and/or community. Follow grant guidelines to the letter. If you fail to do so, no matter the worth of your project, your proposal will be rejected. Think about how you have shown that library goals match those of other decision makers, such as your CEO, your school board, or your mayor. Use the same strategies to match the goals of your proposed project to the priorities of the granting body.

Grant-writing resources include:

- ALA's *Big Book of Library Grant Money*. This biannual guide is a huge directory of foundations with a pattern or interest in giving to libraries.

- Bill Becker's "Library Grant Money on the Web: A Resource Primer," *Searcher* Nov.-Dec. 2003: http://www.infotoday.com/searcher/nov03/becker.shtml. Lists a variety of resources and suggests strategies for their use.

- The Foundation Center: http://fdncenter.org. Part fee, part free, this site assists in locating donors and provides tutorials and information on the best ways to apply for grants, as well as links to other Web sites. Also see their print *Foundation Directory* and *Foundation Grants Index.*

- Library HQ's "Funding and Grant Sources for Libraries:" http://www.libraryhq.com/funding.html. Includes links to articles, Web sites, partnership programs, scholarships, foundations, and suggested print resources.

- Nonprofit Guides: http://www.npguides.org. Provides sample grant applications and information on the type of questions that are typically asked and material that is typically required.

Use your communication and marketing skills, as well as your understanding of your institution's needs, to create effective and compelling grant applications.

Donations

The idea of soliciting donations is most applicable to public, school, and academic libraries. Donations are often best used for one-time purchases, rather than for ongoing programs or services. Think about how best to solicit and utilize donations from your community. Do you have waiting lists for your public Internet terminals? See if a local business council or chamber of commerce may be willing to donate a new station, and place a sign near the terminal thanking them for their generosity. Need to expand your periodical collection? Start a "donate a subscription" program and allow individuals to sponsor magazines of their choice. These sorts of solicitations will be easiest if you have already done the groundwork in establishing good ongoing relationships with your community in the past; if you have done things for your community, it may welcome the opportunity to give something back to you.

Some libraries are using creative methods of soliciting donations to make up for budget shortfalls; Oakland Public Library, for example, used Amazon.com's "wishlist" function to create a list of books they could use, and invited people to donate a copy. Their program took off when mentioned on a popular Web log.

Some libraries can raise funds or receive a large enough donation to establish an endowment. A large endowment can be invested so that your library can use the interest money to fund programs and services without touching the principal. As a library director, you will be responsible for overseeing the investment of endowment funds, with the goal of creating a steady stream of income for the library and allowing it to provide additional or special services. You will need to develop the necessary skills for interpreting the various financial statements and materials associated with your investments. Endowments set up by a single donor may have restrictions on how the funds can be expended. You also want to ensure that endowment funds are not part of your "normal" budget, because this will allow your funding body to remove some regular funding.

You can also start a program that solicits donations and cultivates potential donors—another use for your communication skills. Soliciting donations requires you also to create a program recognizing the gifts and funds the library receives. Be willing to provide recognition for any donor, whether in the form of a bookplate noting that a particular volume is a gift in memory of one of your community members, or a plaque noting that a particularly generous donor has endowed a particular room or section.

Partnerships

Consider setting up some joint programs with other institutions to share the costs and the benefits of these programs. For public libraries, this feeds directly into the idea of the library as crucial in revitalizing community. These partnerships can be particularly helpful when applying for grants, as granting bodies often want to see community cooperation. You can work with local schools to establish after-school homework centers, for example, or to set up a program where you rotate boxes of popular materials through their classrooms. You can work with the Rotary or other community organization to set up a literacy program, perhaps hosting and publicizing it at your institution while the Rotary solicits volunteer tutors. Think about ways in which you can partner with the various groups in your own community or larger institution.

Fee for Service

Many public librarians balk at any idea of charging user fees, since the free flow of information and resources is so fundamental to the principles of public librarianship. Others point out that most institutions have always charged for at least some services (photocopies, late fees), and that adding additional cost-recovery fees merely extends previous practices. Corporate libraries often use fee for service as a matter of course, and academic institutions usually charge fees for copies, nonaffiliated patrons, and so on.

As an administrator or department head, you might be involved in making fee-for-service decisions within your own institution. Should you charge for nonresident access to the Internet? Should you charge video rental fees? Should you charge for classes or programs? Should you establish a book rental program for new best sellers? Should you provide a tiered reference service and charge local businesses for more extensive research by experienced librarians? All of these options have been discussed and implemented in various institutions.

Making Your Case

In making the case for your library and its continued (or increased) funding, take some lessons from the business world, where the concept of Return On Investment (ROI) governs investment. There has been much recent talk about running libraries more like businesses—which, in its best sense, means emphasizing accountability and efficiency in all of your operations. This also means being able to market your services and to demonstrate their value to those who control your library's funding. (See more on marketing, PR, and advocacy in Chapter 10.) As Edward B. Stear writes about corporate libraries: "So what does this mean in the business world? In a nutshell, never relate your projects to *your* needs. Relate your project to management or enterprise benefits using the business terms management understands. Make sure the benefits are real. Make sure they are tangible. Make sure they provide value that is meaningful for the enterprise."[3] These tips apply to any type of library. Focus on those in the organization or community with the power to influence your library's budget and political position. Make an effort to learn what is important to them, and target your message to their interests and needs.

Outline how the library's programs, holdings, and services support their projects and mission.

Marylaine Block outlines some fantastic suggestions for showing people—especially those who control your library's funds—how their dollars are spent. Her bullet points for public libraries include items such as: "X dollars to license X number of databases that provide online access from home or office to articles in thousands of magazines, newspapers, and reference books; X dollars for professional librarians who this year have answered X number of questions, by phone, e-mail, chat, and in person ... "[4] Even if you are in a nonprofit environment, be able to show investors—in this case, taxpayers—the return on their investment. The health of your budget and your continued ability to provide high-quality service requires advocating for your institution and demonstrating the impact of its services.

You will have to be able to advocate for your library, even if this is not in your official job description or if you were assured that funding/priorities were stable before you came on board. Lawrence A. D'Urso, Manager of Adult Services, Mount Prospect Public Library, Illinois, shares his biggest surprise about a previous management position: "I had to establish an identity and credibility for the project and for myself and my one staff person within a very firm and inflexible bureaucracy. I had to do a lot of talking, cajoling, listening, negotiating, pleading, insisting, and not only use all of what interpersonal skills I had but learning some I didn't have. I wasn't expecting to have to sell and get acceptance for the project within the organization that created the project to begin with. It was an interesting time." Another manager survey respondent had a similar surprise, not expecting: "How much of a constant fight it is to educate the resource allocators about what libraries do, what librarians do, and especially the value that library services add to the institution, the community, the nation, and especially the lives and careers of library clients."

Statistics and Performance Measures

Statistics and performance measures appear in this chapter because your library's funding (or lack of funding) will often depend on its perceived performance. This is true whether a referendum fails due to a community's dissatisfaction with existing service, an academic institution chooses to put funding into computer resources rather than a new library building because "everything is online now anyway," or a corporation defunds its research center because of a perceived lack of value to the company. (Find more on marketing your library and its services in Chapter 10.) You will not find detailed instructions on data collection and evaluation here, but rather an overview of the usefulness of statistics and performance measures. There are a number of resources that can help you decide more specifically what to track and how to do so.

Understanding these numbers will also help you allocate resources and engage in strategic planning. (See more on this in Chapter 8.) You cannot work effectively without accurate facts, figures, and statistics—about your library's demographics, about the usage of electronic and other resources, about your department or institution's workflow, or about the costs of individual services. Realize that a number of these statistics are collected for you automatically, and make use of those that are easily at your disposal. Look at the reports your automated circulation system can produce, or at the reports on database usage available from your electronic resource vendors.

You will need to determine both what to track and how to use these statistics to impart an understanding of the institution's value to your larger community or organization. You will also need to translate the raw data, sorting and organizing that which will be most relevant to you. This is true whether you are using this information to make your own decisions or to influence those of your "higher-ups." When providing statistical information to nonlibrary decision makers, be sure to translate this material into terms that make sense to them. Minimize your use of library jargon; show why a particular measure is important and useful; be aware of the tendency of statistics to oversimplify and do not rely entirely on raw numbers.

Take a look at your traditional statistical measures to ensure that they still reflect your library's current reality. Part of adjusting to change includes measuring changed statistics. These include access and usage vs. circulation figures, or availability as opposed to ownership. Some libraries are intended to turn a profit, so you will need in this situation to manage those numbers as well. This involves figuring your cost of providing service (including salaries, your facility, and access to electronic databases), and figuring projected revenues from services for which you charge (including database searches and preparing reports). Even if it is not your intent to turn a profit, showing your value to your institution or community is essential for any type of library. Also use general statistics when making your case. Studies consistently show, for example, that good school libraries are linked to improved test scores. What school media center cannot make use of this news to argue for funding?

A library background is tremendously useful in making sense of these numbers, budgets, and statistics. Without an understanding of the way libraries work and the ability to translate data into meaning, these remain merely numbers. Never let numbers or statistics intimidate you; just look at them in terms of what you and your library already do and where you want to go from here.

Notes

1. Guy St. Clair and Martina J. Reich, "Knowledge Services: Financial Strategies and Budgeting," *Information Outlook*, June 2002: 33.

2. Lisl Zach, "A Librarian's Guide to Speaking the Business Language," *Information Outlook*, June 2002: 19.

3. Edward B. Stear, "Ten Ways to Gain Management Support for Key Projects (Or, All I Need to Know to Manipulate Management I Learned as a Teenager)," *Online*, May 1997. <http://www.infotoday.com/online/MayOL97/manager5.html> 9 November 2003.

4. Marylaine Block, "A Predictable Funding Disaster," *Ex Libris*, July 26, 2002. <http://www.marylaine.com/exlibris/xlib149.html> 8 November 2003.

Recommended Reading

Becker, Bill. "Library Grant Money on the Web: A Resource Primer." *Searcher*, Nov./Dec. 2003. <http://www.infotoday.com/searcher/nov03/becker.shtml> 7 November 2003.

Block, Marylaine. "A Predictable Funding Disaster." *Ex Libris*, July 26, 2002. <http://www.marylaine.com/exlibris/xlib149.html> 8 November 2003.

—. "R.O.I.: The Economic Benefits of Libraries." *Ex Libris*, Aug. 30/Sept. 6, 2003. <http://www.marylaine.com/exlibris/xlib153.html> 8 November 2003.

The Bottom Line: Managing Library Finances. Bradford, England: Emerald Group.

Brownlee, Elaine U. and Neal J. Ney. "Alice B. Toklas and the Liberries: Building a Successful Friends Group." *Library Journal*, Feb. 1, 1988: 41–43.

Business Finance for the Numerically Challenged. Franklin Lakes, NJ: Career Press, 1998.

Business Math for the Numerically Challenged. Franklin Lakes, NJ: Career Press, 1998.

Diedrichs, Carol Pitts. "Off to See the Wizard: Demystifying Your Financial Relationships." *Library Administration & Management* 10:2 (Spring 1996): 105–109.

Hennen, Thomas J. Jr. "Do You Know the Real Value of Your Library?" *Library Journal*, June 15, 2001: 48–50.

Martin, Susan K. "The Changing Role of the Library Director: Fund-Raising and the Academic Library." *Journal of Academic Librarianship* 24:1 (January 1998): 3–10.

Nelson, Sandra, Ellen Altman, and Diane Mayo. *Managing for Results: Effective Resource Allocation for Public Libraries.* Chicago: ALA, 2000.

Paulos, John Allen. *Innumeracy: Mathematical Illiteracy and Its Consequences.* New York: Hill and Wang, 1988.

Prentice, Ann E. *Financial Planning for Libraries, 2nd ed.* Lanham, MD: Scarecrow, 1996.

Rounds, Richard S. *Basic Budgeting Practices for Librarians*, 2nd ed. Chicago: ALA Editions, 1994.

Seer, Gitelle. "Special Library Financial Management: The Essentials of Library Budgeting." *The Bottom Line* 13:4 (2000): 186–192.

Smith, G. Stevenson. *Managerial Accounting for Libraries and Other Not-for-Profit Organizations, 2nd ed.* Chicago: ALA Editions, 2002.

St. Clair, Guy and Martina J. Reich. "Knowledge Services: Financial Strategies and Budgeting." *Information Outlook*, June 2002: 26–27, 29–30, 33.

The Taft Group. *The Big Book of Library Grant Money, 2004–2005.* Chicago: ALA Editions, 2004.

Warner, Alice Sizer. *Budgeting: A How-To-Do-It Manual for Librarians.* New York: Neal-Schuman, 1998.

White, Herbert. "Our Conflicting Responsibilities: To Our Bosses, Our Staff, and Our Profession." *Library Journal*, April 15, 1997: 50, 52.

Zach, Lisl. "A Librarian's Guide to Speaking the Business Language." *Information Outlook*, June 2002: 18–20, 23–24.

Chapter 10

Managing Upward and Outward

We are all managers. Like it or not, each of us is plunked down in the middle of an organizational context—family, friends, neighborhood, school, job, whatever—that requires management skill to achieve a result. The flow of responsibility goes in every direction and uses different sets of tools to match the circumstances.
Rosanne Badowski with Roger Gittines[1]

Libraries exist only in relationship with their larger communities or institutions. In addition to your responsibilities to your staff, serving as a library manager inherently involves responsibilities to and interaction with those above you, such as boards, deans, or vice presidents, as well as to the greater community. Each holds a different sort of influence over you and over your library.

Your job involves a complex web of relationships that each must be carefully tended, both inside and outside of your institution. As librarians, we are in a unique position to appreciate the interrelatedness of all of the parts of our organizations. Effective reference service depends heavily on effective cataloging. Public library children's programs bring parents in, who may stay to check out books on parenting, videos for their weekend entertainment, or resume-writing resources. Our Internet classes help give patrons the skills they need to use modern OPACs and do research in our electronic databases. Every one of our activities works together with every other to create value for our patrons.

As a manager, you will in most cases also be in some sense managed. As a manager, your job performance hinges, not only on your personal performance, but on that of your staff. This is yet another reason to encourage those working for you to realize their potential and to work effectively toward the goals of the institution.

Part of your job as a manager is to serve as a liaison, communicating the intentions of your boss, board, or larger institution to your staff—in terms of the library's mission and of their own responsibilities—and communicating what you learn with your staff to your boss, board, and/or larger institution, system, or consortium. You will need to master various forms and styles of communication in order to talk to each group in their own language, from the perspective of what each sees as important, and in terms of your shared priorities and goals. Your style of communication with your staff, for example, may not fly with a board member, but you must continue to value the free flow of information to each. (See more on communication in Chapter 5.)

Dealing with all of these individuals and groups can be challenging, but also exciting. You have the advantage of multiple perspectives, and get to interact with such a variety of people that your work will never be dull. Interacting with various groups also lets you practice all those people skills they tried to impart in library school! You will, however, face a conflict of loyalties when the different groups and individuals to whom you are responsible take different directions or have different priorities. Look at the larger goals and mission of your institution to help you resolve these conflicts, taking the time to talk to different constituencies and try to balance their competing demands and perspectives. Library managers are responsible not only to their own boss but to their staff, their customers, and the library as a whole. This somewhat surprised David Pauli, Reference and Programming Librarian, Hillsboro Public Library, Oregon: "I knew what I was getting into in general, but wasn't aware of how many interest groups you have to please: public, board, friends group, city officials, staff." One staff survey respondent notes that one of a manager's main roles is: "to strike a balance between the needs of the patrons, the higher ups, and the library staff."

The following sections reflect a somewhat artificial separation among these roles, which must in real life be balanced and carried out simultaneously. Take heart, other professions also engage in this balancing act; reams of business literature address the art of "managing multiple bosses." (See recommended reading at the end of this chapter for some suggestions.) Just remember that with each of these groups, you interact as a representative of the library, and that communication skills are as essential in dealing upward and outward as they are in dealing with library staff. Make a point of acknowledging the contributions of each of these groups; motivation and enthusiasm grow from recognition.

Your Own Manager

Much of your job as a library manager may involve making your own manager's job easier—and, in all honesty, making her look good to the bosses she herself reports to. As an assistant director, for example, your direct reports might include the library's various department heads, freeing the director to deal with the day-to-day issues of running the library. Department heads' smoothly running departments can work together with others toward achieving the library's mission, as set by the institution's administration. In almost any management situation, you will have one (or more) managers. Even the most nonhierarchical organization must employ people with the ultimate responsibility for making executive-level decisions.

In addition to supporting the goals of the institution, your duties often include supporting the goals of your boss. When your goals or philosophies and those of your boss fail to match, or if you feel that your boss's goals are undermining or working against those of the institution, it may be time to move on. With a flexible attitude and mutual willingness to see things from each other's point of view, however, you can eventually develop a useful working relationship with most managers. As Kelly R. McBride, Director, Russell County Public Librarym, Lebanon, Virginia, explains about her first management experience: "Managing my boss was the biggest challenge. Our styles were very different and I had to flex to accommodate and meet his way of doing things." You may need to work to match your boss's communication style, or to assign people in your department to carry out tasks matching her priorities. It is less likely that you will be able to make dramatic changes in your boss's behavior or style than that you will need to make accommodations. This is not to say that anyone needs to put up with an abusive or harassing or just plain insane manager (see Chapter 6 for examples). Dysfunctional situations call for special handling. But clashes or differences in outlook naturally occur between any two differing personalities, and you will need to be prepared for these and open to the ways in which healthy conflict can spike creative solutions.

One of your first steps as a new manager will be to clarify your own manager's goals for your section, department, or institution; use your communication skills again here. Some directors and other upper-level managers are, unfortunately, less than forthcoming, or lack a certain clarity when describing their goals. Communication skills will also be important in learning how your boss prefers to receive information and ideas from you, and in building support for your own initiatives.

You will need to enlist your manager's support for a number of programs, so do your best to develop a good working relationship from the outset. One manager survey respondent says that it is " ... very important to learn what kind of backing you will have from your supervisors. If you don't have their backing, you can achieve nothing; time to look for a new job." Your relationship with your manager will differ from your previous relationships with managers as a nonmanagement employee. You now share management responsibilities in common, which can give you a common perspective on many issues. The power dynamic will change. As a nonmanagement employee, you may previously have at times engaged in the age-old habit of complaining about your boss. Now, as a manager, you may have a different perspective, and should realize that sniping about your boss is generally counterproductive.

Some lucky library managers will find that their own supervisor is their best source of support: Where better to look for a mentor? Kathryn L. Corcoran, Library Services Director, Munson-Williams-Proctor Arts Institute, Utica, New York, suggests: "Develop a good relationship with your supervisor. Use your supervisor as a resource; when I am stuck I never hesitate to take it to my supervisor for advice. As a manager you can use the person you report to as a resource for advice, guidance, etc. They have given me the institutewide perspective that it is easy to lose sight of during the day-to-day management of a unit, guidance in difficult personnel situations, and otherwise been a sounding board and even helped me vent when frustration set in! This may sound obvious but it never hurts to repeat the obvious. Your supervisor will know what issues you are dealing with and as a new manager you will learn more about management as well as about your organization. It's key to know where you fit in and how you can support your organization's mission and goals."

In other library environments, you may find that your nonlibrarian managers have less understanding about the way the library (and its staff) fit into larger institutional goals. In this case, it is your job to educate them. Mary MacKintosh, Librarian, DeVry University, Seattle campus, explains: " … working with nonlibrary managers is more difficult than I expected it to be. They usually don't understand what is required to run a library well, and I found communicating upward to be as challenging as managing the staff below me." Take responsibility in any situation for keeping the lines of communication open between you and your manager. You will need that foundation to work together effectively and to make joint decisions in the future.

Your Peers

Within any library organization, mid-level managers will need to forge effective working relationships with their counterparts in other departments. Library operations are inherently interrelated, and the success of your institution's mission and goals depends on the ability of different departments and teams to work together and support each other. You will need to put forth an extra effort to forge bonds with your fellow managers in cases where the library culture or administration has previously failed to encourage these cooperative relationships.

This is another reason to support cross-training, if permitted by your institution and by any union rules you may be subject to. You will want to acquire a basic familiarity with the operations of the other departments in your institution, which enables you to see how different areas of the library interact. Cross-training also allows you and/or your staff to help out or collaborate when another section is short-handed, or when a special project needs to be completed. A willingness to help out in other areas for the greater good of the organization goes a long way toward building relationships with your colleagues, and new tasks can help keep your mind and skills fresh.

Cultivate relationships even with colleagues who have no direct influence on your section of the library. As Joanna Howard points out, " ... you can save yourself energy by making the assumption that all your relationships can be developmental. ... This means making the assumption that all your working relationships can be mutually beneficial in some way and that you can *always* learn from them."[2] Your behavior with your peers necessarily differs from that with your employees and your own boss; the power relationship is inherently more equal. You can sometimes therefore work together more easily or naturally to resolve problems and to strategize new programs and services for your institution.

Your Community

All types of libraries, not just public libraries, serve a particular community. This community can be defined as those who live within given geographic boundaries, as those who work at a company or in a particular department, or as those who attend or work at a school or church or college. Whether your primary community comprises university students and faculty, your town's residents, the physicians, nurses, students, and patients at your hospital, or the journalists at your news bureau, your institution's principal responsibility is to that main constituency. This group represents both potential and actual library users. As a manager, you can also serve subcommunities, as a liaison to a specific college department, as a team leader of a research group working for one division of a larger company, as a young adult librarian serving the 12-to-18 age group. Your community—your patrons or customers, both actual and potential—are also in one sense your "boss," as their requirements dictate your and your institution's goals and activities. Without customers, your library loses its purpose for existing.

It is all too easy to get wrapped up in our day-to-day activities and forget to look at our work in terms of our larger institutional mission, which, in any library environment, always revolves around meeting the needs of our patrons or customers. You need to determine your core constituency, and then manage outward from there. The success of your institution depends on your staff's ability to provide your community with the information services it needs. If you direct a library, you will need to think about the institution's overall mission and goals in these terms; if you head up a department, you will need to think about how your section's activities help the organization meet these goals.

Engage in additional interaction with your community to promote the library's services. Although most libraries are not businesses, they are nonetheless in competition: for funding, for attention, for customers. Patrons and politicians have to balance competing alternatives; one of your tasks will be to show how your library is a good alternative and worthy of that funding, that attention, those customers. (See the next section for more on marketing your library.) People today have more choices than ever before for meeting their informational needs. Your job is to show them, and to make it true, that their library is their best source for answers. You also need to gain their support for your institution.

Another part of your responsibility as a manager will be to work to convert potential users in your community to actual users. Do this by providing and promoting the programs, customer service, and services that best meet your community's needs. This is in part accomplished by cooperating with groups within your community, asking for outside input in your planning process, and asking for feedback from your library's users (and potential users). Ask your staff; those who work with your library's customers daily will get to know them and their needs. Once you have these programs and services available, you will need to market them to both library users and library nonusers. (See the section on marketing later in this chapter.) Show how the library's programs and services are directly relevant to them and their needs.

Nyama Reed, Branch Librarian, Genesee District Library, Montrose Branch, Michigan, points out that new public library directors should "network with the community as quickly as possible. Especially if it is a small town. Take the editor of the local paper out for coffee or lunch to establish a good rapport. Go to local group meetings (Kiwanis, Elks, school PTA, etc.) and talk about how the library can help them. (For example, if they need a new dishwasher at the Elks Club, offer to help them look up reviews online.) Don't just go to them when there's a problem or just to ask for a donation. Go to local government meetings and get to know the mayor and commissioners. Become a part of the community, not 'just the librarian.'"

In public libraries, this also includes getting to know your elected officials, so that you can show how your institution's activities fit into their priorities. Keep them informed about what your library has accomplished and how it fits with their goals for the community. In an academic library, it means liaising with faculty members (and assigning staff to do so), stocking material in their areas of interest, and pleasing deans. In a medical library, you can target specific services to individual groups, such as physicians, nurses, and the general public.

In many management positions, you will need occasionally to deal with upset customers. Either a disgruntled patron will want to talk to a supervisor, or a situation will escalate beyond your staff's comfort level. As Cessa Vichi, Library Division Manager at the Josephine County Library System, Grants Pass, Oregon, points out: "Many people do not want to deal with uncomfortable situations, managers have to." This is true no matter your library situation, although public libraries, which serve anyone who walks through the door, may be somewhat more susceptible to the "difficult patron" syndrome than others.

Vichi goes on to note that one of the most dispiriting parts of management can be "not getting to have the positive patron interactions! Much of your time is spent with the unhappy or problem patrons. The daily interactions with the happy customers make library work so rewarding. When dealing with all the negative sides, it can become depressing and discouraging." Be prepared to be the go-to person for negative interactions, and proactively work to balance these encounters by building the foundations for positive interactions with others.

Often, a patron's anger will be defused just by being able to talk to someone "in charge." Other times, hearing the explanation of the reasoning behind a given policy can help them see its need. Every interaction you have with a dissatisfied patron is an opportunity to transform that interaction and turn that person into a library supporter. Try to focus on positives, giving patrons options rather than just saying no. ("Our policy is that everyone must present their library card to check out items, but we'd be happy to hold these books at the desk until tomorrow to give you a chance to go home and get yours.")

Spend time on the library floor, so that you become accustomed to the types of patrons and problems that may recur in your institution. If you work each week on the reference desk, for example, you will get to know your regular patrons and their recurring issues. Consider surveying your patrons, asking for suggestions, posting a questionnaire on your Web site, or using similar methods to find out what your community is looking for and where you might improve. If you take feedback via a suggestion box or other means, take the time to respond personally to people's comments.

There are entire works on dealing with difficult patrons; however, a couple of basic points are worth mentioning here. (Also, look back at the communication and conflict management skills discussed in Chapter 5; similar strategies apply to dealing with difficult patrons.) First, extend the same empathy to your customers as you try to extend to your coworkers and staff. Listen carefully and calmly to their complaints, and reflect an understanding for their point of view. It will often be helpful here to reflect their concerns by acknowledging their disappointment and paraphrasing their words in your replies. This shows that you understand their position, and gives them the opportunity to clarify if they are dissatisfied with your understanding of the situation. (This is sometimes referred to as "active listening.") Be sure to find out the actual problem—by the time a patron is referred to you, the situation may have escalated, and both parties may have lost sight of the original issue.

Make your responses sympathetic but clear, and be sure to back up your staff when they are following library policy. As free-lance author and Webmaster Priscilla Shontz says: "It's important for you to stick up for your staff—with your administration, with the public, etc. Never criticize a staff member in front of a patron or in front of another employee if at all possible. Always show a positive, united front to the public. Nothing beats morale down faster than a manager who blames problems on his or her staff, or who doesn't stick up for them and fight for them when dealing with administration. That's not to say that your staff is always right—just that your staff needs to know that you are going to fight for them when it's important, and that they can trust you not to stab them in the back just to please your supervisors." If you always give in to angry customers, you show staff that you will not back them up and that you are more concerned with avoiding conflict than upholding library policy.

If you have set rules, make it clear when staff must follow them and under what special circumstances they can be waived. Be careful of waiving policy in front of the same staff member who was just following the rules, as this does little to enhance good staff/management relations. Make it clear to the patron, however, what you intend to do to resolve the situation, even if you are just reiterating your staff member's point. Make sure that all staff are aware ahead of time that they have some power to be flexible and in what cases they can bend the rules. Empower people to make decisions, in order to avoid creating larger problems than those your policy was originally intended to prevent. Examine other libraries' procedures for dealing with problem patrons; the Alliance Library System in Illinois, for example, has an extensive online manual to guide library employees in handling these types of situations: http://www.alliancelibrarysystem.com/safeharbor/index.cfm.

Just as with library staff, there may be underlying reasons for any patron conflict. Maybe your customer is just having a bad day! This is not to excuse negative behavior, but cultivating empathy for your patrons can go a long way toward resolving these types of situations.

Also, see if you really do need to address recurring issues in your library. Are your staff members being rude to customers? Does the library lack basic information or standard materials on a subject it should cover? Do your policies require patrons to jump through too many hoops to make a simple request? Listen with an open mind to complaints, as these can lead to needed changes. Customers whose complaints are resolved in a satisfactory manner can become your library's most loyal patrons; they understand that you listened to them and that you care.

Dealing with your community in public libraries also means dealing with community groups. Develop and foster relationships with other organizations. You are often working toward similar goals, as when you work with other community groups on grant projects. You can provide services to community groups, for example, by teaching Internet classes at the senior center or by presenting on library business resources at the chamber of commerce. These services are great library public relations as well as an excellent networking tool. You can solicit input from these groups and use their help when planning and creating a new program or service that serves their target population. In academic libraries, you can encourage your staff to teach courses in their area of subject expertise, to participate in the discussion boards for online classes, and to find other ways of getting involved and visible in the life of the institution. Visible librarians are able to integrate themselves into their communities and to show people the value of their library.

Your Institution

Depending on the type of library you work in, members of your larger institution may also be your customers/patrons. You relate to them both as colleagues and as clientele, which can lead to some interesting interactions. You will therefore need to relate with the same people in different ways, depending on the situation.

Libraries that are part of a larger organization may find that other people in the institution need convincing of the value of the library. Those governed by an outside administration will especially need to emphasize the library's benefits and to show its importance to the functioning of the larger institution and to the success of upper management. As one manager survey respondent explains: "Also remember that [the] administration (especially when you have nonlibrary staff administering) will never like being corrected or asked to go out of their way for a library idea, and that you need to present your ideas for change in a proposal that will show them advantages for them." You will need to make a habit of educating upward and outward. Are new employees or faculty members introduced to library resources? Does the library offer classes, targeted intranet pages, or other targeted material? Does it publish a regular newsletter, or subject-specific targeted e-newsletters? Have you identified the needs of decision makers and outlined ways in which you can meet those needs?

Interacting within your institution requires recognition of the ways in which the organizational climate affects your behavior, as well as that of your employees and your own manager. Your choices are to adapt your own behavior to work within the current climate or to work to change it. People may be put off by a serious mismatch between the rest of their institutional environment and your behavior. If the organizational culture is fairly laid back, for example, an authoritarian manager sticks out like a sore thumb. An organizational climate includes all of the unwritten, informal expectations and assumptions about people's behavior and priorities, and it can take some time to catch on to all of these expectations. James LaRue, Library Director, Douglas County Libraries, Colorado, says that his biggest management surprise was: "Stumbling into institutional politics. Learning that there were certain unspoken rules that, being unspoken, are hard to pick up, but easy to run afoul of. There are sacred cows (promote from within!)."

Library Boards

Managing under a library board can test the patience of even the most experienced director. You often need to balance competing priorities and placate widely varying personalities. Familiarize yourself with your board members' different personalities and priorities, and build individual relationships with each. Remember that you are all on the same side, working for the good of the same institution. Remember also that the board likely hired you for a reason (!)—and assume goodwill from the outset. The board members' basic job is to represent the interests of their community. Familiarize yourself with the type of board that governs your institution and with its specific powers—while many public libraries, for example, are operated under a board of trustees that has the power to set policy and to hire and fire the director, others may be government departments that have only an advisory board that lacks the power to set policy, or will be governed by a village board or other body.

Many new directors are surprised at the extent of the issues created by their need to deal with their library board, and some may see the previous note that "you are all on the same side" as laughably idealistic. Without looking at ideal working relations, though, it is hard to understand how a board should function and to build that positive connection. If your board is made up of dysfunctional individuals who seem not to have the good of the institution at heart, or if they have a tendency to micromanage, it may be time to move on. One former library director even had to resort to out-side help to resolve problems with her board, saying: "[The board members] just wanted to be on the board to have the status. Most refused to come to meetings, thus we never had a quorum and couldn't resolve any issues. Had to eventually have the county manager (my boss) reappoint members in a special commission-ers meeting since we could not get enough folks together to OK our budget in time for the commissioners to review before the state's deadline."

One manager survey respondent named her biggest managerial challenge as: "Board micromanagement. Board insensitivity. Boards with personal power priorities, rather than the library as the heart of the community." It can be difficult for some board members, many of whom will be longtime community members with possibly very traditional notions of what a library "should" be, to recognize the need for your institution to adapt to changing cir-cumstances. Because they are not in the library every day seeing new needs and demands, you need to show them how the library's needs are changing and to provide them with the data that they need to make informed decisions. Board members, as much as anyone else, are subject to confirmation bias: the tendency to col-lect and examine data to support one's own worldview and assumptions. Realize that they likely receive no training in their roles as board members, and that they rely on their fellow board members and on you for guidance as to how to proceed. Mary Wilkins Jordan notes: "Often boards, especially in smaller libraries, are made up of good-hearted people who are fuzzy, at best, about what is expected of them. They either ignore you (possibly a bless-ing) or try to manage every last little detail of the library. But they mean well. Hold onto this idea when things get difficult."[3]

Working with a board requires extending your communication skills to keep its members informed about the issues affecting the library, so that they can in turn make informed decisions about the governance of the institution. This requires providing them with full (if concise) information, rather than selecting just the information that supports your own point of view. Be aware of your own biases, and work on basing your recommendations to the board on what will benefit the institution and its constituency, not on what will make you popular or on programs you personally prefer. Balance your recommendations with the understanding of the desires of your board, as well; see the section on politics later in this chapter for more on that. Realize that the board is also, in many cases, your boss.

An active board can be invaluable to the success of your institution, keeping it politically connected, advocating for a referendum when needed, and speaking to and connecting with other community organizations. Think about suggesting gently that board members take advantage of training opportunities for trustees. These are sometimes offered through your state library or state conferences, or you can offer board training in conjunction with a staff in-service day. Some systems, such as Illinois' North Suburban Library System, provide innovative ways (such as online training) to help new trustees settle in. See http://www.nsls.info/ce/trustees.

Unions

It may take all of your communication and leadership skills to interact effectively with your institution's union once you move into management (in some views, the "other side"). If your library is not at this point unionized, realize that it may someday become so, especially if you and other managers are unresponsive to ongoing concerns expressed by librarians and other staff. For example, Washington's King County Library System staff, seeking greater job security, voted to unionize as recently as December 2002.

In institutions with collective bargaining agreements, many of your actions as a manager will be circumscribed by these contracts. Staff pay raises and increases, job duties, and so on are often laid out in such agreements, which leave you little leeway for making unilateral change in these areas. Read and understand your union contracts before making moves to review, transfer, hire, or cross-train your staff; read and understand your union contracts as part of your first moves as a manager.

Work to find common ground with union leaders. You can all, for example, agree that the library needs either to maintain or to increase its funding in order to provide both good levels of service and a living wage for library employees. How can you work together to help secure that funding? You all value staff members' contributions and agree that they should be fairly compensated for these contributions, given the opportunity to learn and grow in their positions, and encouraged to be a part of the institutional culture. When you build on common ground, the question becomes one of allocating funding and prioritizing needs, rather than an "us" vs. "them" situation. If you lay ground work for cooperation, later negotiation in areas on which you may not agree can be less adversarial. Also try to put aside any preconceptions you have about labor unions and union organizers—these may be about as accurate as the stereotypes the public holds about librarians. Labor unions involve far more than strikes and petty rules.

Another key to dealing with unions is consistency. If union support staff or librarians face modest pay increases or cutbacks, giving managers larger raises is a bad way to gain cooperation. If the library has limited funds for travel and professional development opportunities, providing these monies only to upper-level managers is a bad way to apportion scarce resources. Union leaders will appreciate consistency and the recognition that any cutbacks need to affect all equally.

Use your skills as a team builder to create and moderate groups in which union and management representatives can work out issues together. Involve your union leadership in any reassessment of workflow or staffing issues, in order to avoid springing your conclusions on them at a later date. Realize that, if you do make staffing changes or changes in the way work has traditionally been done, this will need to go through the union, especially if you begin rewriting job descriptions. Find out the situations in which you need to negotiate with a union representative rather than talking directly to an employee.

Also be prepared for the eventuality of a union grievance at some point in your managerial career. Your best bet here is of course to resolve issues before they get to the point of a formal grievance; this is another reason to keep those lines of communication open and to keep connected to your staff. Remember also from Chapter 3 the importance of comprehensive record keeping and documentation, especially when you need to reprimand or eventually terminate an employee. Your burden of documentation only increases in a unionized environment. The agreements put in place to protect workers can make it very difficult to let someone go, even when their dismissal seems fully justified. Be prepared for this, and take the time to create the paper trail you need.

Politics

Much of the previous discussion at its heart really focuses on politics—in your institution, in your community, in your system. Politics receives special mention here, because political savvy is one of the most difficult qualities for library managers to develop. It is, however, one of the most essential. Political savvy may come more naturally than you expect once you learn that politics, like librarianship, is all about relationships. In many management situations a large proportion of your work centers around both internal and external politics, as you go about building relationships, influencing decision makers, and freeing up others in your institution to get down to the day-to-day work of keeping the place running. Ignore politics at your peril; today's library manager must be

political in order to ensure the continued well being (or even survival) of his or her institution. Denise A. Garofalo, Library Director,
Astor Home for Children, Rhinebeck, New York, notes that her
biggest challenge at the outset of her managerial career was:
"Learning the politics of the institution at the same time I was learning how to do my job as a library manager." Nyama Reed says that the
biggest challenge she faced as a new manager was simply: "Politics!
Politics! Politics!" This includes both internal and external politics.

Try to build allies and find mentors to help you navigate the
political environment your own institution faces. David Pauli
explains that "I think it really helps to have an ally in city hall (or
the county courthouse, or whatever larger agency you are a part
of). In my case, my mentor/ally was the city clerk, who wielded a
lot of authority in town. She helped me understand the politics
and how to negotiate the rocky shoals of local government."
Another clerk advocate, Amanda E. Standerfer, Library Director,
Helen Matthes Library, Effingham, Illinois, explains: "I received a
lot of help from our city clerk. He is very good with public finance,
and I asked him a lot of questions. He quickly saw that I was going
to try to do things the right way and get the library back on track.
He, then, became a library advocate and has helped us with many
things since then." In any environment, you need to find similar
allies: academic librarians might befriend deans or HR personnel,
corporate librarians, accounting managers or the CEO's reception-
ist, school librarians, secretaries or principals.

Find out who wields the real power and who has the knowledge
that you need. An old business saying suggests always making
friends with the secretary and the janitor; think about the wisdom
of this when identifying those you need to make particular friends
with in your own managerial situation. Treat everyone well, not
only because you never know who might hold the real power, but
because it is the right thing to do and the only way to go about
building effective relationships. Politics, like management, at its

heart boils down to relationships—although in this case the power relationships may be less clearly delineated. Political relationships range from local, state, and national government, to committees, to library systems, to boards, to administrators, to the press, to the law and legislation affecting libraries. No library is an island; each needs its backers and advocates inside and outside of the institution. Your job as manager (especially as a director) includes cultivating and nourishing these relationships, building allies where needed.

In an era when libraries increasingly compete with other services for shrinking dollars and legislation on privacy and information access issues brings us into the spotlight, it is more important than ever to foster these relationships and to build a foundation of mutual respect. One manager survey respondent explains that " … in the public library world, [dealing with politicians] is very important. They are our biggest money sources." Proactively work to build a foundation of support. Keep local politicians or deans or CEOs supplied with information. Learn what they value and show them how your library can help them accomplish their goals. You want local leaders to see your library as essential to revitalizing your downtown, your CEO to see your research center as integral to staying ahead of the competition. You cannot assume that everyone automatically shares your belief in the value of your library and of its services, but must continually demonstrate that value in very personal terms.

Marilyn Gell Mason points out that: " … managing in a political environment is nothing more or less than working with people. Each individual has different sets of goals and values but most try to accomplish good, as defined in very personal terms. These goals and values may not duplicate our own but they are not necessarily in conflict with them. We are more likely to achieve respect and understanding for ourselves and our institutions if we begin with respect and understanding for the people with whom we come in contact."[4]

This involves also respecting and understanding different groups' sometimes deep-rooted affection for pet library projects and perks, adding to the difficulty of creating institutional change and/or reallocating scarce resources. Politics also means facing the reality that all library customers are not created equal. As Judith Siess writes: "Telling the chief executive officer (CEO) (or managing partner or chief of the medical staff or president or mayor or superintendent of schools) that he or she will have to wait while you answer a question from a secretary (or summer intern or resident or clerk or member of the public or teacher) may be egalitarian, but it also may be a shortcut to the unemployment line."[5]

Marketing, PR, and Advocacy

Entire reams of literature address marketing library programs and services, so marketing, PR, and advocacy will be discussed here only briefly in terms of interacting with your larger community. Marketing at its most basic involves finding out what your community members need, providing it for them, and telling them about its availability. You can look at PR as a way of demonstrating your library's value to your various communities, whatever those communities may be, and positively influencing the way that others perceive your institution. Advocacy involves building support among those with the power to support your institution; see also the previous section on politics. You need to target your advocacy efforts toward decision makers, such as your board, your local government, your taxpayers, or your larger institution or company. Every library needs to market and advocate for its services. In corporations, libraries that neither directly create revenue nor habitually emphasize their value can be easy targets for cutbacks. Public libraries depend on the willingness of their constituency for funding.

Academic libraries face the belief among some deans, students, and faculty that "everything is online."

If you have not yet exhausted your zest for planning by creating the strategic plan described in Chapter 8, you should also think about creating a marketing plan for your library that formalizes all of your marketing and public relations efforts. Again, as a library director you may be primarily responsible for this, or as a department head, you may be responsible for providing input on areas that directly affect your department. Larger libraries may employ someone who is solely responsible for publicity. In any library, though, the director and managers are important in developing a focused message and ensuring that the entire library stays on target. You might also either be on or be asked to lead a team charged with creating a marketing plan; each library has its own process here.

Your marketing plan needs to mirror your strategic plan in many ways. It can start by outlining your current circumstances: your library's visibility, your community's demographics, how you are serving your community, and your current marketing efforts. It then needs to talk about the objectives you wish to reach through your marketing plan and to outline the specific requirements, strategies, and timeline for doing so—as well as the ways in which you will measure the results of your marketing activities. Creating a marketing plan is a perfect way to use your skills as a librarian. Instead of the one-on-one user needs that you identify in a reference interview, you are now identifying broader community needs, for example. Instead of researching information for a patron, you are now researching your community's needs and makeup.

Market through all of your activities. The best way to market is simply to be proactive about learning and addressing your users' needs. As a manager, you will need to foster this sort of customer-centered library culture and to ensure that your marketing efforts show specifically how the library meets these needs. Libraries today need to market in order to ensure their continued visibility in a world filled with alternatives. Library managers need to spearhead these marketing efforts, which will only succeed if they permeate the entire institution. Make sure that your staff are all on the same page. Enlist them in creating your marketing plan. Beyond staff, build support for your institution and your message wherever possible. Start or work with your Friends group, and cultivate informal supporters in your conversations with your customers.

The Press

No matter your type of library, positive publicity is always a good thing—both for you and for your larger institution. Make a habit of establishing a good ongoing relationship with the press, whether this is with your local community paper or with the reporter assigned to cover the activities of the multinational corporation of which your library is a part. Keep the lines of communication open, as the press can be a powerful ally in getting the word out about the importance of your library and its services.

Beyond standard press releases, be prepared to provide the library perspective on a number of issues. In some institutions, only library managers are encouraged to talk to the press, or a certain manager or publicity person may be designated as a press liaison. Know the proper procedure at your own library. When creating press releases, know the specific formats and deadlines of your outlet. You can find and modify sample press releases on a number of issues at the ALA Web site, especially if you are joining in one of their regular campaigns (National Library Week, @ Your Library, etc.).

Even a newsletter or e-newsletter can serve as your own internal press, providing another way to reach your customers. This is limited, however, in that you are somewhat preaching to the converted—you have to get people to read your newsletter before it can influence them. Some libraries or library systems, such as the North Suburban Library System (Illinois), sponsor programs on public access TV channels (see: http://www.whatsnewinlibraries.org/ about/index.asp). Do not overlook avenues as simple as letters to the editor, from you, your trustees, or your Friends.

Networking

Harvey Mackay sums it up best, saying that: "No matter how smart you are, no matter how talented, you can't do it alone."[6] You need to foster a number of relationships as a library manager. Those most useful to you and to your career, however, are those with the individuals who become part of your personal network. Successful managers in any environment thrive by drawing on multiple levels of support. Your personal network includes your mentors, people you mentor, colleagues, managers in other institutions, vendors, elected officials, and others that complement the rest. Even new library managers have an existing base of support. As one staff survey respondent explains: "New managers should not be afraid to seek help from their colleagues. No one should have to reinvent the wheel each time, and there is a lot of support out there from other library professionals."

You will eventually need people to write you a recommendation, to mention your name, to help you solve problems, to give you information—and vice versa. Remember that networking is a two-way street. You are here in luck, because a librarian's training and impulse to help and give information comes in handy in any relationship. Keeping professionally active and networking through associations and other avenues also helps you and your library become more well known. This will help you attract job candidates, get to know potential candidates, and find people to work on mutually beneficial projects and programs.

Associations for Library Managers

You can build your network partially by joining and participating in associations targeting library managers. These are often divisions of larger associations, including:

ALA's Library Administration and Management Association (LAMA); http://www.ala.org/lama. Joining LAMA also subscribes you to their useful journal, *Library Administration & Management.*

MLA's Leadership and Management Section: http://www.lms.mlanet.org. Includes a newsletter, e-mail discussion lists, and programming.

SLA's Leadership & Management Division: http:// www.sla.org/division/dlmd. Includes focuses on competitive intelligence, consulting, and knowledge management as well as a quarterly electronic newsletter.

You can also join your state association as well as other specialized or local groups. One manager survey respondent shares: "I also have greatly benefited by actively participating in our state library association. Networking is so important! Collect those business cards! This has been key to having people I can contact when I run into challenges or need some help. Being active in the association also give you excellent organizing experiences and gets your name out in the library community, which is helpful during job searches."

Look for additional opportunities to network as well. If you are in a small, rural, or one-person library, you may feel especially isolated; many institutions lack the funding to send people to conferences and other in-person networking events. Take advantage of opportunities to network online with other managers and librarians. While not a complete replacement for in-person networking, electronic networking can foster a real sense of community, and can provide you with groups of people to draw upon for their advice, support, and expertise. Start with general discussion lists such as Libadmin-L (http://listserv.williams.edu/archives/libadmin -l.html), and then investigate those in your area of specialty or interest. See if your local library system has an administrators' discussion group.

Network, not only with other librarians, but with others in your community with whom you can build mutually supportive personal and professional relationships. This goes back to the preceding sections on politics, your community, and marketing; you want to build ongoing relationships, serve on committees, and help with projects, rather than just showing up to ask for money at budget time.

Your willingness to serve as a mentor (or to seek out mentors to advise you) also helps build your personal network and helps alleviate any feelings of professional isolation. As Lori A. Schwabenbauer, Director of Library Services, Holy Family University, Philadelphia, Pennsylvania, explains: "But the biggest benefit I've gained from all my experience with mentoring—as mentor and mentee—is a boost in confidence. Through mentoring and being mentored I've learned concretely (I always knew it abstractly, but didn't *feel* it) that others have similar issues. I've even learned that there are times when I've done better than I thought."

Library managers' advantages in dealing with multiple groups of people grows out of the understanding of librarianship as a profession that not only provides and finds information, but that cannot effectively do so without building relationships. All of your information-gathering and communication skills come into play.

Notes

1. Rosanne Badowski with Roger Gittines, *Managing UP: How to Forge an Effective Relationship with Those Above You* (New York: Doubleday, 2003) xvi.

2. Joanna Howard, *Managing More With Less* (Oxford: Butterworth-Heinemann, 1998) 72.

3. Mary Wilkins Jordan, "Surviving Your First Year As Library Director," *Public Libraries*, July/Aug. 2003: 215.

4. Marilyn Gell Mason, *Strategic Management for Today's Libraries* (Chicago: ALA Editions, 1999) 62.

5. Judith A. Siess, *The Visible Librarian: Asserting Your Value with Marketing and Advocacy* (Chicago: ALA Editions, 2003) 5.

6. Harvey Mackay, *Dig Your Well Before You're Thirsty: The Only Networking Book You'll Ever Need* (New York: Doubleday, 1997) 11.

Recommended Reading

Badowski, Rosanne with Roger Gittines. *Managing UP: How to Forge an Effective Relationship with Those Above You.* New York: Doubleday, 2003.

Belanger, David. "Board Games: Examining the Trustee/Director Conflict." *Library Journal*, Nov. 15 1995: 38–41.

Block, Marylaine. "Training Our Bosses." *Ex Libris*, March 3, 2000. <http://www.marylaine.com/exlibris/xlib46.html> 8 November 2003.

"Can Unions Solve the Low-Pay Dilemma?" *American Libraries*, Jan. 2002: 65–69.

Corbus, Larry. "Taking Charge of Micromanagers." *American Libraries,* Feb. 1999: 26–28.

Dobb, Linda S. "President's Column." *Library Administration & Management* 17:2 (Spring 2003): 62, 64.

Hilyard, Nann Blaine, column ed. "Our Trusty Trustees." *Public Libraries,* July/Aug. 2003: 220–223.

Kassel, Amelia. "How to Write a Marketing Plan." *Marketing Library Services* June 1999. <http://www.infotoday.com/mls/jun99/how-to.htm> 8 November 2003.

Lee, Deborah. "Marketing Research: Laying the Marketing Foundation." *Library Administration & Management* 17:4 (Fall 2003): 186–188.

Lubit, Roy H. *Coping With Toxic Managers, Subordinates...and Other Difficult People: Using Emotional Intelligence to Survive and Prosper.* Upper Saddle River, NJ: Prentice Hall, 2004.

Marketing Library Services. Medford, NJ: Information Today, Inc.

Mason, Marilyn Gell. "Politics and the Public Library: A Management Guide." *Library Journal,* March 15 1999: 27–32.

Nickerson, Pat. *Managing Multiple Bosses: How to Juggle Priorities, Personalities & Projects—and Make It Look Easy.* New York: AMACOM, 1999.

Reed, Sally Gardner. *Making the Case for Your Library: A How-To-Do-It Manual.* New York: Neal-Schuman, 2001.

Sarkisian, Alexis H. and Anne Rose Johnson. "Forum IV: Funding and Marketing the Essential Library: A Partner-Building Forum." *Library Administration & Management* 17:2 (Spring 2003): 84–86.

Siess, Judith A. *The Visible Librarian: Asserting Your Value with Marketing and Advocacy.* Chicago: ALA Editions, 2003.

Stear, Edward B. "The Successful Manager: Ten Ways to Gain Management Support for Key Projects (Or, All I Need to Know to Manipulate

Management I Learned as a Teenager)." *Online* May 1997. <http://www.infotoday.com/online/MayOL97/manager5.html>. 8 November 2003.

Stratigos, Anthea. "Managing Up." *Online,* July/Aug. 2000: 84–86.

Weigand, Darlene E. *Customer Service Excellence: A Concise Guide for Librarians.* Chicago: ALA Editions, 1997.

White, Herbert. "Librarian Burnout." *Library Journal,* March 15, 1990: 64–65.

Willis, Mark R. *Dealing With Difficult People in the Library.* Chicago: ALA Editions, 1999.

Chapter 11

Theories of Management

New management concepts, from Taylor and Weber through McGregor and Herzberg past Pinchot and Peters to an unknown future, usually contain something digestible, like ballpark peanuts. Also like peanuts, they leave a lot of garbage to be cleaned up. All management concepts are by necessity generalizations, and that is simply because individuals differ and nothing works for everyone. The experienced manager adapts policies to people rather than people to policies.

Herbert S. White[1]

Most accidental library managers never assimilated the formal management theories, principles, and concepts that are taught in management programs or assumed in the literature. Most manage perfectly well without incorporating theory; others blend their own, or are required to subscribe to particular management theories and styles by their administration.

Academia has a concept of "cocktail party knowledge," or of knowing just enough on a given subject to be able to provide the illusion of depth in casual conversation. The descriptions in this chapter will help provide you with a similar veneer of "interview knowledge"—the ability to demonstrate basic familiarity with the management theories, principles, and concepts most likely to come up in your professional reading or in situations from an interview to a conversation with your board, dean, or director. You will also find suggestions for resources for further reading, should you be intrigued by a particular theory or be required to adopt a certain management technique in your institution.

Many library manager survey respondents stress that either they work with no particular theory or they blend elements from a variety of theories to fit their personal management style. A number dismissed the idea of using management theory to any real extent in a working library environment. Cathy Chadwick, Librarian, Washingtonville Senior High School Library, New York, states that: "School is theory; working, in any field, is the reality. Putting theory to work is like trying to nail Jell-o® to a tree." Another respondent says that: "I think the theories I learned about in grad school are sort of silly. I have been in several jobs where they were trying to use a particular theory, and so far I haven't seen the theories do much good."

Most managers pick and choose elements from the theories that either make sense to them, match their management style, or seem to apply to their particular management situation. (This practice is sometimes called "contingency management," since managers here choose from the theories and techniques that match, or are contingent to, a particular situation. Most practitioners, though, never name their style.) In other cases, theory grows out of practice, as managers develop their own to match what they observe and the particular people and organization that surrounds them. Camila Alire notes that: " … common-sense management still drives the way many administrators work with their staff no matter which organizational theory is in place."[2]

Since management at its core deals with the ever-unpredictable variable of people, no one theory or principle fits every situation— and you will note in the following descriptions that even defined theories borrow freely from one another and overlap. Theories also move in and out of vogue, and, as technological, generational, and other changes impact the library workplace, ideas that once seemed relevant can quickly begin to seem dated. In reading the previous chapters, you will no doubt notice where my own prefer-ences lie; every manager, though, must assimilate what is most appropriate for his institution.

Realize also that some theories are more applicable in a corpo-rate environment than in a library setting; again, you may wish to pick and choose from among those elements that seem most appropriate to your environment or that your own administra-tion/institution favors. Theories from the corporate world some-times focus on maximizing profits, whereas the value created by and the missions of many libraries go beyond the monetary. Nonbusiness library managers may wish to choose among those ideas that seem to work in a nonprofit situation. Before dismissing business management theories out of hand, however, realize that many management situations are relatively generic. Most focus on dealing with people, and every organization, profit or nonprofit, library or nonlibrary, is made up of various people and personali-ties. Be sure to check the library literature for examples of how a particular theory has worked in the library environment, and avoid jumping on unproven ideas that may turn into short-lived fads.

Use various theories to help you think about the practices at your own institution and whether they help achieve your library's mission. As Joan Magretta points out: "Good theory ... helps you to make sense of things. It helps you to see patterns, to separate what matters from what doesn't, to ask the right questions."[3] Theory helps you understand the activities of your institution or depart-ment in terms of what the library exists to do.

Management Theories and Principles

Since there is a fine line between the theories, philosophies, and principles of management and the various theories of personality and organizations, you will find each represented to some extent in the following descriptions. A basic familiarity with these will also be useful as you read the library management literature, as authors generally assume some prior knowledge. While certain theories underlie many of the rest of the suggestions and information throughout this book, here you will find each major idea separately delineated. Each is of course tremendously simplified; investigate further by consulting more in-depth resources before deciding to implement a particular theory in your own institution.

Benevolent Neglect

Less a deliberate management theory than a style that grows over time due to managerial laziness or fear of confrontation, benevolent neglect describes situations in which management takes little active interest in the day-to-day running of the library, leaving staff to go their own way. While benevolently neglectful managers never act directly against the interests of their library, the end result is usually problematic. Unresolved conflicts undermine morale, and a lack of planning or push for change allows the institution to stagnate. Being an effective library manager requires the willingness to make decisions and resolve problems.

Chaos Theory (Complexity Theory)

Chaos theory borrows from the physical and natural sciences, emphasizing that seemingly minor changes can have results dramatically out of proportion to the original action. The famous example here is of "the butterfly effect," where a minute change in variables, such as a butterfly flapping its wings in Brazil, theoretically leads to a tornado in the U.S. Chaos theory emphasizes that everything we do, no matter how minor, has an impact, and that the accumulation of minor events leads to major change. Librarians should also appreciate the emphasis that everything we do is interconnected.

Contingency Theory

Contingency managers, rather than choosing one theory and sticking with it, beg and borrow from those that seem most relevant to a given situation. Most managers engage in this to a greater or lesser extent, depending on (or despite) the management philosophies favored by their administration.

Dimensional Model of Behavior

Building on the interpersonal classification system developed by Coffey and Associates in the late 1940s and developed further by the Kaiser Foundation in the 1950s, Robert Lefton and Victor Buzzotta have been promoting and refining this model since the late 1960s. The dimensional model of behavior envisions there being two main dimensions of human behavior—dominance/submission and hostility/warmth—each of which occurs on a continuum represented visually by a line. The two dimensions intersect perpendicularly to form four quadrants: dominant-hostile (autocratic), submissive-hostile (unassertive), submissive-warm (easygoing), and dominant-warm (collaborative). Each of these quadrants describes a main category of human behavior seen in organizations among both managers and staff.

Lefton and Buzzotta argue that using this model can help managers understand both their own behavior and that of their employees. They favor the fourth quadrant, or the dominant-warm (collaborative) category of behavior, which emphasizes the free flow of information, a concern for others, an understanding of people's differences, accountability, a focus on goals, and collaboration.

Diversity Equals Strength

See more on managing and incorporating diversity in Chapter 4. To recap here, however, institutions that embrace the principle that diversity equals strength actively seek to employ a diverse workforce and to include diverse perspectives. The incorporation of diverse perspectives and backgrounds helps an institution to manage change, to innovate, and to resolve problems. Libraries that overtly implement a diversity equals strength philosophy may be more likely to include those serving diverse communities.

Emotional Intelligence

Daniel Goleman's landmark book describes a different way of thinking about intelligence, moving beyond academic expertise to thinking about a person's ability to interact with others and to react in emotionally healthy ways, to "be able to perceive one's own feelings and those of others." It shows that high IQ has little correlation with high achievement, that expertise in a subject is a beginning, not an end, and that emotional intelligence skills are much more important to success than either traditional intelligence or experience. The title talks about EQ, or "emotional quotient," as opposed to IQ, and posits that a high EQ allows managers to recognize the effect their emotions have on others and the effect of others' emotions in influencing their behavior. Emotional intelligence includes self-awareness, motivation, self-regulation, empathy, and adeptness in relationships.

FISH!

The FISH! program, based on a series of best sellers that glean management techniques from the philosophy of Seattle's playful, efficient, and energetic Pike Place fishmongers, is gaining popularity in many types of libraries. One manager survey respondent mentions that this "is a terrific tool for motivating staff." See more on the first FISH! book in the management classics section later in this chapter, and on the program at http://www.fishphilosophy. com. FISH! aims to bring energy and passion to the workplace. It appeals because of its playful prose and emphasis that work should be fun. FISH! trainers often use little fish beanbags, posters, cutouts, and so on to engage in hands-on activities that help library staff regain enthusiasm.

Franklin-Covey (7 *Habits of Highly Effective People*)

Library managers are occasionally sent to Franklin-Covey leadership seminars to learn how to manage proactively, create vision, and lead from their principles. The original book, *7 Habits of Highly Effective People*, emphasizes leadership in both personal and professional life. It shows that true leadership comes from a shift in personal outlook and habits, and that success requires questioning our own assumptions, setting priorities, and moving toward personal and professional goals. Leadership grows out of our personal values, and requires an ability to prioritize, to create mutually beneficial relationships, to listen, and to engage in life-long learning.

The seven habits are: be proactive; begin with the end in mind; put first things first; think win-win; seek first to understand, then seek to be understood; synergize; and sharpen the saw.

The Golden Rule

Simply stated, the golden rule says: "Do unto others as you would have them do unto you." The beauty of this one is that it works equally well for your staff, your patrons, your board, your dean, or anyone else you need to deal with in your capacity as a library manager. Some version of the golden rule appears in nearly every religion and culture, due largely to its basic common sense. Why would you not always treat others the way you yourself would like to be treated?

The golden rule principle can also be useful in developing a customer service philosophy within your institution. How would you like to be treated, and what might you expect, as a patron of your own library? Work from there. The inherent danger of the golden rule is that it can be oversimplified—each person is an individual and the same methods do not work equally well with everyone. Some managers modify the concept to treat each person the way *he or she* (rather than *you*) would like to be treated, recognizing these differences. Each person will respond to different motivations, communication styles, and so on; the trick here is to apply the golden rule broadly, treating others as you would like to be treated in the sense of managing them in the best way for them, just as you would like to be managed in the best way for you.

Herzberg's Theory of Motivation

In the late 1950s, Frederick Herzberg postulated that people are motivated by two basic groups of needs: those relating to their work environment and those relating to their job satisfaction. The factors that motivate employees are completely separate from those that lead to job dissatisfaction. He shows that factors in people's work environment, including company policy and administration, supervision, salary, interpersonal relations, and working conditions, are most often negative motivators ("dissatisfiers"). People are more likely to be unhappy and unmotivated in their work when dissatisfied by one of these conditions than they are to be motivated when these conditions are met.

People's job satisfaction and motivation includes a separate set of needs that are less related to the work environment. These include achievement, recognition, the work itself, responsibility, and growth or advancement. These are "satisfiers," factors that serve as positive motivators for employees. (See more on motivation in Chapter 5.) People are motivated by interesting work that lets them grow and learn while still serving organizational goals.

Jazz Combo

A cute metaphor for a specific type of teamwork, in which every member's knowledge of the others' individual strengths creates enormous flexibility, as the team can lean on different members depending on varying circumstances. A jazz combo team must by its nature be small, so that each member can develop knowledge of and bonds with the others. It also requires that each member take responsibility for his own actions, rather than in a "symphony," where each group of instruments is specifically directed by a conductor. Leadership in a jazz combo team is shared and fluid, each member stepping up as her individual strengths are needed. Each has a certain amount of independence, but with the responsibility to turn individual accomplishments toward common goals and harmony.

ISO 9000

ISO stands for the International Organization for Standardization, and 9000 refers to a particular set (or "family") of five international quality-management and quality-assurance standards. These standards are intended to apply across the board in various types of businesses, and to ensure customers that the products or services they get from ISO 9000 organizations are up to the standards they expect. While these standards are most often used in manufacturing, some larger libraries or their parent institutions are ISO 9000 organizations; organizations can apply for ISO 9000 certification. You may see the year 2000 ISO 9000 revisions referred to as ISO 9000:2000. Find more at http://standardsgroup.asq.org.

Lead by Example

One common complaint of library staff—or those in almost any organization—is that managers are too removed from the day-to-day work of the place and that they employ a "do as I say, not as I do" approach to management. (See Chapter 6 for more on staff's dissatisfaction with this approach.) Those who lead by example display their willingness to step in, show by example that they understand and can do the work of their library or department, and earn the respect of their staff. This is not to imply that managers should spend all of their time doing the same work as their staff, but that they need to show that they understand and respect that work and that they are willing to pitch in when needed.

Learning Organizations

John Buzas, Branch Manager, Norfolk Public Library explains, Norfolk, Virginia: "For years I have followed the ideas of Peter Senge in espousing an understanding of systems and modeling as the foundation for what he calls a Learning Organization. All too few librarians I have met think about their libraries as systems or have an appreciation for the dynamic complexities that interact to make them work effectively, or, in too many cases, to fail to work."

The Fifth Discipline, by Peter Senge, outlines five "learning disciplines:" personal mastery, mental models, shared vision, team learning, and systems thinking (see discussion under "Systems Theory"). The Management Classics section later in this chapter provides additional explanation of these learning disciplines. Senge defines a learning organization as "a group of people working together to collectively enhance their capabilities to create results they truly care about." Learning organizations subscribe to the value of communication (supporting the disciplines of team learning and shared vision, among others), and strive to decentralize decision making. Many libraries, consciously or not, subscribe to some form of learning-organization theory—many knowledge and information workers do their best work under a less authoritarian structure where they have a stake in the results of their decisions and actions.

Management by Objectives (MBO)

Management by Objectives emphasizes results, laying out specific organizational goals and focusing organizational efforts on achieving those goals. Managers and their employees then create individual goals that support the larger organizational goals, and set specific courses of action to achieve them. The advantage here is that each employee has clear goals to strive toward, and knows exactly how he will be evaluated. Each staff member knows where her library and/or department are headed. Reviews can be linked to specific achievements; performance evaluations can depend on mutually agreed upon goals.

Management by Walking Around

Lori A. Schwabenbauer, Director of Library Services at Holy Family University notes that "MBWA (Management By Walking Around) really has been useful at times. I learn things that way about my library's needs, my staff, and my clients, that I wouldn't learn otherwise." In libraries, management by walking around also means "walking around" by your customers—getting in there, interacting with them, and listening to what they have to say. Management by walking around emphasizes that managers need to be present in the daily life of the organization and need to interact with both employees and patrons. See also Lead by Example.

Maslow's Hierarchy of Needs

Maslow outlined a hierarchy of human needs, starting with the most basic physiological level and moving step-by-step up to the pinnacle, self-actualization. He notes that basic needs must be met before people are able to worry about the needs further up the hierarchy—people who are starving are not necessarily interested in worrying about becoming self-actualized.

Some libraries extend their use of Maslow's hierarchy to customer needs as well. The first level, physiological needs, might seem less applicable in the library environment, but you can think about the application of your other services when basic needs are not met. A homeless customer that asks for an area list of shelters, or an unemployed patron seeking job search information, are very focused on these immediate needs. The other levels can also be matched up with library services and activities. Maslow's next level of needs, security, corresponds with the way library facilities are built, organized, and maintained and how security is maintained, providing patrons with a stable and comfortable environment in which to research, read, interact. Moving up, the need for love and belonging is filled by a friendly, welcoming, caring, and customer-centered staff, as well as by the opportunity to interact with others during library programs, events, classes, and other functions. The next level, esteem, can also be addressed by offering classes and resources through which your customers can achieve goals and master tasks. The last level, self-actualization, is more personal, but the library here again can provide resources that help their users "be all that they can be."

McGregor's Theory of X and Y

Douglas McGregor's 1960 *The Human Side of Enterprise* posited that there are two basic approaches to managing people—you guessed it, X and Y. Theory X typifies the authoritarian, or "tough," management style, in which employees are assumed to dislike work and thus have a tendency to avoid it if possible. Theory X managers believe that employees need extensive direction, avoid responsibility, lack ambition, value security above all else, and must sometimes be threatened with punishment in order that they work toward organizational objectives.

Theory Y (preferred by McGregor), exemplifies the participative management style (see description later in this chapter). Theory Y managers believe that work can be as natural as play, that people who feel a commitment to an organization and are satisfied in their jobs will work in a self-directed manner toward organizational objectives without extensive direction or the threat of punishment, and that the creativity and intellectual ability of most employees are underutilized and can benefit the organization when allowed to flourish. If employees are treated as responsible and valuable, then they will in turn act as responsible and valuable members of the organization. McGregor's Theory Y is based heavily on Maslow's hierarchy of needs (see previous description). His theories assume that employees' behavior depends largely on the management style of their managers.

Library staff generally demonstrate a strong preference for theory Y managers. John Lubans Jr. outlines a fascinating experiment he does in management workshops, where he tests participants both on how they see themselves as managers and how they would themselves wish to be managed. Although managers rank themselves as supervisors anywhere from extreme theory X to extreme theory Y, most shift to the theory Y side of the room when it comes to how they would themselves like to be supervised. As he notes: "Those with a strong theory X inclination in supervising others find themselves wondering, 'Why am I the boss that I would not want?'"[4] (See also Chapter 6 for more on library staff's dislike of micromanagement.)

Myers-Briggs

There are a number of Myers-Briggs type surveys online, which you can examine for an overview of this personality inventory (e.g., the Keirsey Temperament Sorter at http://www.keirsey.com). For actual use in your organization, though, these are best done with a trained interpreter/facilitator. The Myers-Briggs personality type indicator uses a variety of questions to measure people's level of introversion and extroversion. An understanding of our own personality type and strengths and how these typically interact with those of others in our library then lets us carry out those interactions more effectively. Myers-Briggs results can also be used to help managers form functional teams that contain complementary personality types, allowing members to balance out each others strengths and weaknesses and to work together with less conflict.

The Pareto Principle (The 80/20 Rule, Pareto's Law)

A little more than 100 years ago, Italian economist and sociologist Vilfredo Pareto was examining patterns of wealth and income in England. He found that the distribution of wealth across the population was imbalanced; some 20 percent of people owned 80 percent of the wealth. When examining other time periods and places, he noted that this imbalanced pattern remained constant. Others then began to extrapolate this imbalance to the principle that, in most endeavors, 80 percent of your results come from 20 percent of your endeavors.

This principle has been generalized over the years by business writers who have realized the Pareto Principle's applicability to any number of situations. For example, 80 percent of a company's sales often come from 20 percent of its customers, 20 percent of our effort creates 80 percent of our results. In the late 1940s, George Zipf expanded Pareto's ideas to create the "Principle of Least Effort," which noted that people (and other resources) organize themselves to minimize work— thus 20 percent of a given resource accounts for 80 percent of a given activity.

The 80/20 rule goes against our belief as librarians that patrons are equally valuable, that all reference questions are equally important. Recognizing the value of the principle requires us to think about resource allocation in terms of what will have the most impact.

Therefore, where this principle most often comes into play in library management is as a tool in deciding where to set priorities or allocate scarce resources—money, assets, or people—within an organization. If 20 percent of your library's users account for 80 percent of your checkouts, should you concentrate on pleasing that core 20 percent, or should you see this as a sign you need to branch out and attract a bigger pool of users? If 80 percent of your time is spent dealing with the 20 percent of your employees who are "difficult," how will you resolve the situation so you can reallocate your efforts more equitably? Are 80 percent of your complaints revolving around the same 20 percent of issues? Resolve these problems for a happier customer base.

Participatory Management

Participatory management involves getting nonmanagerial and nonsupervisory staff members involved in librarywide decision making. Institutions that emphasize participatory management often support team building and group input into decision making, as committees, teams, or groups charged with looking into an issue and making recommendations to the library administration. Participatory management recognizes that leadership is not necessarily concentrated in managers, and that frontline people often have knowledge and experience from their day-to-day work that managers lack.

One manager survey respondent points out that: "Participatory management is beneficial to getting staff to feel they have a say in library operations; however, a manager must follow through with the group decision or face legitimate complaints. Meetings become a waste of time when management decides another course of action, especially without giving a reasonable explanation."

Participatory management recognizes that when people provide input into their organization's operations, they develop a personal stake in the organization's success. When library staff are encouraged to give input on decision making, you get a better buy-in for change and for the policies and practices influenced by their ideas.

The Peter Principle

The Peter Principle (named after its creator, Laurence Peter) points out that people are often promoted to their "highest level of incompetence," there to languish indefinitely. It recognizes that the skills that serve individuals well in one position do not necessarily translate into success at the next rung up the traditional career ladder. A world-class cataloger, for example, that is promoted to assistant head of technical services may not have the management and people skills to exceed in her new position. She is thus never again promoted, stuck at a level where she does not perform well. Keep the Peter Principle in mind when you think about which staff members to promote, and when looking at your own management performance.

Ranganathan's Laws

In the early 1930s, Indian mathematician and librarian S. R. Ranganathan developed five basic laws of library science:

1. Books are for use
2. Every reader his book
3. Every book its reader
4. Save the time of the reader
5. A library is a growing organism

A number of modern thinkers have created their own updates or modifications of these laws, but each emphasizes the underlying ethic of service to library users. Ranganathan also invented the Colon Classification for library materials.

Reverse Hierarchy

Traditional organizational structures envisioned a top-down pyramid, with directors at the very top, perhaps an assistant director next, department heads underneath, followed by supervisors, then staff, then customers. Reverse hierarchy turns the pyramid over, places the "customer" first, and recognizes that the frontline staff that interact directly with patrons really are the ones who define the institution to its customers. It emphasizes that every action occurs for the benefit of the customer, not for anyone inside the library itself. Inverting the traditional hierarchy also places more power into the hands of frontline staff and supervisors than in top-down organizations, recognizing the need to empower them to be flexible, and make decisions and to provide them with the training they need to give effective service to customers and accommodate patron needs. Total Quality Management (TQM;

see later section) also emphasizes inverting the organizational pyramid.

Risk Management

Less a management theory than a strategy for prioritization and decision making, risk management involves looking at the long- and short-term risks of activities in order to make an informed decision. When engaging in risk management, you try to identify the impact of events and actions so that you can minimize their negative consequences, hence minimizing the risk to your organization. Risk management involves accepting certain risks given the probability of a greater gain, and eliminating others that threaten your organization's existence or health.

Scientific Management

While Taylor's principles of scientific management may seem irrelevant to today's knowledge workers, his work revolutionized the management and productivity of factory labor at the time he was writing. Taylor's principles show that making manual workers more productive involves looking at the tasks they are doing, recording each task step-by-step, eliminating any wasteful elements, and deciding on the best tools for the job. These manual tasks can then be set up so that they can be accomplished in the simplest, least wasteful, and quickest manner, rather than in the way they had traditionally been done. The focus here is on planning, standardization, minimizing waste, and maximizing efficiency.

Another big name in scientific management, Henry L. Gantt, lends his name to the Gantt chart, still popular in some libraries today to calculate work schedules and manage projects. Scientific management involves strict control over workers and their every task, and assumes that workers' primary motivation is financial. The theory has less impact today: People are seeking more challenge and less routine in their work, and we know that there are a number of motivating factors.

Servant Leadership

First discussed in Robert K. Greenleaf's *The Servant as Leader* in the early 1970s, servant leadership stresses that leaders must first serve their staff and their organizations, while their aspirations to lead then grow out of that service. Optimally, leaders are not imposed from above, but are chosen by the people they serve. Servant leadership emphasizes a personal relationship with employees, a commitment to helping them grow as individuals, and a commitment to creating an ethical and caring organization.

Six Sigma

The six sigma quality initiative originated in the 1980s at Motorola, and was later popularized by GE's Jack Welch. Corporate libraries will be more likely to use six sigma than others. At its core, six sigma focuses on improving both the effectiveness and the efficiency of everyone in an organization, leading to satisfied customers and a decreased cost of doing business. It differs from other quality initiatives in that it focuses on how an organization is managed from the top down, not just on the ways its employees carry out their jobs.

Six sigma points out that dissatisfied customers are likely to take their business elsewhere (which is perhaps especially relevant to libraries in an age of Barnes & Noble and Google on every desktop). Companies must therefore keep their customers satisfied, but not at the expense of profits—or they will go out of business. Any improvement therefore has to focus both on effectiveness and efficiency, and must begin by looking at what the customer wants and how to satisfy his needs.

The term six sigma itself refers to a near-perfect measure of performance, or customer satisfaction. It equates to just 3.4 bad customer experiences out of every million customer opportunities, and insists on keeping perfectly consistent at providing quality goods and service, with no variation. "Sigma" refers to the symbol that represents one standard deviation; most companies appear to run at around three sigma, or performing at 97 percent. The six sigma cycle? Define, Measure, Analyze, Improve, and Control.

Strategic Management

See also the section on strategic planning in Chapter 8. Strategic management involves creating a vision of the future of your institution (or department). Then, you need to set objectives and lay out the day-to-day activities needed to reach this vision. In order to achieve your goals you will need to communicate the organization's vision to others and to inspire your employees to "buy in" to change, while ensuring that any innovation is implemented smoothly. Strategic management always focuses on these future goals, and requires that you periodically evaluate to see how well you are meeting your objectives and working toward organizational goals.

Systems Theory

Systems thinking emphasizes the importance of looking at our work in terms of the larger system of which we are a part, focusing on our relationships as individuals, as members of groups, and as affected by our external environment. Senge's theory of a learning organization includes systems thinking, which emphasizes that any organizational endeavor is a system made up of interrelated actions and that we need to look at the root causes of difficulties and at repeating patterns (or archetypes) to find real solutions to organizational problems. Changes in any part of the organization or any one of our activities inherently affect the other parts of the organization.

Team-Based Management (Teamwork)

Successful team management recognizes that teams are nothing new and that the current vogue only formalizes these sorts of extant working relationships. Peter F. Drucker says that there are three kinds of teams: baseball, in which a team does one task and then passes it on to another team and in which each member has a fixed position to "play"; football, in which members work in parallel, each having his position to play but all working simultaneously; and tennis doubles (or "jazz combo," see earlier discussion), in which team members have a primary position to play but can also move to cover their teammates' weaknesses and adjust to changing demands. Teams work best when they are not overly large—five to seven members is often suggested as a happy medium.

In many situations, working in teams allows people to join their abilities and resources to accomplish more and work more effectively than they could individually. Teams can be short-lived (set up to accomplish a specific project) or permanent, yet strive toward a common purpose. Teams may draw on individuals from various library departments in order to bring together the right combination of skills to achieve a particular goal. Managers of teams need to help enable team members to work together, help lead them toward their common goal, and give them the tools they need to achieve that goal. Temporary teams may also need to help even define their own goal.

Total Quality Management (TQM)

American statistician W. Edwards Deming's post-WWII work with Japanese manufacturers popularized total quality management, which involves continuous improvement in an organization's ability to meet its customers' needs. In the Japanese environment, this resulted in the transformation of a reputation for cheap and shoddy goods to the reputation for quality (and accompanying profitability!) that persists today. In the library environment, TQM translates into an ongoing effort to continually increase the quality and effectiveness of our services and offerings, in terms of what patrons actually want from our institution. It assumes that patrons always have alternatives, and therefore we must provide them with top-notch service lest they go elsewhere to meet their informational needs.

TQM libraries make a point of asking for patron input and feedback to determine their customers' true wants and needs. TQM involves never assuming that you are doing a good job of meeting people's needs, as well as never assuming the reasons behind patron's use or nonuse of our services, but finding out first-hand (through surveys and other methods of data collection) and figuring out how to improve our offerings. "Quality" is defined by how well we meet, or even exceed, our customers' needs and expectations, and by how quickly we shift to meet, and even to anticipate, their changing requirements. Given Deming's background in statistics, it is unsurprising that TQM relies upon gathering and analyzing data that describes how we are doing our jobs and meeting patrons' needs.

True TQM library environments involve employees on all levels in their quality initiatives, realizing that it takes the involvement of the entire institution to provide quality service and an environment of continuous improvement. TQM defines "customers" broadly, including the internal customers that are your fellow staff members. It counts among its goals the breaking down of barriers between departments and the empowerment of employees to create improved service and solve problems on their own initiative. This also means that all employees share the responsibility for providing quality service to library customers, rather than this being just the responsibility of top management. TQM posits that people have a natural tendency to care about the quality of their work.

Some TQM institutions also implement what are known as "quality circles," in which small groups of people who are doing similar work start regularly meeting to identify and thoroughly evaluate problems that affect their work. They then recommend or implement solutions to these issues. The idea is that people who are directly affected by a problem will be those best able to come up with a workable solution, and that employees who are directly involved with improving their working environment will be more motivated and satisfied. Members of a quality circle can discuss a number of issues, but these should be limited to those that directly affect their daily work—otherwise you run the risk of these merely becoming gripe sessions about salary and other perennial library issues. Beyond quality circles, TQM emphasizes the importance of cross-functional teams, helping bring together people from the different (yet interdependent) parts of the organization.

Classic Management Titles

Beyond some of the specific theories and principles of management, you will also want to have a sense of the "big names" in the management arena. Following, you will find brief summaries of several management classics, allowing you to turn to those that intrigue you. The focus is on the general management literature, for two reasons. First, library administrations tend to borrow freely from the general literature, and, secondly, familiarity with these will translate to any library or nonlibrary management situation in your future.

The term "management classics" is here somewhat loosely defined. Some fairly recent titles (with apparent popularity and staying power) are included in the list, as are titles that may not originally have been intended as management texts but nonetheless have been adopted as useful tools by library managers. This is a less-than-inclusive list; it merely provides a sense of those that are at the moment most often cited and discussed, and the exclusion of any particular writer should not be interpreted as a dismissal of his ideas. Additional titles are mentioned in the preceding descriptions of various management theories.

Again, many of these works are specifically intended for use in the corporate environment, and some of their ideas may be more or less applicable in those libraries that are nonprofit or governmental institutions. Modify, pick, and choose among these and others to suit your own situation.

The Fifth Discipline by Peter Senge

Senge and his colleagues at MIT's Center for Organizational Learning popularized the idea of the "learning organization." Senge's 1990 work defines a learning organization as one in which change and new ways of thinking are nurtured and our ability to collaborate and to aspire are set free, one in which we are able to continually grow and learn as individuals and improve our ability to create results by working together. The five "core disciplines" in a learning organization are: personal mastery, mental models, shared vision, team learning, and systems thinking. The last discipline, systems thinking, integrates the other four.

FISH! by Stephen C. Lundin, Harry Paul, and John Christensen

FISH! is quite popular as a management theory in many libraries, and is especially popular during in-service days and workshops. The FISH! folks produce videos and other materials for just this purpose. The FISH! parable focuses on Seattle's famous Pike Place Fish Market, and outlines four strategies to prevent burnout and increase excitement in any organization. These are: 1) Choose your attitude, 2) Play, 3) Make their day, 4) Be present. Find more at http://www.fishphilosophy.com.

How to Win Friends and Influence People by Dale Carnegie

Carnegie originally wrote *How to Win* back in 1936. Its longevity can be attributed to its nine universal, practical, and evergreen principles on how to understand other people, get along with others, and get people to subscribe to your ideas. These principles range from: "give honest, sincere appreciation" to "make the other person happy about doing the thing you suggest." Each is discussed and illustrated with pertinent anecdotes. Although often used by salespeople, Carnegie's principles also are useful to leaders in any organization.

In Search of Excellence: Lessons from America's Best-Run Companies by Tom Peters and Robert Waterman

In the early 1980s, coauthors Peters and Waterman researched 62 American companies, and outlined the qualities common to the best-run. Its eight basic principles for successful management are a bias for action; close to the customer; autonomy and entrepreneurship; productivity through people; hands-on, value-driven; stick to the knitting; simple form, lean staff; simultaneous loose-tight properties. Successful companies focus on the needs of both customers and employees, and emphasize giving people a personal stake in the organization and the autonomy to do their jobs.

The One Minute Manager by Kenneth Blanchard and Spencer Johnson

Coauthors Kenneth Blanchard and Spencer Johnson (see *Who Moved My Cheese*) emphasize that it takes little time to get big results from employees. The book's secrets? One-minute goal setting, where you mutually agree on responsibilities and expectations. Praise—immediately and clearly letting people know what they are doing well and encouraging them to do more of the same. Reprimands—clearly and immediately letting people know what they are doing poorly, and then moving on.

Blanchard has also written a number of additional "One Minute" books as well as other titles on coaching, leadership, and other aspects of management. He advocates such timeless principles as open communication, ongoing learning, and a focus on customer results (see http://www.blanchardtraining.com).

The Practice of Management by Peter F. Drucker

Drucker's 1954 classic introductory text was one of the first to talk about management as a cohesive discipline. He began in the 1940s by studying General Motors from the inside out, and ended up emphasizing the importance of developing a marketing perspective in which businesses look through their customers' eyes to determine what they truly value. Understanding who your customers are and what they value allows you to focus on meeting their needs. Peter Drucker's name is by now nearly synonymous with the term management. His copious writings on the subject address nearly every aspect of the discipline, but library managers may be especially interested in his writings on change and on non-profit organizations.

The Principles of Scientific Management by Frederick Taylor

Taylor's classic 1911 tome emerged from his experience as a consultant at Bethlehem Steel. His thesis: Any task can be studied scientifically to determine the one best way of doing it; implementing these "best ways" inevitably increases productivity and decreases costs. Scientific management emphasizes the importance of looking beyond the way a company has always done things to find ways in which these things could be done better.

Thriving on Chaos: Handbook for a Management Revolution by Tom Peters

Tom Peters' classic *Thriving on Chaos* advises looking at "chaos", that is, constant change and uncertainty, as an opportunity to thrive. Janine Reid, District Librarian, Delta County Public Library District, Colorado, notes that: "*Thriving on Chaos*, by Tom Peters, is my bible. The concepts within that I try to emphasize include being responsive to our patrons, working in a participatory management environment as a team, loving change, and demanding total integrity." While Peters addresses issues in the business environment, some of his principles can transfer to libraries, and he does provide "public parallels" for those that he believes will be most difficult to translate to the public sector. The book outlines a number of principles (or "prescriptions") in five major areas: customer responsiveness, innovation, partnership and empowerment, openness to and the ability to effect change, and systems (including a passion for communication throughout an organization and measurement of the "right things"). Peters is also the coauthor of the classic *In Search of Excellence,* many of whose ideas are expanded on here.

Up the Organization: How to Stop the Corporation From Stifling People and Strangling Profits by Robert Townsend

Townsend, famous for turning around Avis in the early 1960s, here irreverently attacks bureaucracy and emphasizes the importance of delegating important tasks so that employees feel real ownership in the organization. He emphasizes treating employees as people rather than "personnel," of leadership rather than administration.

Who Moved My Cheese? by Spencer Johnson

Spencer Johnson's little parable about mice in a maze struck a chord everywhere. (See http://www.whomovedmycheese.com.) Basically, this tiny title uses metaphor to underscore the importance of being able to accept change.

Working With Emotional Intelligence by Daniel Goleman

Goleman followed up his popular *Emotional Intelligence,* which talked about "a different way of being smart," by providing specific applications to the world of work. The premise is that specific technical skills or knowledge are less important in most positions, especially leadership positions, than those involving "emotional intelligence" (which, in part, involves the ability to successfully relate to those around you, what we might think of as people skills). The title makes the case for the importance of emotional intelligence, talks about different emotional competencies, discusses the importance of self-mastery in getting ahead, outlines important relationship skills, shows how to improve your own emotional intelligence, and looks at emotional intelligence from an organizational perspective. In a similar vein, Goleman has coauthored a newer title specifically for leaders: *Primal Leadership: Realizing the Power of Emotional Intelligence.*

Library managers that want or need to implement any of these (or other) various management theories in their institutions can use their skills as researchers to assimilate information on each, from researching the literature, to consulting an expert, to asking colleagues in other institutions what has worked well for them. Realize that the true test of your management efforts, however, will be in your people, their performance, and the results for your organization, regardless of what—if any—theory underlies your actions.

Notes

1. Herbert S. White, "The Library Implications of Individual and Team Empowerment," *Library Journal*, June 15, 1993: 47.

2. Camila Alire, "Two Intriguing Practices to Library Management Theory," *Library Administration & Management* 18:1 (Winter 2004): 41.

3. Joan Magretta and Nan Stone, *What Management Is: How It Works and Why It's Everyone's Business* (New York: The Free Press, 2002) 10.

4. John Lubans Jr., "She Took Everything But the Blame: The Bad Boss is Back," *Library Administration & Management* 16:3 (Summer 2002): 157.

Recommended Reading

Additional suggestions of reading material on specific theories can be found interspersed in the appropriate sections throughout the chapter.

Alire, Camila. "Two Intriguing Practices to Library Management Theory." *Library Administration & Management* 18:1 (Winter 2004): 39–41.

Crawford, Walt. "Exceptional Institutions: Libraries and the Pareto Principle." *American Libraries,* June/July 2001: 72–74.

Drucker, Peter F. *Managing the Nonprofit Organization: Principles and Practices.* New York: HarperCollins, 1990.

Euster, Joanne R. "The New Hierarchy: Where's the Boss?" *Library Journal,* May 1, 1990: 40–44.

Herzberg, Frederick. "One More Time: How Do You Motivate Employees?" *Harvard Business Review,* Jan. 2003: 87–96.

Kirth, Thomas G. Jr. "The Role of Management Theory in Day-To-Day Management Practices of a College Library Director." *Library Administration & Management* 18:1 (Winter 2004): 35–38.

Koch, Richard. *The 80/20 Principle: The Secret of Achieving More With Less.* New York: Doubleday, 1998.

Lefton, Robert E. and Victor R. Buzzotta. *Leadership Through People Skills: Using the Dimensional Model of Behavior to Help Managers.* New York: McGraw-Hill, 2004.

Line, Maurice B. "How Do Managers Learn to Manage?" *Library Management* 23:3 (2002): 166–167.

Lundin, Stephen C., Harry Paul, and John Christensen. *FISH!* New York: Hyperion, 2000.

Lynch, Beverly P., ed. *Management Strategies for Libraries.* New York: Neal-Schuman, 1985.

Mason, Marilyn Gell. *Strategic Management for Today's Libraries.* Chicago: ALA Editions, 1999.

Miller, Danny and Jon Hartwick. "Spotting Management Fads." *Harvard Business Review,* Oct. 2002: 26–27.

O'Neil, Rosanna M., ed. *Total Quality Management in Libraries: A Sourcebook.* Englewood, CO: Libraries Unlimited, 1994.

Peters, Tom. *The Pursuit of WOW! Every Person's Guide to Topsy-Turvy Times.* New York: Vintage Books, 1994.

Pryor, Sherrill. "Library Media Centers That Learn: Applying the Fifth Discipline." *Book Report,* Sept./Oct. 2001: 20–22.

Scherdin, Mary Jane, ed. *Discovering Librarians: Profiles of a Profession.* Chicago: ACRL, 1994.

Stueart, Robert D. and Barbara B. Moran. *Library and Information Center Management, 6th ed.* Greenwood Village, CO: Libraries Unlimited, 2002.

Taylor, Merrily E. "Participatory Management and the New Librarian Model." *The Journal of Academic Librarianship* 10:4 (Sept. 1984): 201–203.

White, Herbert S. "The Library Implications of Individual and Team Empowerment." *Library Journal,* June 15, 1993: 47–48.

Worrell, Diane. "The Learning Organization: Management Theory for the Information Age or New Age Fad?" *The Journal of Academic Librarianship* 21:5 (Sept. 1995): 351–357.

Chapter 12

Philosophical, Legal, and Ethical Issues

Because today's American society is actively
litigious, we feel it is necessary for libraries to learn
how to practice defensive law. Like defensive
driving, this method is meant to prevent accidents
—in this case, legal accidents—by anticipating a
problem and taking affirmative steps to avoid it.
Arlene Bielefield and Lawrence Cheeseman[1]

Library managers are inevitably called upon to make ethical decisions in their institutions. These decisions need to be based upon the philosophical foundation you have built up through your education, experiences, and entire career as a librarian. As a manager, however, you will also need to balance both philosophical concerns and your personal convictions with the practical and legal issues involved in pleasing and serving all of your institution's constituencies. This can be an especially hard lesson if you enter a management position freshly out of library school. Academia, LIS schools included, generally tends to emphasize theory and philosophical extremes; interacting in a real-world library environment with its varied personalities and requirements, however, can be much different.

Try as much as possible, though, to carry out your duties in a way that is in sync with your own value system. Too much disconnect between your actions and values at work and your personal values can tear you apart. Given the number of libraries serving various communities and encouraging various philosophies, you can find one that is a good fit with your own values. Alternatively, you can work to make your own institution a better fit. Also consider the wider implications of your decisions and actions as a library manager. One specific action that seems on the surface to run contrary to your personal principles may be an inevitable step, given the larger purposes and goals you and your institution hold dear.

The sections in this chapter discuss just a few of the main philosophical, legal, and ethical issues you may encounter as a library manager, showing examples of the types of issues you might need to address. The coverage here is of course less than comprehensive; libraries and library managers face myriad policies, requirements, and ethical issues on a daily basis. Many are really issues that affect librarianship as a whole and librarians as individuals, specifically impacting managers mainly in terms of decision making. You will need to be prepared to make these decisions in your own environment, every day of your managerial career. Philosophical and ethical issues in many cases overlap legal issues, and you may on occasion be put in a position where your personal and professional beliefs conflict with the legal or other requirements of your job. Legal issues are addressed briefly here; discussions are also included in the appropriate sections of each topical chapter. More general legal issues are left for more thorough discussions elsewhere, and coverage of legal issues in this chapter reflects only the climate in the U.S.

Of course, much of the discussion in this book has already included—or at least touched upon—the various legal issues affecting today's libraries. Any library manager, however, should remain connected to a source of competent legal advice, most likely through an attorney or law firm retained by your library or by your larger institution. Realize that I am not a lawyer; neither the author nor Information Today, Inc. can be liable for damages incurred by following the advice in this book. Ensure that whomever you retain or consult on legal issues is familiar with library law and with the specific situations you are likely to encounter. Realize also that the laws governing your library will vary, depending on your location and type of institution.

You will be called on to make legal, ethical, and philosophical decisions in your institution because in most cases it is your staff's responsibility to follow policy, yours to help create that policy and to make decisions as to when to allow policies to bend. (Ask your staff—they will say that this is "why they pay you the big bucks!") You should as a library manager—especially as a director or upper-level administrator—familiarize yourself at least broadly with some of the issues you are most likely to encounter in your specific institution.

Privacy

From the provisions of the USA PATRIOT (Uniting And Strengthening America by Providing Appropriate Tools Required to Intercept and Obstruct Terrorism) Act to everyday reference service, privacy issues affect every library. While rank-and-file librarians face their own dilemmas, as a manager you will need to balance privacy concerns with legal considerations. You will need to be prepared to create policy, to handle issues referred to you by your staff, and to know when to consult your library's attorney. Privacy law also varies widely from state to state; you are responsible for finding out what applies to your institution.

The PATRIOT Act, one part of which allows federal agents to check library records, and bars librarians from telling patrons (or anyone else) that their information has been requested, has resulted in some of the more interesting decisions in libraries in recent years. Prohibited by law from telling individual patrons if federal agents have requested their checkout records or Internet logs, managers at institutions such as the Santa Cruz Public Library, CA, for example, posted signs warning their visitors to be aware that agents can secretly request their records and information at any time. Other libraries instituted a policy of regularly destroying records, including checkout histories, Internet signup lists, Web server logs, browser histories, cookies, and so on. This is an extension, of course, of many libraries' previous policies of erasing checkout and other patron-specific information; but expanded technological capabilities and new legislation make the issue somewhat more pressing and increase the number and types of records your library needs to consider keeping or destroying. As a library manager you may be involved in creating or providing input for such policies in your own institution.

For more on the act and related issues, see ALA's Web site at http://www.ala.org/alaorg/oif/guidelineslibrary.html, or attorney Mary Minow's useful chart at http://www.llrx.com/features/libraryrecords.htm. While other specific statutes and requirements may arise by the time you are reading this, patron privacy is a perennial topic and the issues involved in protecting it remain constant. Libraries have traditionally upheld the principle of patrons' rights to privacy and confidentiality, and you as manager may feel a particular responsibility to continue to do so in the face of outside pressures. You will need to educate all library staff members, from circulation clerks to reference personnel, on their responsibility to safeguard patron privacy as well. Ensure that they understand the need to refer requests for information to managers and that they know under what circumstances to do so.

Privacy issues include concerns pertaining to children and teens, as well. Some states and municipalities, as well as individual library boards, for example, have passed laws or created policies requiring public libraries to turn over minors' checkout records to their parents or legal guardians. In those areas that do not, you may be faced with an angry parent who is responsible for his child's fines, but cannot be told the title of the item that incurred the fines. Be prepared to be consistent and to follow your library's policies on such issues, and be prepared to explain the reasoning behind the rules.

Privacy issues can also encompass times when a patron requests ethically questionable material. If a teen asks a young adult librarian for materials on how to commit suicide, what is that librarian's obligation to the teen? To that teen's parents? If a patron asks for assistance on locating material on building bombs, maps of the local area, and the locations of all local police stations, what is the librarian's obligation? How value-neutral should your staff remain? If your staff comes to you seeking guidance on these types of questions, how will you be prepared to respond?

Business Ethics

As a corporate library manager or solo researcher, you will encounter special ethical situations affecting business librarians. These include confidentiality, competitive intelligence, and pulling information from your competitors. Your responsibility as a corporate librarian is to the institution you work for, so you may need sometimes to compromise your principles as a librarian in favor of the company's needs. For example, you will not be able to freely provide information to all, but only to your own corporate colleagues—or to select colleagues whose departments are paying for your services. You will not be able to provide information outside of the organization, partially because of the potential that an inquiry could come from a competitor. You will need to keep proprietary information confidential.

Ethics also come into play when dealing with vendors. When you are selecting a new electronic database or automation system, for example, vendors may wish to "wine and dine" you at conferences—inviting you to parties, taking you to lunch. You need to make your purchasing decisions based on what will be best for your company, not based on a personal relationship with the vendor or on the freebies they throw your way.

Intellectual Freedom and Censorship

More virtual ink may have been spilled over the Internet filtering issue in the past few years than on any other library-related issue. Filtering has become one of those hot-button topics that tend to make some librarians weary just hearing the word. As a manager, however—particularly as a youth services head, school media specialist, or public library director—you will need to be able to make the "to filter or not to filter" decision (or to provide input into your administration's position), and to back up your position either way. You will also need to keep up-to-date on the alphabet soup of legal decisions that may affect your library's Internet policy and practices, another reason to keep up with your professional reading. Public and school libraries choosing not to filter all of their terminals as of this writing, for example, forego their E-rate and certain LSTA funding under the Children's Internet Protection Act (CIPA). Some states and municipalities are creating their own local, sometimes more stringent versions. For libraries dependent on this funding, financial considerations, of course factoring in the cost of the filtering software itself, therefore come into play.

Beyond filtering, there are a number of intellectual freedom issues that concern today's library managers. If you are in a public institution, for instance, you may face the specter of controversial or hate groups wanting to use your meeting room. Public libraries' meeting spaces have been defined as public forums, necessarily open to groups espousing any point of view. If a controversial group books the meeting room for an event, you might find yourself paying for extra security and facing a barrage of bad publicity. If you ban the group, you might find yourself facing a lawsuit on First Amendment grounds, as well as a conflict with your own freedom of speech principles. The Anti-Defamation League has a handy guide online at http://www.adl.org/civil_rights/library_extremists.asp to help you work through some of these questions.

You also want to be sure to maintain clear collection development policies, both to ensure a balanced and useful collection and have available to refer to when an item in your library is challenged. This is a more pressing issue for public and school libraries, which will wish to provide a clear and streamlined process and to make staff aware of the channels through which patrons can file a complaint about library materials. (See more on collection management in Chapter 6.) As a department head, you may be the first person to hear a complaint about or challenge to an item in the library's collection. As a director, you may be the first line of decision-making authority on dealing with a challenged item, or you may be responsible for bringing that challenge to the library board. Be sure to have a clear policy before the situation arises.

As a collection development manager or department head, you will also be responsible for selecting materials that balance out your collection, avoiding the temptation to purchase only those that support your own points of view. Learn to separate censorship, or not purchasing or eliminating items due to personal distaste, from selection, or picking the best available material for your institution's purposes.

Copyright

Library managers need to concern themselves with copyright compliance both by their patrons and by the institution as a whole. This concern includes ensuring that your library or department refrains from using copyrighted material (from articles to images) without permission on its Web site, publicity materials, and other library-produced items, and that it refrains during library programs from showing videos or DVDs for which you have not purchased public performance rights. Although librarians should have a special understanding of and respect for copyright, many institutions sometimes play loose with the rules on the assumption that no one will find out or that they are not big enough for copyright holders to go after. You as a library manager need to assume the responsibility for educating your staff about copyright and ensuring compliance.

You will also need to look at copyright in terms of what your institution does for its patrons and what patrons are doing in your institution. Your library likely has signage posted near its copy machines, for example, explaining the concept of fair use to patrons before they proceed with photocopying library materials. You will need to comply with copyright rules in your interlibrary loan procedures (governed by section 108, the "library exception" portion of the Copyright Revision Act), and, if you are in an academic institution, in the ways in which you create and hold course reserve material. You will need to think about what patrons may be doing on your public PCs, and whether to allow activities such as peer-to-peer networking and file downloads. Your larger institution may have strict copyright compliance procedures that you will be bound to follow.

Think also about how you can protect the copyright of library-produced works. Do you mind if another library copies one of your brochures word-for-word and puts its own name on the bottom? How will you prevent another institution from pulling material from your Web site and rebranding it as its own?

ALA conducts periodic courses on copyright in the library environment, some available via e-mail. If you are involved with copyright compliance in your institution, you may wish to investigate ALA's or other institutions' continuing education opportunities. The University of Texas has a clearly written "crash course" online at http://www.utsystem.edu/ogc/intellectualproperty/cprtindx.htm, and, of course, the U.S. Copyright Office provides its own discussion at http://www.copyright.gov.

Personnel/Labor Law Issues

Beyond making decisions about whether to filter public-access computers, you may also need to develop policies that regulate e-mail and Internet use by staff. More libraries (especially in the corporate sector) are emulating a number of companies in beginning to monitor employees' Internet and e-mail usage. Some filtering software (such as WebSense), which libraries have installed to comply with CIPA (or otherwise) also has these capabilities built in, whether your library chooses to use them or not.

Your library also will be subject to legislation on labor and wage issues. In nonpublic institutions, this includes a ban on "comp" time for exempt employees. Exempt here means exempt from the provisions of the Fair Labor Standards Act, and salaried, full-time employees are generally exempt and cannot accrue comp time, except at public institutions (such as public libraries and schools) where a comp time agreement exists.

U.S. legislation that affects your hiring and staffing process also includes the Americans With Disabilities Act (ADA); see Chapter 4. You will want to familiarize yourself with the other major legislation governing civil rights, equal pay, age discrimination, and so on. The Equal Employment Opportunity Commission (EEOC) governs these issues in the U.S., and these various pieces of legislation basically prohibit employers from discriminating on the basis of race, religion, sex, national origin, age, disability, and so on. This carries through from interviewing through hiring to promotion to on-the-job discrimination. Various states have their own local EEOC equivalents. (For more on interviews, reviewing, and firing, see Chapter 3; for more on managing diverse groups, see Chapter 4.)

If your library employs minors, you will also need to become familiar with the laws covering the number of hours a day under-age employees can work when school is in session, at night, and so on. This will affect your library if you employ minors as pages, as interns, or as assistants during your summer reading program.

As a director, personnel manager, or assistant director in the U.S., you will also have to concern yourself with Occupational Safety and Health Administration (OSHA) compliance. OSHA creates guidelines governing workplace safety policies and accident minimization strategies. You will be responsible for creating a safe workplace for all library employees and for responding to their concerns. As a middle manager or supervisor, you may be responsible for implementing safety guidelines and for conveying staff concerns to higher-level administrators or to HR. Other countries have their own equivalent agencies; if you manage staff, familiarize yourself with the safety issues and regulations in your own environment. In libraries, workplace safety issues can range from ergonomics to the availability of first-aid supplies. Find more information on OSHA compliance assistance at http://www.osha.gov/dcsp/compliance_assistance.

Managing Legal Issues

Depending on the type of institution in which you work, you may also be subject to various other pieces of law and legislation. Public libraries, for example, fall under the Freedom of Information Act (FOIA), which allows individuals to request and receive access to documents held by government agencies. As a manager, you might be responsible for responding to such requests, determining whether a certain request is "reasonable," or ensuring that a request is fulfilled in a timely manner.

An earlier section mentioned the need for most libraries to retain or have access to legal counsel. Your lawyer will also prove invaluable in the unfortunate event that someone chooses to sue your institution (or you and/or library board members personally). Some libraries can claim governmental immunity from certain types of lawsuits; again, this depends on your organization's situation.

Setting Policies

You can forestall a number of difficulties, legal and otherwise, by preemptively setting clear and consistent policies in your library. As a manager, you should be involved in formulating and/or reviewing those that are pertinent to your department or institution. If unexpected but similar situations continue to crop up, it may be time to revisit your existing policies and to build in a defined mechanism for dealing with these recurring situations.

You will need, again, to use those communication skills to ensure that your staff members are familiar with and able to reinforce library policies clearly and consistently. To aid in this, make them clear and understandable, using as little legal and library jargon as possible. Involve affected staff in drafting or revising policies if at all possible.

Examples of situations that might require written policies include public Internet access, unattended children in the library, materials challenges, those governing who may remove materials from your facility, and so on. Public, school, and academic libraries may need to establish rules of conduct for visitors. Ensure that these apply equally to everyone and that they are not specifically directed against one class of patron (such as the homeless or mentally ill). Focus on desired behavior, rather than on specific groups.

You will also need to establish policies that govern staff behavior and lay out procedures for library staff to follow in completing common tasks. Consistency is essential, and the free flow of information again is crucial here.

ALA has a number of suggested policies, statements, and codes of ethics available to guide librarians in setting policy and making ethical decisions. These range from the Library Bill of Rights to its Code of Ethics to its Policy on Confidentiality of Library Records. You can find pertinent policies at the ALA Web site when you have a question, or need guidance in resolving an issue. Association subgroups and specialized associations also have similar sets of documents; consult yours for guidance. These, however, are only guidelines rather than legal documents, and individual libraries can choose the extent to which they follow the association's suggestions.

Again, library managers' research skills will come in handy when they need to comply with legislation, guidelines, or procedures, or to investigate the legal ramifications of their institution's actions. Managers' networking and information-seeking skills come to the forefront when developing policies for their library. Their understanding of the profession is essential in creating consistent policies that line up with our professional principles. Our core values define the direction of our profession, and must underlie our day-to-day decisions.

Notes

1. Arlene Bielefield and Lawrence Cheeseman, *Library Patrons and the Law* (New York: Neal-Schuman, 1995) 1.

Recommended Reading

Bielefield, Arlene and Lawrence Cheeseman. *Library Patrons and the Law.* New York: Neal-Schuman, 1995.

Gorman, Michael. *Our Enduring Values: Librarianship in the 21st Century.* Chicago: ALA Editions, 2000.

Hannabus, Stuart. "Being Negligent and Liable: A Challenge for Information Professionals." *Library Management* 21:6 (2000): 316–329.

Hauptman, Robert. *Ethics and Librarianship.* Jefferson, NC: McFarland, 2002.

Michigan Electronic Library (MEL): *Laws Affecting Libraries.* <http://mel.org/viewtopic.jsp?id=1165> 24 April 2004.

Minow, Mary. LibraryLaw.com. 2003 <http://www.librarylaw.com> 28 June 2003.

Minow, Mary and Tomas A. Lipinski. *The Library's Legal Answer Book.* Chicago: ALA Editions, 2003.

Peck, Robert S. *The First Amendment and Cyberspace: What You Need to Know.* Chicago: ALA Editions, 2000.

Rodgers, Joey. "Core Values: Our Common Ground." *American Libraries,* Oct. 1998: 68–71.

Symons, Ann K. and Carla J. Stoffle. "When Values Conflict." *American Libraries,* May 1998: 56–58.

University of Maryland College of Information Studies and School of Public Affairs. Center for Information Policy. <http://www.cip.umd.edu> 1 May 2004.

Chapter 13

Where to Go from Here

Lore has it that a person without a compass,
tramping a long distance in the wilderness, will
slowly veer sideways, make a circle, and end up
where she began.

Arlie Russell Hochschild[1]

Although you will spend most of your time as a library manager taking care of your staff's and institution's needs, you need also to continue taking care of yourself. Many library managers feel the stress of their positions strongly, and run the risk of burning out or losing the love of librarianship that originally spurred them to enter the profession. Focusing on others' needs at the expense of your own hurts both you and your workplace. Take care of yourself along with taking care of your work-related responsibilities; avoid becoming a workaholic, neglecting your life outside your institution, or unduly obsessing about your work situation.

The same skills that serve you well in managing people and helping them grow professionally will also serve you well in nurturing your own career. Be as patient with yourself as you would with your staff; set goals for yourself and follow up; pay attention to your own lifelong learning and professional development; work on your own ability to accept change and on managing your own stress. You may not have a manager, boss, or mentor looking after your interests, so you will need to accept that responsibility for yourself.

Part of looking after yourself requires looking after both your career and your personal goals. Chapter 1 talked about keeping your mind, outlook, and skills fresh through lifelong learning. When you establish personal goals, you can use everything you have learned—on the job, about yourself, through training, networking, mentoring, and classes—to figure out where to go from here. Try to identify your own levels of ambition and of competence, your own strengths and weaknesses. All the learning in the world means nothing if you fail to assimilate your accumulated knowledge and understanding into your outlook and decision-making processes.

Every one of your experiences as a library manager will help you grow and will open up additional possibilities for your future. Although you may have "accidentally" ended up in management, you can now afford to spend some time planning the next steps in your career with more deliberation—while still remaining open to happy accidents. However you decide to proceed, work on developing a plan for your own personal and professional future that fits your vision of who you are and where you want to be. As Anthea Stratigos writes: " ... if you follow your heart, you'll be successful in whatever role you choose, evolving roles or not. It sounds a little bit like motherhood and apple pie, but the trick is to identify what brings you success and joy and then put yourself in an environment where it's possible."[2] Many librarians originally entered the field to make a difference; for many managers, their new responsibilities give them the power to make even more of a difference in their own institution and community.

Defining Goals

Ask yourself a number of questions when developing goals for yourself and your own career. Now that you have found yourself in a management position, how do you wish to proceed? Do you want to move up the career ladder? Can you see yourself settling at your current level for quite some time? Do you want to try a different type of library, a different type of management, a different type of career altogether? Are you coming to the reluctant realization that management is not really for you, and that you miss the activities involved in a frontline library position?

Now, think about creating a career development plan for yourself. Focus the bulk of your formal and informal learning and your career moves on your long-term goals. Write down these goals, and be willing to come back to revise them and to evaluate your own progress as needed. By defining long-term goals and working toward them, even if these goals do not seem to relate directly to your current job, you paradoxically can become more effective in your current position. When you can see a path forward, a potential for growth, and possibilities for change, it is impossible to feel "stuck" and to start phoning it in on your current career. Knowledge acquired through lifelong learning, further, can be useful when you least expect.

Selected Professional Development Opportunities for Library Managers

Formal continuing education and certification opportunities for library managers and upcoming leaders range from those sponsored by state and national associations to general management workshops. Selected opportunities are listed here to show the types of programs available; check with your own state, system, or associations for more ideas.

ACRL Harvard Leadership Institute: http://www.gse. harvard.edu/~ppe/programs/acrl/program.html. This prestigious six-day leadership program prepares librarians to run academic libraries in director-level positions.

ARL's Leadership and Career Development Program: http://www.arl.org/diversity/lcdp/index.html. Aims to help members of underrepresented groups become more competitive in the academic promotion process, increasing their numbers in leadership positions in research libraries.

Frye Leadership Institute: http://www.fryeinstitute. org. An intensive two-week residential leadership program held at Emory University.

Library Leadership Ohio: http://www.camls.org/ce/ ce_LLOhio.asp. A biennial residential, experiential program to help groom future leaders with 2–10 years post-MLS experience in Ohio libraries.

MPLA Leadership Institute: http://www.usd.edu/ mpla/leadership. Assists 30 emerging library leaders with fewer than 10 years of post-MLS library experience who work in the 12-state Mountain Plains Library Association region.

Urban Libraries Council (ULC) Executive Leadership Institute: http://www.urbanlibraries.org/eli.html. Prepares aspiring leaders for the challenges currently facing large American public libraries through a combination of seminars, personal coaching, and work on "leadership challenges."

YSLead Massachusetts: http://www.wmrls.org/YS Lead. Intended for Massachusetts school or public library youth services staff, helping nurture their leadership, recruitment, and mentoring capabilities.

The following sections outline a number of the main career options open to library managers. Your personal career goals may fit into one or another of these categories, or you may see yourself branching out in an unexpected direction. Career goals are, by their very nature, quite personal decisions.

Stepping Back

After some time on the job as a library manager, you may discover that you are not after all suited for a management position. This is not a decision to be made, though, after the first day, week, or month in your new job—while you are still suffering the pains of settling in. As Whitman Air Force Base Public Services, Missouri, Librarian Stephanie DeClue counsels: "Give it a year. You'll be so much more confident and relaxed the second year and more so every year after that. Don't freak out in the first few months thinking you can't do it."

After a reasonable period of time, however, stepping back can eventually be a practical and reachable decision for many librarians. As one manager survey respondent stresses, "If you discover management isn't for you, get out and move on. Life is too short to be unhappy for eight hours per day." While moving back is always a risk, you can think of staying in a position where you are unhappy as a risk in itself—to your mental well-being, life balance, and/or long-term goals.

Those manager survey respondents who have chosen to move out of library management and back into frontline positions offer a variety of reasons for their decision. Some chose to remain in their frontline positions, others took a break and then moved back into management:

- "I realized that I wasn't ready to give up doing the things I really enjoyed as a Children's Librarian. While I was a manager I worked for a city that required me to attend many city meetings, on topics such as setting long-range plans. I found that I was away so often at these irrelevant meetings that I found it hard to get my actual library work done. I moved to a noncity library into a nonmanagerial position and am back to doing the things I love."

- "I consciously sought out a new position that involved little or no management of others. I found management to be wholly unrewarding. The extra salary and authority did not begin to make up for the stress and grief of supervising others. I loathed the idea of being evaluated on the work of others when I had no real ability to force them to properly perform their jobs. Whether it hurt or helped my career is a matter of opinion. It has closed me off from 'moving up the ladder,' but I very much enjoy my current position and have no desire to 'move up.' I am much happier in a nonmanagement role."

- "I did [step back] for a time and am now back as a manager. Stepping back was really a step forward. ... It helped build a base of support within the organization that I believe has helped preserve my position at the library during difficult budget times."

- "I moved back to my home state to deal with family issues and did not find a management job. But I did secure employment as a reference librarian, and I don't regret it. I make a bit less money, but have none of the kind of headaches I had as a director."

- "I gave up management for 10 years when I started working part time after the birth of my child. I found that being supervised was wonderful, but would not pay the bills, so I went back to management."

- "I decided I preferred system work to management. Computer problems are much less stressful than personnel problems and it's a better fit for my personality. I took a $10,000 pay cut when I moved from a private to a public university and from management to systems. I have never regretted leaving management."

- The job I took after leaving my department head position (my current job) is nonmanagerial. I don't consider it a step back, because even though I got a lot of useful experience at my old job, the library was understaffed, and I was severely underpaid. In my current nonmanagerial job, I'm getting paid $15K more a year and am not going crazy juggling too many responsibilities. What's to complain about?"

- "My next (and current) job was a nonmanagement position. I am able to do things I didn't have time for when I was a manager. I have less headaches and stress. I was also lucky enough to find a nonmanagement position that paid more money than my previous management position, so I didn't have to contend with a pay cut."

- "The issues with upper management in the library got so awful that the job stress was unbearable. I transferred out of there into a nonmanagement position (from the library to document management). It was heavenly—I was extremely well-respected there for my library capabilities. I don't think it affected my career adversely—in fact I was making a higher salary there than in the library."

Only you can determine your own path, but the above reasons show some of the variety of experiences and thinking that characterize library managers' career moves "backward."

Interview with Priscilla Shontz
Priscilla K. Shontz is editor/Webmaster of LIScareer. com
and a freelance author

Please explain the type of management position you were in, and your reasons for leaving.

I have held several management positions, including managing the access services department at a private university; managing a two-person medical library in a children's hospital; and managing a public library branch.

I first chose to quit a high-stress position as a public library branch manager, partially because I wasn't a good fit for that particular job, because I had had a miscarriage, and because I wanted to lower the stress in my life for a while. I then worked in a one-person library for a year, while working on a book, until I had my first child. I then chose to quit working altogether so that I could stay home with our children when we started our family. I hope to stay home until our youngest is about three years old or so.

Do you intend to return to a library management job when your children are older? Why?

Management is not a specific goal of mine, but I'm open to management opportunities that might come along. I enjoyed managing, particularly being able to interact with a variety of employees and being involved in planning and implementing interesting projects. I think I would be interested in management positions because they would be stimulating and challenging. However, I imagine I would have to consider the time commitment involved in a management position more carefully because my family will be my top priority.

What impact do you feel that stepping back has had on your career as a whole?

I don't know that I will really know this until I return to the workplace, but I hope that by staying active professionally I will be able to step back into library work without too many problems. I think that most employers understand that a mother may choose to take some time away from work to raise young children.

What advice would you have about how others who step back from management can remain professionally active and marketable?

Some of the suggestions I made in the article "A Librarian without a Library: Staying Professionally Active While Unemployed" (http://liscareer.com/shontz_activeunemployment.htm) include read professional literature, keep up with trends and news, stay in touch with your contacts, make new contacts, attend workshops or conferences, visit local libraries, volunteer or work part time, participate in discussion lists, work on professional projects.

Is there anything else you would like to share about stepping back?

I think that if you explain your reasoning for stepping back from a management position, or from work in general, clearly in your cover letter or interview, a potential employer will understand your reasoning for stepping back for any reason. For example, many librarians choose to step back into a frontline reference position because they tire of the stress of management or they miss the daily interaction with patrons.

I have certainly not regretted taking time away from the workplace to be home with my children. Watching my children grow and learn is more rewarding and fun than I could have imagined.

If you do think about leaving your management position, realize that you are far from alone. Many current managers confess to at least occasionally feeling the temptation to give up their management responsibilities. (One manager survey respondent mentioned that "now and then I daydream about it," another that "I am certainly thinking about it. I have about had it with the stress of this position.")

Realize also that, while moving into management is the only viable way of increasing your compensation at many libraries, financial considerations should not be your only reason for remaining a manager. Doing so when your heart lies elsewhere is unfair, not only to your staff and institution, but to yourself. Think realistically about your alternatives and about whether you and management are a good fit. Consider whether you could reasonably acquire technical or other skills that would enable you to earn a similar salary in a nonmanagement position, or whether a monetary tradeoff would be worthwhile due to lower stress, more time to spend with your family, or other personal reasons. Emphasize to yourself that you always have choices, and that the only right career path for you comes from your priorities and what you value.

We tend to an unfortunate extent to define ourselves by our jobs, so think about how much of your desire to stay in management stems from the desire to call yourself a manager, to tell friends and family you are a supervisor, to see your title on your business card. Ann Snoeyenbos, Librarian for West European Social Science, New York University, reflects: "I'd rather be good at solo work than mediocre at supervising. Librarianship has too many bad administrators already. Because becoming a manager is the only way to make more money in our profession, people who hate it and/or have no talent for it actively pursue management positions. It's a shame, and detrimental to the profession overall."

Many also find it possible to move in and out of management positions. You can consider taking a break from your management responsibilities and later coming back refreshed to a similar role to the one you left behind. Be prepared, however, to provide future employers with a reasonable explanation for your desire to return to library management. (Try a straightforward statement like: "I felt it was time to try something different, but my experience as a ___ has made me realize that I miss the challenge of helping my staff and organization reach their full potential as a supervisor.") Sometimes, taking a break can help you see if you are truly suited for management after all. One manager survey respondent explains: "I found that I really missed many of the management functions that I had done in previous jobs and was actually quite happy to return to a management position."

If after careful consideration you do decide to step back and seek a nonmanagement role, realize that others may not understand your rationale. Moving back or stepping down are not options on the traditionally envisioned librarian career path. When hunting for a nonmanagerial position, you again need to be particularly prepared to offer a clear explanation in your cover letter, as well as to search committees, hiring managers, and interviewers who might be concerned about your propensity to jump ship in the future for another higher-level position. Any departure from the traditional path straight up the career ladder may make them wonder about your reasons and commitment.

Staying Put

As long as your current managerial position continues to offer you opportunities for growth and the chance to impact the direction of your library, do not feel compelled to seek opportunities elsewhere. Many libraries function as well as they do because of a wealth of institutional memory held by long-term librarians—you could eventually become one of these institutional treasures. In an era where job-hopping is common, though, be prepared to explain your decision to stay put to well-meaning family members and colleagues. ("Aren't you tired of that place yet?" "Couldn't you make more money somewhere else?") Again, any decision to stray from the established route up the career ladder can throw people for a loop.

Long-term management at a single institution can offer benefits such as:

- A long-term perspective that allows you to see the bigger picture and envision (as well as experience!) the future benefits of your actions

- A level of comfort in your position, in your work, and with your coworkers and community that comes from long familiarity

- A familiarity with and knowledge of the institution, its community, and its environment that allows you to do your best work

- The satisfaction of seeing your programs and services bear fruit over the years

- The opportunity to mentor younger/newer librarians and library workers in your institution

"Plateauing" is often seen as a negative, implying that people are growing stagnant in their careers and lack a dynamic future. Yet a conscious commitment to personal growth—and the recognition of libraries as constantly changing institutions that present new challenges and new opportunities, even absent new job titles or promotions—can allow many library managers to remain indefinitely content and stimulated in their existing positions. Take advantage of professional development and cross-training opportunities; learn to grow along with the inevitable changes in your institutional environment. Consider broadening your contributions to librarianship as a field by writing, presenting, mentoring, or through other activities that help keep your mind fresh and your options open. Apply for a sabbatical, if your institution offers this option. Realize that eventually every manager will plateau, that is, will come to a point where she has no reasonable opportunity or need or desire for promotion or career change. Just make sure you are comfortable with the level at which you have settled.

Lateral Moves

A traditional library career path involves moving step-by-step up the career ladder. For example, one might progress from entry-level librarian, to supervisor, to department head, to assistant director, to director. In some cases, though, it may be expedient to move to another position and assume a similar position to the one you currently hold. Various reasons for making a lateral move include increased salary, relative institutional prestige, a chance to do some different things, future opportunity for advancement, and a feeling that you are stagnating in your current position. You can move laterally now, and later make a move in a more traditionally upward direction, after you have gained some different skills or a fresh perspective or entered an institution with more room for advancement.

As Nancy J. Agafitei, Branch Librarian, Barbara Bush Branch, Harris County Public Library, Texas, notes: "Sometimes, when you can't go forward as planned, you have to find a way to go around." Think about the gaps in your career, skills, and knowledge, and whether these could be filled by moving into a different position at a similar level—helping achieve your long-term career goals by providing you with new perspectives and experiences.

Moving Up

The much ballyhooed "graying" of the library profession is projected to translate into an upcoming glut of upper-level management positions, as the older librarians currently holding these jobs begin to retire. This is good news if you are a younger library manager who has developed a taste for management and the ambition to move up and take on new challenges. This is especially good news if you have taken the time to nurture your own professional development. One manager survey respondent has this advice: "What's your competitive edge, when you apply for library management positions? For special libraries, consider getting an MBA—or at least taking a considerable number of classes toward an MBA. If you are interested in public libraries, consider getting a Master's in Public Administration. If you are interested in college libraries, make certain that you have an advanced subject degree!"

Although you may not need to stack up multiple degrees for most library management positions, any evidence that you have worked to further your own knowledge and management abilities will serve you well. Think, not only about how such self-improvement can serve you in your current position, but about how it will be helpful in the future.

Interview with Mary Pergander

Mary Pergander is currently Head Librarian at Lake Bluff
Public Library, Lake Bluff, Illinois

When did you set your sights on becoming a library director, and what made you do so?

I had been in healthcare administration for 20 years, and knew it was time for me to move on. For several years I had secretly considered becoming a librarian. By the time I left healthcare, I knew that my next career goal was to lead a public library. I felt it would be a way to use my talents and skills to make a difference, and that was very important to me. I carried a lot of idealism about libraries as bastions of freedom and being the heart of the community. Libraries had had a big role in my life, and I wanted not only to be part of it all but to step up to the plate as well. Knowing my goal early on helped me be very deliberate in choosing coursework, and selecting mentors and networks that would help me fast-track my experiences into opportunities.

What specific steps did you take to achieve your goal?

First, I interviewed 10 or more people who had done what I intended to do: Become a library director within two years of obtaining my master's. I spoke to those who had done so deliberately, as well as those thrust unwillingly into the role. I asked what went well, what didn't, how they prepared for their role, what they wished they had done, and so on. From this I began to see what lay before me, and planned how to navigate the challenges.

When I went back to school, I sought out and developed a network of mentors from whom I sought advice and direction. They helped me identify what I needed to learn.

At that time, I also found a job nearby as Manager, Youth Services under library director Kelly Sigman. Kelly is zany, energetic, with a strong and cutting-edge vision. I went after that job with all the creativity I could muster, because I could see that I would learn things from her that I may never again see done. Fortunately, she took a chance on me. I actually took notes those two years because I wanted to remember how she approached things. She has a style very different from mine, and there was so much that I learned. At the same time, I got involved with North Suburban Library System (Illinois) and its terrific leadership team. I invited various leaders to lunch and asked for their thoughts about becoming a strong library leader. I tested ideas with them, and listened carefully when they gave feedback. I also contacted other directors I admired and asked to interview them about their styles and philosophies. These one-on-one conversations were very precious to me, and really opened my eyes to the realities of libraryland. I also saw the varieties of ways diverse leaders face similar problems and challenges, and the many definitions of good results. I really believe this approach to deliberate mentoring helped me learn in two years what I may not have learned in eight!

When I was nearing graduation, several local director positions were opening up. I called my contacts and received inside information about several. I was warned away from a few, and given valuable information on others. I identified two that I thought would be a good marriage of my talents and their needs. But I really only applied for my top choice at first. My lack of library leading experience was offset by my years of healthcare management experience. I wanted a small library where I could continue to develop my library skills, which would later build credibility with staff in a larger library. I was somewhat scared by what I still didn't know about levies, funding, library law, etc.

I carefully researched the library I wanted. I even learned the names of all the board members so I could greet them by name and know something about them in the interview. I visited the library before the interview, and identified three specific ways I felt the library could improve and how we could accomplish this together. I drove around the whole town and walked the main streets and shops to feel the culture of the place. I wanted that job with a white-hot passion. I got it. Afterward, I made a point of thanking those who had helped me by sending out notes and taking them to lunch. That was actually suggested by a mentor, and I am glad I followed through.

Whether one becomes a manager accidentally or deliberately, negotiating a fair salary is an important skill to learn and apply. Dr. Leigh Estabrook at the University of Illinois has a short seminar, available online, about salary negotiation. This helped me immensely. Know what you are worth, know what the job is worth, and learn how to find out what the organization will pay. Very rarely is it the same as what you are initially offered. As someone who has hired managers in the past, I know there were many times people asked for much less, sometimes as much as $10,000 less, than what I would have been able to pay them. Yes, library jobs as a rule pay less than some other professions, but there is nothing noble about not asking for what you know you are worth!

What advice would you have for those wishing to emulate your success?

Be deliberate about it, know what you want. Learn from many sources. Build a network, or "mastermind group" of people with stronger skills, more knowledge, better relationships, more contacts than you have. Watch for opportunities and evaluate them—then *go!* Remember to also help others get what they want, share the knowledge and experience you gain, and mentor others.

What advice would you have for those who end up in upper-level library management positions, without originally having had management as their goal?

Learn all you can about management *and* leadership. They are not the same thing. You can take classes, attend seminars, read books, interview those who have successfully mastered what you need to learn. I do not believe they can best be learned only from on-the-job experience, but that is certainly part of it! Learn from nonlibrary sources. Allen Meyers at Vernon Area District Library, Lincolnshire, Illinois, suggested joining the American Management Association. Get involved with other librarians, not just directors, and build a strong network. Develop those relationships and rely on one another for growth. Rely on your library system for help, guidance, and to lend an ear. They have the insight that comes from seeing it done a hundred different ways. Participate in professional associations. Attend sessions regularly and identify at least three ideas you will begin to implement on Monday.

Learn about building strong boards. If you are not the director, attend every board meeting you can. Ask yourself, "How would I have handled that? How would I help grow this board? How would I present that to get to *yes*?" Practice thinking up a level from where you are. Get on boards yourself in other organizations so you experience it from the other side.

Rely on the strengths of your employees. Learn from them, no matter how long you have been in the business. Help them reach their goals, and beyond. And reward them with what is important to them. If you don't want to be there, don't let it eat you alive. There are always alternatives. Whether you stay or go, choose to be happy.

*Is there anything else you would like to share about
moving into library administration?*

See this (library leadership) for the privilege that it is.
We are vital community leaders. Our organizations can
provide the heartbeat of the community. We are smack-
dab in the middle of the crossroads between our past
and our future of both our profession and our libraries
as institutions. Let's not squander this opportunity. Let's
use it to redefine for ourselves, the profession, and the
nation what it means to be a public library in a demo-
cratic society, entrusted with the resources for which we
are stewards. And in this redefining moment, let's lead
the way into the future.

Work on your ability to promote yourself and your own managerial accomplishments. Many librarians and library managers
find it more natural to promote their institution than to market
themselves. If you, in contrast, master the art of self-promotion,
you will stand out among your peers when opportunities open up.
Get known within your organization, the local library community,
and in the profession as a whole; get your name in front of decision
makers. Even if you are not currently planning on moving from
your current position, you never know if at some point you may
find that you feel as if you are stagnating and do need to take
action to progress in your career.

Whenever you move to a higher-level managerial position, you
will encounter new challenges. Realize, though, that this is often
really a difference in scale. Many of the same skills that served you
well in managing a department of four, for example, will prove useful in managing a department of 16 employees. The same political
skills apply in any environment.

Changing Fields

The fluidity of the modern information economy and the evolution of library school curricula to meet contemporary technological needs allow more librarians than ever to transfer their skills to other fields. Combine your library expertise with your management experience, and your options expand even further. Keep an open mind, and your career can only benefit from expanded opportunities. Librarianship is truly the Swiss army knife of professions, providing you with the tools to do (or learn to do) almost anything, all wrapped up in one handy field.

You can move in and out of the library field at different points in your career, using the skills you have picked up elsewhere to improve your library career. All of your experiences, inside or outside of librarianship, have the potential to enhance your abilities as a library manager. As Tracy Bushell, City Librarian, City of Mandurah, Australia, notes: "I think, if anything, working outside the field has given me alternative viewpoints and a different method of viewing problems and opportunities."

As library schools transform themselves into schools of information, merge with other departments, and encompass classes and focuses unheard of even a few years ago, librarians and information professionals recognize that the field is expanding and changing as never before. Even if you choose to move out of what is formally considered "librarianship," you may be using your library and management skills and doing knowledge or information-related work. Never get hung up on job titles; look at the actual duties and responsibilities of a given job.

Going Solo

Some of the skills that define good library managers are equally useful to those who make the jump to becoming an independent consultant, information broker, or other independent professional. As an independent information professional, you truly manage the zoo—your own business, and your own self! This requires building on the marketing and communication skills you have developed throughout your managerial career, as well as your skills in managing yourself and your own time.

As with solo librarians in corporations (see Chapter 2), networking is especially important to independent librarians. Look into joining an organization such as the Association of Independent Information Professionals (AIIP; http://www.aiip.org). Any independent information professional should also consult Mary Ellen Bates' *Building and Running a Successful Research Business: A Guide For the Independent Information Professional* (Medford, NJ: Information Today, 2003).

Managing Stress and Burnout

The challenge of balancing multiple, and sometimes competing, roles can stress even the best library manager. Realize, first, that you are not alone! Every good managerial librarian feels the stresses of her position; an unnecessary feeling of isolation only adds to these feelings. Making proactive decisions about your career, as previously outlined, can be the most useful way to minimize your own stress.

Be aware also that the constant small, everyday stresses involved in library management can be more difficult to overcome than the type of one-time stress caused by dramatic events. At least with major deadlines or events, there is an end or a resolution to the occasion—and your adrenaline may have kicked in to help you along. There is no tidy resolution to the day-to-day minor stresses of just being a manager, which include the usual librarian worry of too much to do in too little time, along with the stresses of increased responsibility, dealing with your reports, and so on.

To minimize your own stress:

- Overcome a tendency toward perfectionism. You will never be able to make things "perfect," and unexpected events upset even the most carefully laid plans. Learn to live with discrepancies; set realistic expectations for both yourself and your staff.

- Stay organized. Librarians of all people should have a handle on this! Think about how poorly your library would run with an ineffective system of cataloging and/or shelving—now, apply the same principles to your office and your inbox. Try the "touch every piece of paper only once" rule, and immediately file, deal with, or toss each sheet that comes across your desk.

- Learn to prioritize. This will become easier with experience. As a library manager, you likely have too much to do in too little time. If you view all of these tasks as equally important, the prospect of completing them can seem overwhelming. Identify the best uses of your time, and concentrate the bulk of your efforts there.

- Learn to multitask. This includes learning what tasks lend themselves to multitasking and when you need to step back, think about, and devote uninterrupted blocks of time to a project. Build the potential for uninterrupted time into your own work life by multitasking, prioritizing, and organizing in the areas that lend themselves to this. Break large projects into manageable pieces, which you can work on simultaneously or individually as their nature dictates.

- Empower your staff. Resist the urge to micromanage, and learn how to delegate tasks and responsibility. (See more on delegation in Chapter 5.) Spend some time figuring out what logically and realistically can be done by others.

- Cultivate outside interests. While your job is important (after all, this whole book is devoted to it!), never let your life revolve around work. Deliberately create balance in your life, and never spend all of your off-work hours dwelling on library issues. As Colorado State University Digital Projects Librarian Michelle Mach suggests: "Be sure to take time out for yourself and your life away from work. You will be happier and healthier in the long run if your management position is just part of your life and not your entire reason for being." Realize that imbalance has a way of creeping in gradually, and be alert to the possibility.

- Plan ahead. Build stability into your own day. Remember from the discussion of change in Chapter 8 the importance of a stable foundation in handling the changes and transitions inevitable in a library career, and work to create your own continuity.

- Recognize the warning signs and head off your own stress. Take a short walk around the building, have some chocolate, or just take some deep breaths. One manager survey respondent explains: "I also discovered how critical it is to do nice things for yourself on a regular basis to avoid burnout."

- Focus on the positive. If your managerial position begins to feel like a series of putting out fires, step back for a moment and look at the broader picture. What have you, your staff, your department, your library achieved in the past year? What successes can you look back on? Building on a foundation of success can help you think long-term and feel that your work truly has an impact.

- Overcome procrastination. Often we create much of our own stress by leaving things until the last minute, then feeling the pressures of multiple deadlines and projects. Look for your own tendencies to put off tasks, especially to put off the duties you find less pleasant. Insist on and create manageable deadlines for yourself and your staff.

- Learn to find the humor in situations. There is a reason that many library job ads specify "a sense of humor" as a desirable quality in candidates, and part of your job as a manager is to bring some enjoyment into the workplace for you and your staff.

- Learn to network. Stress shared seems less dire, and talking and sharing solutions with others in similar positions can prove therapeutic. See suggestions in Chapter 10.

- Learn to identify the situations that are most stressful for you. Some may be unavoidable, but some can be minimized. When you stop feeling any stress at all, however, it might be a sign that you no longer care! Small stresses can be motivating, while ongoing or larger stresses can become debilitating. The key here is to balance the unavoidable stresses inherent in your job with an underlying sense of control. Think also about the physical aspects of stress. There are any number of guides that talk about the importance of exercise, ergonomics, healthy sleep habits, and so on. Get up and move around to get your mind moving again; learn to leave work at work.

Think about ways in which you could reenergize yourself and refresh your energy for your career. Academic institutions may offer the option of a sabbatical, for instance; a public library's administration might be open to your taking a leave of absence. (This may be more palatable to administrators if you save up for an unpaid leave of absence, or if you accumulate enough sick and vacation time to cover at least part of your time away.) Sometimes, merely taking a break will renew your strength and give you ideas for strategies to implement upon your return, allow you time to work on personal and professional projects, or make you realize that you miss being in a leadership role. One manager survey respondent emphasizes: "Take comp time! It's a job, not your life!"

Chapter 5 talked about the importance of learning to use delegation as a tool. You do need to leave yourself adequate time to fulfill your main duties as a manager, and effective delegation can be a key tool in minimizing your own stress. Keeping your hand in by spending some time as a frontline library employee, however—doing what originally attracted you to the field—can also be an important factor in achieving balance and avoiding burnout in your career. If you were promoted to head of adult services from a reference librarian position, for example, consider scheduling yourself to cover the reference desk at least one afternoon a week. If you were promoted to head of circulation from a circulation clerk position, schedule yourself regular time to keep working with the public. Lesley Moyo, Head, Gateway Libraries, Penn State University, shares: "Sometimes I felt I had to remind myself that I'm a librarian, and not an administrator. I had to create extra time to do the professional stuff I enjoyed: reference and user education, research, scholarship, etc."

Keeping your hand in also has the additional benefit of allowing you a first-hand look into the issues faced by your staff, and lets them see you as a part of the day-to-day running of the library rather than as a completely separate member of the management team with nothing to do with them and their concerns. Doing some of the same work allows you to demonstrate that you hold yourself to the same standards, and also gives you first-hand experience that enables you to more accurately evaluate your staff. Roxanne Corbin, Clinical Knowledge Specialist, at Medstat, a healthcare information company in Ann Arbor, Michigan, suggests: "Don't just plan on being in charge, lead by example. The best managers are those who are willing to put their hand to any task that needs doing rather than waiting for a subordinate to become available." Chrissie Anderson Peters, Librarian, Basler Library, Northeast State Community College, Bloutville, Tennessee, concurs, saying: "Don't ever expect your staff to do things that you are not willing and *able* to do yourself. Getting out there and 'working in the trenches' with your staff can give you a whole new perspective on things, a new respect for what those you supervise do on a regular basis, and goes a long way in helping you earn the staff's respect and cooperation."

Lastly, combat stress and burnout with careful attention to your own professional development. Continuous learning keeps you energized and can result in a sense of your own options. Chapter 3 talked about motivation and goal-setting for employees—now, what motivates you? You face the same need to grow in your position and to have goals to strive toward. These can include anything from specific goals you want to accomplish at your library, to personal goals about your own career path, to goals about your own managerial behavior. Try to attend conferences, participate in online discussions, and/or contribute to the profession via speaking or writing or mentoring.

When deciding where to go from here, remember that your library background is unshakable and transferable. One wondrous aspect of librarianship is that every bit of information and experience is someday of use; translate all of the knowledge you hold into planning your own career path.

Notes

1. Arlie Russell Hochschild, *The Commercialization of Intimate Life: Notes From Home and Work* (Berkeley: University of California Press, 2003) 1.

2. Anthea Stratigos, "Choose Your Future," *Online*, Jan./Feb. 2000: 65–66.

Recommended Reading

Blake, Julie C. "The (D)evolution of a Director." *American Libraries*, Oct. 2002: 62–63.

Bronson, Po. *What Should I Do With My Life? The True Story of People Who Answered the Ultimate Question.* New York: Random, 2002.

Klaus, Peggy. *Brag! The Art of Tooting Your Own Horn Without Blowing It.* New York: Warner, 2003.

May, Eloise. "How I Got a Life." *American Libraries,* Oct. 1998: 59–61.

Montgomery, Denise L. "Happily Ever After: Plateauing as a Means for Long-Term Career Satisfaction." *Library Trends* 50:4 (Spring 2002): 702–716.

Siess, Judith A. *Time Management, Planning, and Prioritization for Librarians.* Lanham, MD: Scarecrow Press, 2002.

Stratigos, Anthea. "Choose Your Future." *Online,* Jan./Feb. 2000: 64–66.

Tieger, Paul D. and Barbara Barron-Tieger. *Do What You Are: Discover the Perfect Career for You Through the Secrets of Personality Type.* Boston: Little, Brown: 2001 ed.

Conclusion

"...it becomes clear that the transition to manager is not limited to acquiring competencies and building relationships. Rather, it constitutes a profound transformation, as individuals learn to think, feel, and value as managers ..."

Linda A. Hill[1]

New library managers feeling insecure in their positions should take heart. The quotes and comments throughout this book should make it clear that you are not alone! One manager survey respondent even notes that her biggest surprise was: "How unprepared for management library school had left me," and her feelings are echoed by countless others. Regardless, most accidental library managers successfully grow into their positions, assimilating the necessary skills and knowledge along the way.

As the preceding discussions show, anyone can learn to serve successfully in a library management position; a little common sense and empathy for others goes far. Most library managers lack real-world preparation for their new duties, and the question becomes whether it is even possible to prepare someone to become a manager without actually setting them loose in a managerial position. Julie Farnsworth, Director, Pleasanton City Library, California, explains that: " ... trying to prepare someone for management is like trying to prepare someone for having a baby—honesty inspires terror while the good parts are very hard to explain."

It is entirely possible that parts of your own managerial duties have been given short shrift. The wonderful diversity of the library field translates into a diversity of managerial responsibilities and activities. The preceding discussions, however, build a foundation for any managerial position, while your networking and research skills let you progress further. Confidence, dedication, and empathy for others are the building blocks of your successful library management career.

Also, you can turn to specific titles for help in specific fields. See my previous book, *The Accidental Systems Librarian* (Medford, NJ: Information Today, 2003), for example, if you manage technology. Look at Peggy Johnson's *Fundamentals of Collection Management* (Chicago: ALA Editions, 2004) if you have collection development responsibilities. Use your skills as a librarian to locate the resources you need for your own career; use your accumulated experiences and expertise to succeed.

Notes

1. Linda A. Hill, *Becoming a Manager: Mastery of a New Identity* (Boston: Harvard Business School, 1992) 5.

Appendix A

Library Management Surveys

Survey for Library Managers

The survey for library managers was posted as an online form at the library careers site Lisjobs.com during the summer of 2003. Announcements were posted on a number of library-related e-mail lists and Weblogs, as well as in the associated *Info Career Trends* electronic newsletter.

Selected Manager Survey Statistics

Out of 244 total respondents*

- Female: 194 (80%) / Male: 49 (20%)

- Average age at which respondents began their first management position: 33. (This was the same for both male and female respondents.)

- Average age of respondents now: 43

- MLS: 214 (88%) / Non-MLS: 30 (12%)

- 77 (31%) indicated that they hold at least one other advanced degree, but some seem to have misunderstood the question and listed a BA. These degrees range from liberal arts MAs (history, English), to JDs, to MBAs.

---

* Some respondents left certain questions blank, so not all totals add up to 244. Percentages were calculated from the total number of usable answers, and rounded to the nearest percent.

Respondents are self-described library managers. This is not a scientific survey; responses merely provide a snapshot of the lives and experiences of working library managers.

Questions

Thanks for taking the time to complete this short survey about your experiences as a library manager. By filling out this survey, you are giving your permission to be quoted in a forthcoming book from Information Today, Inc., as well as in supporting material (articles, promotional materials, etc.). If you would like to remain anonymous, please note that below. Identifying details about your institution will then be deleted from any quoted answers as well. If questions do not apply, please leave them blank.

Your Name:

Your E-mail address:

Your Sex:

Your Age:

Age at which you entered your first library management position:

Title and institution of your first library management position:

Current job title and institution:

Would you prefer that your responses remain anonymous if quoted in the book or elsewhere? (Y/N)

Do you have an MLS? (Y/N)

If yes, when/where did you receive your degree?

Do you have other advanced degrees?

If yes, when/where did you receive them?

Please describe how it came about that you accepted your first library management position/took on management responsibilities.

What was the biggest surprise about becoming a library manager?

What one piece of advice would you give to others entering library management?

What were the biggest challenges you faced as a new library manager?

Do you feel that library school (if applicable) adequately prepared you to take on management responsibilities? What else could your school have done to help prepare you for management?

Have you ever received any formal management training outside of library school? If so, when and where? How did it help you fulfill your responsibilities as a library manager?

Have you ever served in a non-library management position? If so, did it help prepare you for your library management responsibilities? How?

Have you ever participated in a library mentorship program? Please describe and explain whether or not it was useful to you as a library manager.

What other resources or training were most helpful to you as you settled into your library management responsibilities?

Is there a specific theory of management that has proven useful to you as a library manager? If yes, how so?

Have you ever given up management responsibilities and moved back into a non-management position? If so, why? How did stepping back impact you and your career?

Is there anything else you'd like to share with newer/potential managers about serving successfully in a library management position?

Would you like to be informed via e-mail when the book is published? (Y/N)

Survey for Library Staff

The survey for library staff was posted as an online form at the library careers site Lisjobs.com during the spring of 2004. Announcements were posted on a number of library-related e-mail lists and Weblogs, as well as in the associated *Info Career Trends* electronic newsletter. Some survey statistics and further discussion can be found in Chapter 6.

Questions

Your Name:

Your E-mail Address:

Your Current Job Title:

Your Institution:

Would you prefer that your responses remain anonymous if quoted in the book or elsewhere? (Y/N)

Do you have an MLS? (Y/N)

Are you in a "professional" position in your library?

Think back to the best library manager you ever had. What made him or her special?

Think back to the worst library manager you ever had. What made him or her especially difficult to work for?

What qualities would you most appreciate in your own manager?

What do you see as the most important responsibilities of library managers?

What one piece of advice would you like to give to new library managers?

Do you have any other comments about library management or managers in general?

Would you like to be informed via e-mail when the book is published? (Y/N)

Web Sites

Appendix B: Web Sites

http://www.lisjobs.com/talm

Chapter 1

LAMA: http://www.ala.org/lama

American Libraries: http://www.ala.org/alonline

Library Journal: http://www.libraryjournal.com

Emerald Now: http://www.emeraldinsight.com/now

The Informed Librarian: http://www.informedlibrarian.com

Chapter 2

Steve McKinzie article: http://www.webpages.uidaho.edu/~mbolin/mckinzie.htm

SOLOLIB-L: http://listserv.silverplatter.com/archives/soarcmsg.html

The One-Person Library: http://www.ibi-opl.com/newsletter

Chicago-Area Solo Librarians: http://casl.chilibsys.org

AIIP: http://www.aiip.org

Gantt and PERT charts: http://www.doc.mmu.ac.uk/online/SAD/T04/projman.htm

Chapter 3

The Contrarian Librarian: http://groups.yahoo.com/group/contrarianlibrarian

Lisjobs.com: http://www.lisjobs.com

Yale Library HR Dept. Interview Questions: http://www.library.yale.edu/jobs/Employment/interviewguidelines.html

Indiana University Interview Questions: http://www.indiana.edu/~libpers/interview.html

Competencies for Information Professionals of the 21st Century: http://www.sla.org/content/learn/comp2003/index.cfm

Core Competencies for Librarians: http://www.njla.org/resources/competencies.html

Core Competencies for Libraries and Library Staff: http://archive.ala.org/editions/samplers/sampler_pdfs/avery.pdf

Tampa Bay Library Consortium: Core Competencies: http://www.tblc.org/training/competencies.shtml

Ahead of the Curve: http://www.infotoday.com/cil2004/presentations/ballard.pps

CLENERT: http://www.ala.org/ala/clenert/clenert.htm

Chapter 4

ALA Diversity Recruitment Tips: http://www.ala.org/ala/diversity/divrecruitment/recruitmentdiversity.htm

Sample Diversity Training Program: http://www.lib.utk.edu/~training/diversity

REFORMA: http://www.reforma.org

BCALA: http://www.bcala.org

SLA Gay & Lesbian Issues Caucus: http://www.sla.org/caucus/kglic

ALA Office for Diversity: http://www.ala.org/diversity

National Diversity in Libraries Conference: http://www.library diversity.org

COLT: http://colt.ucr.edu

SSIRT: http://www.ala.org/ssirt

LIBSUP-L: http://listserv.delta.edu/archives/libsup-l.html

Chapter 6

Contrarian Librarian: http://groups.yahoo.com/group/ contrarianlibrarian

AFPL Watch: http://www.afplwatch.com

Chapter 7

Technology Plans: http://www.ilsr.com/tech.htm

TechAtlas: http://webjunction.org/do/Display?contentPage=/ static/NPower_tools.html

SOLINET Disaster Planning: http://www.solinet.net/preservation

Planning/Building Bibliography: http://www.slais.ubc.ca/ resources/architecture/readingsright.htm

Libris DESIGN: http://www.librisdesign.org

ALA Outsourcing Checklist: http://www.ala.org/ala/oif/ iftoolkits/outsourcing/Default2446.htm

Chapter 8

CLENERT: http://www.ala.org/clenert

NJLA Technical Competencies: http://www.njla.org/resources/ techcompetencies.html

WebJunction.org: http://www.webjunction.org

Chapter 9

GASB: http://haplr-index.com/gasb34faq.htm

GASB: http://www.accounting.rutgers.edu/raw/gasb/index.html

Depreciating Books: http://www.lla.state.la.us/gasb34/Libcoll.pdf

ALA Grants: http://www.ala.org/work/awards

LAMA Fundraising Section: http://www.ala.org/ala/lama/
lamacommunity/lamacommittees/fundraisingb/fundraising
financial.htm

Coffman Panel: http://www.infotoday.com/il2003/presentations

Shoppes of Library Lane: http://www.mitbc.org/librarylane

Friends of the Library: http://www.folusa.org

Library Grant Money on the Web: http://www.infotoday.com/
searcher/nov03/becker.shtml

The Foundation Center: http://fdncenter.org

Funding and Grant Sources for Libraries: http://www.libraryhq.
com/funding.html

Non-Profit Guides: http://www.npguides.org

Chapter 10

Alliance Library System Policy Manual: http://www.alliance
librarysystem.com/safeharbor/index.cfm

NSLS Trustee Training: http://www.nsls.info/ce/trustees

NSLS What's New in Libraries: http://www.whatsnewinlibraries.
org/about/index.asp

LAMA: http://www.ala.org/lama

MLA Leadership & Management Section: http://www.lms.mlanet.
org

SLA Leadership & Management Division: http://www.sla.org/
division/dlmd

Libadmin-L: http://listserv.williams.edu/archives/lib
admin-l.html

Chapter 11

FISH!: http://www.fishphilosophy.com

ISO 9000: http://standardsgroup.asq.org

Keirsey Temperament Sorter: http://www.keirsey.com

Kenneth Blanchard: http://www.blanchardtraining.com

Who Moved My Cheese: http://www.whomovedmycheese.com

Chapter 12

ALA's PATRIOT Act Guidelines: http://www.ala.org/alaorg/oif/
guidelineslibrary.html

Mary Minow's PATRIOT Act Chart: http://www.llrx.com/
features/libraryrecords.htm

Anti-Defamation League: Library Extremists: http://www.adl.org/
civil_rights/library_extremists.asp

UT Copyright Crash Course: http://www.utsystem.edu/ogc/
intellectualproperty/cprtindx.htm

U.S. Copyright Office: http://www.copyright.gov

OSHA Compliance: http://www.osha.gov/dcsp/compliance_
assistance

Chapter 13

Harvard Leadership Institute: http://www.gse.harvard.edu/~ppe/programs/acrl/program.html

ARL Leadership and Career Development Program: http://www.arl.org/diversity/lcdp/index.html

Frye Leadership Institute: http://www.fryeinstitute.org

Library Leadership Ohio: http://www.camls.org/ce/ce_LL Ohio.asp

MPLA Leadership Institute: http://www.usd.edu/mpla/leadership

ULC Executive Leadership Institute: http://www.urbanlibraries.org/eli.html

YSLead Massachusetts: http://www.wmrls.org/YSLead

A Librarian Without A Library: http://liscareer.com/shontz_activeunemployment.htm

AIIP: http://www.aiip.org

About the Author

Rachel Singer Gordon is the former Head of Computer Services at the Franklin Park (Illinois) Public Library. She is the founder and Webmaster of the library career site Lisjobs.com, from which she also publishes *Info Career Trends,* a free, bimonthly electronic newsletter on career development issues for librarians. With Sarah Johnson, Rachel maintains "Beyond the Job," a professional development Web log for information professionals. Rachel also writes the monthly "Computer Media" and "NextGen" columns for *Library Journal.*

Rachel has written and presented widely on career development issues for librarians. Her published work includes *The Information Professional's Guide to Career Development Online* (with Sarah Nesbeitt, Information Today, Inc., 2002), *The Accidental Systems Librarian* (Information Today, Inc., 2003), and *The Librarian's Guide to Writing for Publication* (Scarecrow, 2004). She holds an MLIS from Dominican University and an MA from Northwestern University.

Index

H

I

More Great Books from Information Today, Inc.

The Accidental Webmaster

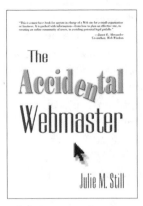

By Julie Still

Here is a lifeline for the individual who has not been trained as a Webmaster, but who—whether by choice or under duress—has become one nonetheless. While most Webmastering books focus on programming and related technical issues, *The Accidental Webmaster* helps readers deal with the full range of challenges they face on the job. Author, librarian, and accidental Webmaster Julie Still offers advice on getting started, setting policies, working with ISPs, designing home pages, selecting content, drawing site traffic, gaining user feedback, fundraising, avoiding copyright problems, and much more.

2003/softbound/ISBN 1-57387-164-8 $29.50

The Accidental Systems Librarian

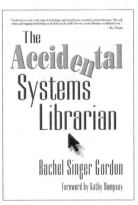

By Rachel Singer Gordon

Author Rachel Singer Gordon believes that anyone with a solid foundation in the practices and principles of librarianship and a willingness to confront changing technology can serve effectively in a library technology position—with or without formal computer training. Gordon's advice on using research, organizational, and bibliographic skills to solve various systems problems helps "accidental" systems librarians develop the skills they need to succeed.

2003/softbound/ISBN 1-57387-104-4 $29.50

The Web Library

**Building a World Class Personal Library
with Free Web Resources**

By Nicholas G. Tomaiuolo
Edited by Barbara Quint

With this remarkable, eye-opening book and its companion Web site, Nicholas G. (Nick) Tomaiuolo shows how anyone can create a comprehensive personal library using no-cost Web resources. This is an easy-to-use guide, with chapters corresponding to departments in a physical library. *The Web Library* provides a wealth of URLs and examples of free material you can start using right away, but, best of all, it offers techniques for finding and collecting new content as the Web evolves. Start building your personal Web library today!

2003/softbound/ISBN 0-910965-67-6 • $29.95

The Information Professional's Guide to Career Development Online

*By Rachel Singer Gordon and
Sarah L. Nesbeitt*

This book is designed to meet the needs of librarians interested in using online tools to advance their careers. It offers practical advice on topics ranging from current awareness services and personal Web pages to distance education, electronic resumes, and online job searches. New librarians will learn how to use the Internet to research education opportunities, and experienced info pros will learn ways to network through online conferences and discussion lists. Supported by a Web page.

2002/softbound/ISBN 1-57387-124-9 $29.50